Surv

GLOBAL POLITICS AND STRATEGY

Volume 64 Number 6 | December 2022–January 2023

'In recent years, MbS has cultivated strong ties with Putin, seeing him as more decisive and reliable than US Democratic presidents, whom he has judged to be sanctimonious and fickle. Converging interests on oil policy have been crucial in cementing the relationship.'

Emile Hokayem, Fraught Relations: Saudi Ambitions and American Anger, p. 10.

'Russia lacks most preconditions for liberalisation and democratisation, and a 30-year Western bet on normalising relations has ended horrendously and unequivocally. Instead, a resolutely revanchist Russia may well emerge, determined to rebuild its military power.'

Michael Jonsson and Johan Norberg, Russia's War Against Ukraine: Military Scenarios and Outcomes, p. 110.

'To use a popular Persian expression, "the knife reached the bone" when a woman could be arrested, humiliated and killed simply for the way she wore a headscarf.'

Mahsa Rouhi, Woman, Life, Freedom in Iran, p. 193.

Survival

GLOBAL POLITICS AND STRATEGY

Volume 64 Number 6 | December 2022–January 2023

Contents

Cover: Getty

On the cover
Saudi Crown Prince Muhammad bin Salman welcomes US President Joe Biden to Al Salam Royal Palace in Jeddah, Saudi Arabia, on 15 July 2022.

On the web
Visit www.iiss.org/publications/survival for brief notices on new books on the United States, Europe, and Counter-terrorism and Intelligence.

Survival **editors' blog**
For ideas and commentary from *Survival* editors and contributors, visit www.iiss.org/blogs/survival-blog.

Putin's World

Review Essay

Book Reviews

Closing Argument

Survival
GLOBAL POLITICS AND STRATEGY

The International Institute for Strategic Studies

2121 K Street, NW | Suite 600 | Washington DC 20037 | USA
Tel +1 202 659 1490   Fax +1 202 659 1499   E-mail survival@iiss.org   Web www.iiss.org

Arundel House | 6 Temple Place | London | WC2R 2PG | UK
Tel +44 (0)20 7379 7676   Fax +44 (0)20 7836 3108   E-mail iiss@iiss.org

14th Floor, GBCorp Tower | Bahrain Financial Harbour | Manama | Kingdom of Bahrain
Tel +973 1718 1155   Fax +973 1710 0155   E-mail iiss-middleeast@iiss.org

9 Raffles Place | #49-01 Republic Plaza | Singapore 048619
Tel +65 6499 0055   Fax +65 6499 0059   E-mail iiss-asia@iiss.org

Pariser Platz 6A | 10117 Berlin | Germany
Tel +49 30 311 99 300   E-mail iiss-europe@iiss.org

Survival Online www.tandfonline.com/survival and www.iiss.org/publications/survival

Aims and Scope *Survival* is one of the world's leading forums for analysis and debate of international and strategic affairs. Shaped by its editors to be both timely and forward thinking, the journal encourages writers to challenge conventional wisdom and bring fresh, often controversial, perspectives to bear on the strategic issues of the moment. With a diverse range of authors, *Survival* aims to be scholarly in depth while vivid, well written and policy-relevant in approach. Through commentary, analytical articles, case studies, forums, review essays, reviews and letters to the editor, the journal promotes lively, critical debate on issues of international politics and strategy.

Editor **Dana Allin**
Managing Editor **Jonathan Stevenson**
Associate Editor **Carolyn West**
Editorial Assistant **Charlie Zawadzki**
Production and Cartography **Jade Panganiban, Kelly Verity**

Published for the IISS by
Routledge Journals, an imprint of Taylor & Francis, an Informa business.

Copyright © 2022 The International Institute for Strategic Studies. All rights reserved. No part of this publication may be reproduced, stored, transmitted or disseminated, in any form, or by any means, without prior written permission from Taylor & Francis, to whom all requests to reproduce copyright material should be directed, in writing.

About the IISS The IISS, a registered charity with offices in Washington, London, Manama, Singapore and Berlin, is the world's leading authority on political–military conflict. It is the primary independent source of accurate, objective information on international strategic issues. Publications include *The Military Balance*, an annual reference work on each nation's defence capabilities; *Strategic Survey*, an annual review of world affairs; *Survival*, a bimonthly journal on international affairs; *Strategic Comments*, an online analysis of topical issues in international affairs; and the *Adelphi* series of books on issues of international security.

Director-General and Chief Executive
John Chipman

Chair of the Trustees
Bill Emmott

Chair of the Council
Chung Min Lee

Trustees
Caroline Atkinson
Neha Aviral
John O. Brennan
Chris Jones
Kurt Lauk
Catherine Roe
Grace R. Skaugen
Matt Symonds
Matthew Symonds
Jens Tholstrup

IISS Advisory Council
Joanne de Asis
Caroline Atkinson
Shobhana Bhartia
Linden P. Blue
Garvin Brown
Alejandro Santo Domingo
Thomas Enders
Michael Fullilove
Yoichi Funabashi
Alia Hatoug-Bouran
Badr Jafar
Bilahari Kausikan

Thomas Lembong
Eric Li
Peter Maurer
Charles Powell
George Robertson
Andrés Rozental
Mark Sedwill
Grace R. Skaugen
Debra Soon
Heizo Takenaka
Marcus Wallenberg

SUBMISSIONS

To submit an article, authors are advised to follow these guidelines:

- *Survival* articles are around 4,000–10,000 words long including endnotes. A word count should be included with a draft.
- All text, including endnotes, should be double-spaced with wide margins.
- Any tables or artwork should be supplied in separate files, ideally not embedded in the document or linked to text around it.
- All *Survival* articles are expected to include endnote references. These should be complete and include first and last names of authors, titles of articles (even from newspapers), place of publication, publisher, exact publication dates, volume and issue number (if from a journal) and page numbers. Web sources should include complete URLs and DOIs if available.
- A summary of up to 150 words should be included with the article. The summary should state the main argument clearly and concisely, not simply say what the article is about.
- A short author's biography of one or two lines should also be included. This information will appear at the foot of the first page of the article.

Please note that *Survival* has a strict policy of listing multiple authors in alphabetical order.

Submissions should be made by email, in Microsoft Word format, to survival@iiss.org. Alternatively, hard copies may be sent to *Survival*, IISS–US, 2121 K Street NW, Suite 801, Washington, DC 20037, USA.

The editorial review process can take up to three months. *Survival*'s acceptance rate for unsolicited manuscripts is less than 20%. *Survival* does not normally provide referees' comments in the event of rejection. Authors are permitted to submit simultaneously elsewhere so long as this is consistent with the policy of the other publication and the Editors of *Survival* are informed of the dual submission.

Readers are encouraged to comment on articles from the previous issue. Letters should be concise, no longer than 750 words and relate directly to the argument or points made in the original article.

Survival: Global Politics and Strategy (Print ISSN 0039-6338, Online ISSN 1468-2699) is published bimonthly for a total of 6 issues per year by Taylor & Francis Group, 4 Park Square, Milton Park, Abingdon, Oxon, OX14 4RN, UK. Periodicals postage paid (Permit no. 13095) at Brooklyn, NY 11256.

Airfreight and mailing in the USA by agent named World Container Inc., c/o BBT 150-15, 183rd Street, Jamaica, NY 11413, USA.

US Postmaster: Send address changes to Survival, World Container Inc., c/o BBT 150-15, 183rd Street, Jamaica, NY 11413, USA.

Subscription records are maintained at Taylor & Francis Group, 4 Park Square, Milton Park, Abingdon, OX14 4RN, UK.

Subscription information: For more information and subscription rates, please see tandfonline.com/pricing/journal/TSUR. Taylor & Francis journals are available in a range of different packages, designed to suit every library's needs and budget. This journal is available for institutional subscriptions with online-only or print & online options. This journal may also be available as part of our libraries, subject collections or archives. For more information on our sales packages, please visit librarianresources.taylorandfrancis.com.

For support with any institutional subscription, please visit help.tandfonline.com or email our dedicated team at subscriptions@tandf.co.uk.

Subscriptions purchased at the personal rate are strictly for personal, non-commercial use only. The reselling of personal subscriptions is prohibited. Personal subscriptions must be purchased with a personal cheque, credit card or BAC/wire transfer. Proof of personal status may be requested.

Back issues: Taylor & Francis Group retains a current and one-year back-issue stock of journals. Older volumes are held by our official stockists to whom all orders and enquiries should be addressed: Periodicals Service Company, 351 Fairview Avenue, Suite 300, Hudson, NY 12534, USA. Tel: +1 518 537 4700; email psc@periodicals.com.

Ordering information: To subscribe to the journal, please contact T&F Customer Services, Informa UK Ltd, Sheepen Place, Colchester, Essex, CO3 3LP, UK. Tel: +44 (0) 20 8052 2030; email subscriptions@tandf.co.uk.

Taylor & Francis journals are priced in USD, GBP and EUR (as well as AUD and CAD for a limited number of journals). All subscriptions are charged depending on where the end customer is based. If you are unsure which rate applies to you, please contact Customer Services. All subscriptions are payable in advance and all rates include postage. We are required to charge applicable VAT/GST on all print and online combination subscriptions, in addition to our online-only journals. Subscriptions are entered on an annual basis, i.e., January to December. Payment may be made by sterling cheque, dollar cheque, euro cheque, international money order, National Giro or credit cards (Amex, Visa and Mastercard).

Disclaimer: The International Institute for Strategic Studies (IISS) and our publisher Informa UK Limited, trading as Taylor & Francis Group ('T&F'), make every effort to ensure the accuracy of all the information (the 'Content') contained in our publications. However, IISS and our publisher T&F, our agents and our licensors make no representations or warranties whatsoever as to the accuracy, completeness or suitability for any purpose of the Content. Any opinions and views expressed in this publication are the opinions and views of the authors, and are not the views of or endorsed by IISS or our publisher T&F. The accuracy of the Content should not be relied upon and should be independently verified with primary sources of information, and any reliance on the Content is at your own risk. IISS and our publisher T&F make no representations, warranties or guarantees, whether express or implied, that the Content is accurate, complete or up to date. IISS and our publisher T&F shall not be liable for any losses, actions, claims, proceedings, demands, costs, expenses, damages and other liabilities whatsoever or howsoever caused arising directly or indirectly in connection with, in relation to or arising out of the use of the Content. Full Terms & Conditions of access and use can be found at http://www.tandfonline.com/page/terms-and-conditions.

Informa UK Limited, trading as Taylor & Francis Group, grants authorisation for individuals to photocopy copyright material for private research use, on the sole basis that requests for such use are referred directly to the requestor's local Reproduction Rights Organization (RRO). The copyright fee is exclusive of any charge or fee levied. In order to contact your local RRO, please contact International Federation of Reproduction Rights Organizations (IFRRO), rue du Prince Royal, 87, B-1050 Brussels, Belgium; email ifrro@skynet.be; Copyright Clearance Center Inc., 222 Rosewood Drive, Danvers, MA 01923, USA; email info@copyright.com; or Copyright Licensing Agency, 90 Tottenham Court Road, London, W1P 0LP, UK; email cla@cla.co.uk. This authorisation does not extend to any other kind of copying, by any means, in any form, for any purpose other than private research use.

Submission information: See https://www.tandfonline.com/journals/tsur20

Advertising: See https://taylorandfrancis.com/contact/advertising/

Permissions: See help.tandfonline.com/Librarian/s/article/Permissions

All Taylor & Francis Group journals are printed on paper from renewable sources by accredited partners.

December 2022–January 2023

THE ADELPHI SERIES

THE DIGITAL
SILK ROAD

China's Technological Rise and the Geopolitics of Cyberspace

David Gordon and Meia Nouwens

available at

amazon

OR

R Routledge
Taylor & Francis Group

Adelphi 487–489; published November 2022; 234x156; 224pp; Paperback: 978-1-032-48687-1

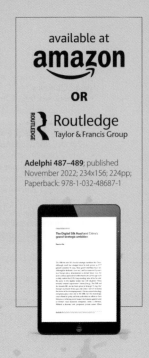

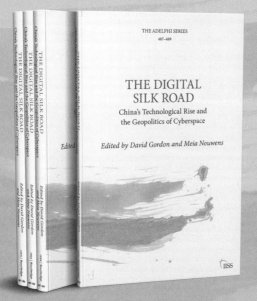

Beijing has grasped the opportunity to leverage the entrepreneurial strengths of its private tech sector to gain prominence in the world's digital ecosystem. But the more interventionist Beijing becomes, the more Chinese firms will be seen as instruments of the state, and the greater the pushback against Chinese technology and the DSR may be. To achieve great-power status and global centrality, Beijing might ultimately need to change tack. How it innovates in further rolling out Chinese tech across the world, and what the DSR will then look like, will have far-reaching impacts on global economics, politics and security.

'China's role in cyberspace is one of the most important international issues of the 2020s and 2030s. This book provides a deeply expert, sober and thoughtful interpretation of this issue, and will be essential reading for policymakers.'

Rana Mitter, Professor of the History and Politics of Modern China, University of Oxford

IISS THE INTERNATIONAL INSTITUTE FOR STRATEGIC STUDIES   www.iiss.org/publications/adelphi

Fraught Relations: Saudi Ambitions and American Anger

Emile Hokayem

On 5 October 2022, the OPEC+ group of 24 oil-exporting countries, led by Russia and Saudi Arabia, announced a cut in oil-production levels of two million barrels per day. Amid setbacks in its campaign in Ukraine, Moscow's rationale was clear. Higher oil prices would not only increase Russian oil revenues, they would also inflict significant economic pain on Western rivals ahead of a hard winter in Europe and hotly contested midterm elections in the United States. With respect to countries supportive of the Ukrainian government, this Russian scheme fit well with Moscow's weaponisation of energy since the beginning of the conflict.

Insofar as the Saudi move came on the heels of a controversial visit by US President Joe Biden to Jeddah in July that was meant to reset the US–Saudi relationship, many in Washington considered it perfidious. To them, Riyadh appeared to be using oil to empower Russia and to afford Republicans an advantage in the midterms.[1]

A ferocious war of words followed. After Biden promised 'consequences', the White House issued a statement: 'We are re-evaluating our relationship with Saudi Arabia in light of these actions, and will continue to look for signs about where they stand in combatting Russian aggression.'[2] Chuck Schumer, the Senate majority leader and its top Democrat, warned: 'What

Emile Hokayem is IISS Senior Fellow for Middle East Security. This article is adapted from an essay that appears in the 2022 edition of *Strategic Survey* (Routledge for the IISS).

Survival | vol. 64 no. 6 | December 2022–January 2023 | pp. 7–22   https://doi.org/10.1080/00396338.2022.2150422

Saudi Arabia did to help [Russian President Vladimir] Putin continue to wage his despicable, vicious war against Ukraine will long be remembered by Americans.'[3] Riyadh pushed back forcefully. An extraordinary statement from the Foreign Ministry expressed 'its total rejection of [US] statements that are not based on facts'.[4]

Saudi officials contended that the production cut was premised on concern that a looming recession in Western economies and the COVID-related slowdown in China would reduce demand and lower prices. After years of economic travails that had raised questions about the viability of Crown Prince Muhammad bin Salman's (MbS) transformation plans, the Saudi economy had recovered thanks to higher oil prices, and was expected to grow by 7.6% in 2022, up from 3.2% the year before.[5] Businesses and investors have been finding their way back to the Kingdom, as demonstrated by the attendance of senior Western executives at the flagship Future Investment Initiative conference in October. In 2021, foreign direct investment (FDI) into Saudi Arabia reached nearly $20 billion, more than the cumulative FDI between 2017 and 2020. For Saudi leaders, depressed oil prices would put a halt to this salutary streak. When Biden visited Jeddah in July, the price of Brent crude stood at $110 a barrel. Between June and September, the price of oil fell by 30%. By the time of the OPEC+ decision, it stood at $94. Saudi calculations suggested a downward trajectory unless action was taken. The current Saudi budget is based on a break-even price of $76. Although the US government's release of oil from its Strategic Petroleum Reserve and a mild autumn in the Northern Hemisphere sped the downward trend in oil prices, the Saudis have credited the cut in oil production for stabilising them.[6]

While a US suspension or cancellation of arms sales or downgrading of defence cooperation is possible, a crackdown on OPEC+ features highest among potential American punitive measures. A Republican senator, Chuck Grassley, introduced the 'NOPEC' (No Oil Producing and Exporting Cartels) bill in October aimed at reducing OPEC's power. It was worrying for Riyadh that an essentially mainstream Republican had manifested such firm discontent with Saudi policies. This bill received bipartisan support, including from prominent progressive and centrist Democrats. In turn, Saudi officials floated retaliatory ideas such as pricing oil sales to China in Chinese yuan instead of US dollars or selling Saudi-held US Treasury bonds.

A deteriorating relationship

This episode clearly indicated the precarious state of the US–Saudi relationship. Riyadh surely would have known that Washington would not welcome production cuts. In the weeks preceding it, senior US envoys had lobbied Saudi officials to reject, or at least delay, such cuts. Such pleading failed to sway Saudi decision-makers, who were focused on economic concerns, anticipating a massive financial windfall and confident that the US would not retaliate in any significant manner. The US and Saudi Arabia interpreted each other's decisions in the worst possible way, reflecting the loss of trust and the transformation of the relationship into a cold, transactional one.

Relations between the two countries have hit an all-time low. Strategic divergence over Iran, regional security and global competition has intensified, with the gap growing between what Riyadh expects from Washington and what Washington is ready to offer. While US businesses have an enormous appetite for opportunities in Saudi Arabia, energy itself is no longer the glue holding the relationship together. According to the Economist Intelligence Unit, in 2021 5% of Saudi exports (overwhelmingly oil) went to the US, 10% to the European Union and a staggering 50% to China, Japan, India and South Korea.[7] This points to the fundamental strategic challenge faced by Saudi Arabia: its security lies in the West, its prosperity in the East.

Worse still, tensions have taken on a strongly personal flavour. In 2019, then-candidate Biden said he saw 'very little social redeeming value in the present government in Saudi Arabia', which he described as a 'pariah state'. In turn, MbS, when asked in 2022 about Biden's opinion of him, dismissively answered, 'Simply, I do not care'. He coldly added, 'It's up to [Biden] to think about the interests of America'.[8]

This brand of acrimony is a departure from the standard tone of bilateral relations in the past. Even in the aftermath of the 9/11 attacks, when Saudi Arabia was vilified because most of the hijackers, as well as al-Qaeda leader Osama bin Laden, were Saudi citizens and Riyadh had past ties with bin Laden, leaders of each country managed to maintain a cordial rapport. The relationship began to deteriorate during the administration of Barack Obama. Saudi monarchs assumed incorrectly that Washington would grant them special access, attention and deference, and American leaders wrongly supposed that Riyadh would unconditionally align itself with the US on strategic and energy issues. The further souring of relations has to some extent been a function of diminished expectations. Personal animosity is accelerating what is essentially a growing strategic divergence based on changing geopolitical and geo-economic orientations in both countries.

In recent years, MbS has cultivated strong ties with Putin, seeing him as more decisive and reliable than US Democratic presidents, whom he has judged to be sanctimonious and fickle. Converging interests on oil policy have been crucial in cementing the relationship: starting in 2016, OPEC+ became Saudi Arabia and Russia's most important mechanism for market stability. The two leaders' high-five at the 2018 G20 summit, after MbS had been internationally ostracised due to his apparent authorisation of the assassination of dissident Saudi journalist Jamal Khashoggi, was emblematic of this rapprochement.

As the personal relationship developed, Saudi Arabia's appreciation of Russian power grew. Upset by the United States' reluctance to provide defensive systems to counter Iranian and Houthi air attacks, Riyadh floated the possibility of buying advanced Russian S-400 air-defence systems. MbS began cultivating relations with individuals close to Putin, such as Kirill Dmitriev, CEO of the Russian Direct Investment Fund, and Chechen strongman Ramzan Kadyrov.

Russia's war in Ukraine has widened the gap. Along with many Middle Eastern states, Saudi Arabia has been reluctant to overtly condemn Moscow. In line with Arab elite opinion, Riyadh anticipated a quick Russian victory due to Russia's presumed military superiority and the West's fecklessness – a view reinforced by its recent failures in Iraq and especially Afghanistan. Even short of outright victory, the Saudis figured, a frozen conflict or a war of attrition would benefit Moscow. They did not seriously entertain the prospect of Ukraine's buoyant morale, operational prowess and fierce resistance, or that of sustained Western commitment to its defence. Saudi businesses, no doubt prompted by the Royal Court, even saw opportunities in Russia: Kingdom Holding – a company owned by Prince Al Waleed and the MbS-controlled Public Investment Fund (PIF) – invested $500 million in major Russian energy companies just as Western sanctions were slapped on them.

This conduct, cynical though it may be, does not amount to Saudi support for Russia. Riyadh purports to view the conflict as a regional rather than a global security matter, pointedly reciprocating what it regards as the Western stance on Iran. Riyadh emphasises that it voted to condemn the Russian annexation of Ukrainian territory at the United Nations General Assembly a few days after the OPEC+ decision. Stung by Western criticism, it sent humanitarian assistance amounting to $400m to Ukraine. MbS also used his influence with Putin to negotiate a deal whereby Western prisoners were released from Russian captivity. In addition, there is anxiety in Riyadh over Moscow's developing defence relationship with Iran, demonstrated by Iran's provision of uninhabited aerial vehicles (UAVs) to Russia. The Saudis hope that through ongoing engagement with the Russians they can constrain Russia's alignment with Tehran and prevent its transfer of military technology to Iran.

Riyadh's policy recalibration

After years of economic pain and political isolation from the West, Saudi Arabia has rebounded spectacularly. Energy-market turbulence has played a key role: the Western scramble for oil and gas resulting from the war in Ukraine has reminded the world of the Kingdom's centrality to energy politics, and has improved the country's economic outlook. Emboldened by this development, MbS has intensified his efforts to recast Saudi Arabia as a modern global power, jettisoning or at least challenging some of the standard assumptions and pillars of Saudi foreign policy and looking to transcend its traditional role as the self-declared champion of the Islamic and Arab worlds. This recalibration has yet to deliver tangible and durable results. And it has shaken up the country's diplomacy, inducing anxiety as well as excitement inside and outside the Kingdom.

As part of his frenetic modernisation drive, MbS has been keen to reduce the ideological and geopolitical baggage that comes with Saudi Arabia's traditional claims to Islamic and Arab leadership, which he sees as convenient but also as limiting and costly. Ideally, from his point of view, considerations of Islamic and Arab solidarity should no longer routinely constrain Saudi policies. Traditional regions of Saudi interest should cease expecting automatic Saudi attention and largesse. Instead, Saudi Arabia should review its legacy entanglements, and prioritise its geo-economic and geopolitical interests in the service of the Kingdom's transformation.

In this regard, MbS is shaping and also reflecting the priorities of a new generation of Saudi leaders who do not share attachments to issues that have consumed and frustrated their predecessors. For this new elite, the focus on regional relationships has squandered attention and resources, and often been uncoordinated, with senior royals taking responsibility for separate portfolios without an integrated view of national interests. It has also created dependencies and expectations abroad, sometimes miring the Kingdom in reputation-damaging controversies. And it has politicised – in some cases, radicalised – Saudi subjects more invested in regional conflicts than in embracing national identity and modernising their country.

There is an overwhelming sense in Riyadh that legacy relationships from Pakistan to Lebanon have not delivered the expected returns. Saudi generosity did not secure Egyptian or Pakistani participation when its campaign in Yemen began in 2015. Long a special project of Saudi leaders, Lebanon has become a source of disappointment and an exporter of threats to the Kingdom via Hizbullah, the Lebanese Shia militant group whose ideology and activities now target Saudi Arabia as much as Israel. Saudi Arabia was one of only three countries to recognise Taliban rule in Afghanistan in 1996, only to see al-Qaeda plotting operations against the royal family from Afghanistan. Saudi backing for Syrian rebels fighting President Bashar al-Assad generated accusations that the Kingdom effectively supported the Islamic State (ISIS). For MbS, even the imperative to intervene in Yemen could be traced to an ill-judged Saudi policy, as Yemeni political and tribal leaders whom Riyadh had cultivated at great cost proved weak and duplicitous.

Such assessments have had significant impacts, particularly in the Levant, where Saudi Arabia had long been a major actor. The Kingdom's attachment to Jordan, Lebanon and Syria had been personal as well as strategic, Saudi royals having established friendships with national leaders. MbS took an unsentimental view of these relationships. In his view, they did not serve the Kingdom's interests because Saudi Arabia's friends and partners had underdelivered or underperformed. In Lebanon, the Saudi-backed Hariri political dynasty had failed to contain Hizbullah. As a result, Saudi Arabia had effectively disengaged in 2016. The Trump administration's rejection of the Israeli–Palestinian peace process had undercut Jordan, which, though long dependent on Saudi largesse, now felt threatened by Saudi ambitions. Indeed, Riyadh toyed briefly with the idea of replacing Jordanian trusteeship of the Muslim religious sites in Jerusalem.[9] Jordanian leaders complained that Saudi financial and energy assistance had dried up, causing major economic and budgetary damage. In Syria, the Kingdom was frustrated by its inability to unseat Assad and by the dominance of rivals Turkey and Iran there. Seeing no way to re-establish influence, MbS preferred to cut the Kingdom's losses and extract Saudi Arabia from the Syrian crisis.

Riyadh has backed Beijing's narrative

Elsewhere, Riyadh signalled that it would no longer automatically champion Muslim causes. When India altered the constitutional status of the disputed region of Kashmir in 2019, the Saudi response was relatively muted, drawing Pakistani ire. In a historic reversal, Riyadh prioritised the cultivation of economic and defence relations with a rising New Delhi over alignment with Islamabad, which had been a close if ambivalent and needy security partner for decades. No less revealing was Saudi Arabia's support for China over the Uighur community: in the face of Western criticism of China, Riyadh has backed Beijing's narrative of counter-terrorism and religious reform, signing letters in 2019 at the UN to this effect. Once the Arab state most opposed to communism during the Cold War, Saudi Arabia now sees courting China as essential to its prosperity and security, and wants to avoid being forced to choose between Washington and Beijing. In April 2022, MbS told Chinese President Xi Jinping that the Kingdom would 'staunchly support China's legitimate position on such issues concerning core interests as Xinjiang, resolutely oppose any interference in China's internal affairs and firmly safeguard the rights of all countries to choose their own political and human rights paths independently'.[10]

Closer by, the Kingdom has started paying more attention to the Red Sea region, which it had once largely ignored. For Riyadh, which had long prioritised development in the Najd hinterland and on the Gulf coast, the Red Sea coast now appears secure and economically promising. The grandest of MbS's projects is the $500bn new city of NEOM on the northwest coast, and there has also been infrastructure development – including pipelines, railways, tourist facilities and ports – along the littoral. To secure this endeavour, Saudi Arabia recovered the islands of Tiran and Sanafir from Egypt and established a Red Sea Council to bring together littoral states. This ambition has unnerved out-of-region states such as Turkey and the United Arab Emirates (UAE), as well as Egypt, the Arab state once dominant in the area. In parallel, Saudi Arabia has cultivated good relations with Ethiopia despite the latter's dispute with Egypt over the construction of the Grand Ethiopian Renaissance Dam, which will significantly reduce downstream Nile River water flows into Egypt.

Domestically, MbS deemed tighter control of religious organisations and the promotion of a more tolerant brand of Islam essential to modernisation. A wide crackdown ensued on clerics with radical or reformist inclinations who had been tolerated in the past. In addition to quelling dissent, this shift was also an important means of burnishing the Kingdom's international image and credibility, which had suffered since 9/11. Consequently, government spending for proselytising abroad has been slashed and Saudi religious leaders have pursued outreach to non-Islamic faiths. The head of the Mecca-based Muslim World League, the Saudi organisation once in charge of propagating Salafi-Wahhabi teachings worldwide, has held meetings with Christian, Jewish, Hindu and other religious figures to promote tolerance.

Surviving ostracism

MbS has strived to position Saudi Arabia as a modern nation intent on deploying geo-economic and geopolitical power globally. Instead of being a leader of poor, weak and dependent countries, Saudi Arabia should be equal to First World nations. In his view, nurturing relations with leading

economies not only makes geopolitical sense but is also essential to the fulfil-
ment of the Kingdom's ambitions. No forum could provide better validation
of Saudi Arabia's new ambitions than the G20, composed of the world's 20
largest economies.

The success of Vision 2030, MbS's epic transformation plan, depends not
only on an overhaul of the Saudi economy but also on a significant upgrad-
ing of political and economic relations with major powers. Instead of being
merely an exporter of commodities and an importer of high-value consumer
goods, the Kingdom now aspires to become a full-spectrum economic
power that is embedded in global supply chains as both a manufacturer
and a logistical hub; a producer of both traditional and renewable energies;
a destination for foreign investment; an allocator of capital to key sectors;
and a partner of choice for major companies.

Developing such capacities has required the Kingdom to conduct more
sophisticated statecraft than in the past, when energy was the only potent
Saudi card. Having concentrated power to an unprecedented degree, MbS is
forcing the Kingdom's foreign, defence and economic policies into stronger
alignment. For example, the establishment of a production line for Chinese
UAVs in Saudi Arabia is meant not only to advance defence cooperation
with Beijing, but also to foster the development of an indigenous defence
industry, secure technology transfers and eventually allow the Kingdom
to become an exporter of weapons systems.[11] MbS has also transformed the
once-sleepy PIF into a driver of domestic economic development as well as
an instrument of international investment and influence.

Such an expansive and transformative plan has necessitated, to an
extent, a retooling of Saudi diplomacy. Prince Saud al-Faisal, the formidable
foreign minister who embodied Saudi diplomacy for 40 years, died in 2015,
a few months after relinquishing his position. In 2018, his successor, Adel
al-Jubeir, a protégé of the late King Abdullah bin Abdulaziz Al Saud associated with 'old' diplomacy, was demoted from his job as foreign minister
and replaced with Ibrahim al-Assaf, a veteran economist who had served as
finance minister. A year later, Assaf himself was replaced by Prince Faisal
bin Farhan, a young prince aligned with MbS. While the management of the
US–Saudi relationship has remained in the hands of MbS and his brother

Prince Khaled, Prince Faisal has been charged with diversifying Saudi relations, tasking Saudi ambassadors in major capitals with more aggressive economic outreach. Tellingly, Khalid al-Falih, the investment minister who previously served as CEO of the state-owned oil company Saudi Aramco and as energy minister, became the point man for China and for Japan, which was the country most involved in the implementation of Vision 2030. In early 2020, Abe Shinzo, then Japan's prime minister, was the first G7 leader to visit Riyadh since the assassination of Khashoggi.

Further, MbS has revamped Saudi energy policy, establishing royal control over a sector that had been left to bureaucrats for decades. In 2015, MbS was appointed chair of the Supreme Council of Saudi Aramco, which had been largely shielded from direct royal control. MbS also installed Yasir al-Rumayyan, the head of the PIF and his right-hand man, as Saudi Aramco chair. In 2019, Prince Abdulaziz bin Salman, a half-brother of MbS, became the first royal to head the energy ministry. The public listing of Saudi Aramco in 2019, which MbS hoped would be in London, New York or Tokyo but ultimately occurred in Riyadh, was an essential element of his economic plan but also a symbol of Saudi economic power.

As the October OPEC+ decision showed, MbS is willing to use oil production as an instrument of influence. The goal of Saudi policy since the 2000s had been to stabilise energy markets by ensuring that oil prices did not climb to a degree that would unduly dampen demand, thus jeopardising the main source of Saudi income in the long term. MbS has proved more willing to favour short-term economic interests (the listing of Saudi Aramco) or strategic objectives (upholding the OPEC+ agreement to cut oil production despite Western demands for greater production after the pandemic peaked). Although the October OPEC+ decision distressed the United States, under MbS Riyadh has also assertively defended its energy interests against Russia, defying Moscow's attempt in 2020 to compel it to cut production amid falling demand at the beginning of the pandemic.

In 2018, the Khashoggi assassination reinforced widespread perceptions of Saudi aggressiveness and overreach, already fuelled by the calamitous war in Yemen. The resulting spotlight on the Kingdom inhibited MbS's modernising efforts. In the US, although Donald Trump himself and certain of his advisers were disposed to give MbS a pass on the Khashoggi hit, progressives, diplomats, intelligence professionals and others sought to isolate him. In turn, he tried to consolidate power at home by cracking down on dissent. The message was that there was no alternative to MbS. The young prince was destined to become king regardless of Western concerns. In September 2022, MbS was named prime minister, making him officially the country's chief executive. Riyadh secured the support of Egypt, the UAE and other Arab nations that were also displeased with US policy.

Calculating that only Western leaders would attempt to marginalise him, MbS doubled down on strategic diversification. He sought closer relationships with autocratic and populist figures in China, India, Russia and elsewhere. At the 2018 G20 summit in Argentina, he was able to mingle, if uncomfortably, with international leaders. Saudi Arabia was slated to host the summit in 2020. This prospect had caused headaches in Western capitals intent on shunning the young prince. Fortuitously, however, the global suspension of travel due to the pandemic kept international leaders from visiting the Kingdom, allowing Saudi Arabia to dodge the embarrassment of poor attendance. The summit was held virtually and focused on the management of the pandemic and economic recovery – relatively safe topics for all concerned.

Ups and downs with the US

Of the many relationships MbS sought to transform and solidify, the one with the US was central. Relatively unknown in Washington when he emerged in 2015, he was seen by some as the moderniser that the Kingdom dearly needed to escape its social conservatism and reshape its economy. Others, notably in the intelligence community, preferred the then-crown prince Muhammad bin Nayef, who had proven a reliable counter-terrorism partner, even though many Saudis regarded him as unable and unwilling to transform the country.

Unlike some of his siblings, MbS had not studied in Western countries and had minimal contacts in the West. But his fascination with the US was on display when he embarked on a three-week tour in 2018, during which he visited Hollywood and Silicon Valley and met US economic, cultural and political elites. In contrast, his visits to China, India and Russia lasted a few days. Strategically, however, MbS had seen the US under Obama as an ungrateful and wobbly partner. Its hesitant support in Yemen, eager diplomacy with Iran, pivot to Asia and dithering in Syria suggested that heavy Saudi dependence on Washington was risky and that accelerating strategic diversification was necessary.

Trump's surprise victory in 2016 gave rise to optimism in Riyadh about a more pliant America. MbS's active courtship of Trump delivered a spectacular first visit to Riyadh in 2017 and apparent alignment on a host of regional issues. These hopes were dashed when it became clear that US policy would not necessarily reflect Trump's personal preferences, as it did not when the US opposed Saudi Arabia's isolation of Qatar and, strikingly, when it declined to retaliate for the 2019 Iranian drone attacks on major Saudi oil facilities.

Trump's victory gave rise to optimism

By late 2020, Saudi Arabia was failing to achieve important goals. Oil prices hovered below $45 a barrel, under the fiscal break-even point for the Kingdom. US 'maximum pressure' on Iran, a strategy the Kingdom strongly supported, did not deliver the crushing blow that the Trump administration had promised. The Saudi-led boycott of Qatar had failed to weaken the small emirate. The Houthi insurgency in Yemen was making military gains at Saudi Arabia's mounting political, military and reputational expense. The election of Biden, amid intensifying criticism of Riyadh in US media and across the political spectrum, seemed to guarantee tense relations. Biden had promised to revive diplomacy with Iran, treat the Kingdom as a pariah, pressure countries over their ties with Russia and China, and promote human rights.

Estrangement from the US imposed a practical cost on the Kingdom. The intensification of Houthi aerial attacks from Yemen and the 2019 Iranian strikes exposed Saudi physical vulnerabilities, putting civilians at risk and embarrassing the country's leadership. The only substantive US response was the supply of intelligence, surveillance and reconnaissance (ISR) and defence systems to Saudi Arabia. But they were limited in number, and US redeployment of assets out of the region heightened concerns in the Kingdom about US reliability.

MbS prudently changed tack, pursuing a less bellicose agenda that prioritised economic modernisation and regional de-escalation. Reconciliation with Qatar occurred during a summit in Saudi Arabia in early 2021, with political and economic normalisation ensuing briskly. Relations with Oman, which had been testy during Sultan Qaboos's rule, improved markedly when Sultan Haitham succeeded him. In April 2022, MbS also hosted Turkish President Recep Tayyip Erdoğan, who in recent years had emerged as a fierce rival. MbS saw Erdoğan as a threat because of his regional ambitions and his support for Islamist movements. Erdoğan also possessed probative intelligence about the Khashoggi assassination and initially allowed the case to be tried in Turkey, at considerable embarrassment to MbS. Erdoğan now endorsed the transfer of the Khashoggi murder trial to Saudi Arabia, and tensions between the two regional powers diminished.

In spring 2021, Riyadh began a dialogue with Tehran in Baghdad. Ostensibly intended to de-escalate the conflict in Yemen, this track was also meant to demonstrate to Washington that Riyadh was more flexible than portrayed. Saudi Arabia was eager to appear as the reasonable and pragmatic party, with an eye to reducing its involvement and exposure in a protracted conflict. Riyadh defined down its objectives in the country, worked with US and UN envoys to reach a ceasefire, and in 2022 forced its main Yemeni client, the ineffectual and controversial president Abd Rabbo Mansour Hadi, to resign. It was the Houthis, not Saudi Arabia, who opposed the renewal of the ceasefire in October.

These moves relieved pressure on the Kingdom but failed to sway the US. Biden maintained a tough line, refusing to talk to MbS and delegating the management of the relationship to cabinet-level advisers. The Russian invasion of Ukraine dramatically changed this dynamic. Saudi Arabia's reluctance to support Western diplomacy and to break the OPEC+ agreement enraged Western officials. As oil prices increased from $60 a barrel in April 2021 to $120 a barrel a year later, generating enormous revenues for the Kingdom after years of low income, Saudi Arabia refused to be the swing state, in contrast to its response to the oil-price spike in 2008. In spring 2022, Riyadh agreed only to small production increases in line with the OPEC+ agreement and its own spare capacity, which appeared to be more limited than expected. The resulting tensions in the oil market were politically useful in that they demonstrated the enduring pivotal role of Saudi Arabia and its value to its traditional partners. Riyadh relished the spectacle of Biden, French President Emmanuel Macron and Boris Johnson, then prime minister of the United Kingdom, courting him in the hope of greater production levels. All three, however, appeared resigned to the fact that MbS would not distance himself from Putin.

After months of diplomacy, Biden came to the realisation that US interests called for a detente with the Kingdom. He flew to Jeddah with low expectations. His visit was meant to reassure US partners in the Middle East that American military power would still underpin regional security. If the visit rehabilitated the Saudi leadership, it also served as a reminder that despite any aspirations towards autonomy from its major Western partner and any desire to diversify its foreign relations, Riyadh remained eager to secure US attention and protection. The October crisis illustrates that Riyadh is willing to prioritise its economic interests and influence over energy markets, in partnership with Russia, at the risk of momentarily upsetting Washington. In the short term, Saudi Arabia is probably right that security cooperation with the US will survive this disagreement.

*   *   *

MbS has been able to articulate a foreign policy that is more independent of the interests of Saudi Arabia's traditional partners and less constrained domestically. He has done so in a context of American retrenchment and contested geopolitics, and in the name of his modernisation project. But his recalibration has not been wholly successful. The constraints on Saudi policy have remained significant. His attempt to build closer relations with Israel, which Trump encouraged and which culminated in a secret meeting between MbS and Israel's then-prime minister Benjamin Netanyahu in NEOM in 2020, has been checked by King Salman bin Abdulaziz Al Saud's continued attachment to the Palestinian cause and by MbS's embarrassment over Netanyahu's revelation of the meeting. The price that Saudi leaders, including MbS, place on eventual recognition of Israel is considerably higher than the one calculated by the Emirati and Bahraini leaderships, who agreed to normalise relations in 2020 by way of the Abraham Accords. This applies to Syria as well: while Riyadh is not opposed to normalisation with the Assad regime, the price it expects in return is greater than what Bahrain and the UAE have agreed to. Burnt by its previous dealings with Assad, Saudi Arabia will want a demonstrable (if unlikely) reduction in Iranian–Syrian relations, especially as Damascus hosts groups that are vocally opposed to Riyadh, such as the Houthis. Barring that, Saudi Arabia will try to align its interests with those of Russia, seen as the most able to contain Iranian influence. And the close relationship MbS cultivated with the Abu Dhabi crown prince and now UAE president Sheikh Mohammed bin Zayed Al Nahyan has not evolved into the full-fledged alliance once envisioned. While the two countries share similar geopolitical perspectives and political mindsets, they remain economic competitors: the UAE is concerned that Saudi ambitions may jeopardise the UAE's own economic and political positions. Saudi ambitions may jeopardise the UAE's hard-earned leading positions in trade, finance, logistics, industry and tourism, as well as its remarkable autonomy in foreign and defence policy. Indeed, many across the Gulf continue to worry about Saudi hegemonic designs, especially if the US were to reduce its role.

It remains unclear whether Saudi Arabia's new orientation can blunt the Iranian challenge, which Saudi officials insist is the gravest the country faces. Most of the countries Riyadh is courting are unwilling or unable to act as security providers and are averse to taking sides. At its moment of extreme vulnerability after the Iranian and Houthi attacks on Saudi oil infrastructure, only the US and France sent defensive systems. This underscored Saudi reliance on its traditional Western partners. Fundamentally, Saudi Arabia's claim to leadership of the Arab and Islamic worlds is central to its global standing. While it ensures the attention and courtship of foreign powers, it also confers heavy responsibilities and obligations. Riyadh's once-privileged relationship with the US was another source of power. As the October crisis suggests, Riyadh is confident that it can maintain its security relationship with the United States even as it reorients its foreign policy, relying on its growing geo-economic influence to shape and benefit from what it sees as a new global order.

Notes

1   See Mark Mazzetti, Edward Wong and Adam Entous, 'U.S. Officials Had a Secret Oil Deal With the Saudis. Or So They Thought', *New York Times*, 25 October 2022, https://www.nytimes.com/2022/10/25/us/politics/us-saudi-oil-deal.html.

2   Quoted in Ben Hubbard, 'Saudi Arabia and U.S. Trade Accusations Over Oil Cuts', *New York Times*, 13 October 2022, https://www.nytimes.com/2022/10/13/world/middleeast/us-saudi-oil-production.html.

3   Chuck Schumer (@SenSchumer), tweet, 6 October 2022, https://twitter.com/SenSchumer/status/1578142595795939330.

4   Embassy of the Kingdom of Saudi Arabia, 'A Statement from the Ministry of Foreign Affairs Regarding the Statements Issued About the Kingdom Following the OPEC+ Decision', Washington DC, 12 October 2022, https://www.saudiembassy.net/statements/statement-ministry-foreign-affairs-regarding-statements-issued-about-kingdom-following.

5   Amine Mati and Sidra Rehman, 'Saudi Arabia to Grow at Fastest Pace in a Decade', International Monetary Fund, 17 August 2022, https://www.imf.org/en/News/Articles/2022/08/09/CF-Saudi-Arabia-to-grow-at-fastest-pace.

6   See 'Saudi Govt Hails OPEC+'s Pivotal Role in Achieving Balance, Stability in Oil Markets', *Asahrq Al-Awsat*, 11 October 2022, https://english.aawsat.com/home/article/3925451/saudi-govt-hails-opec%E2%80%99s-pivotal-role-achieving-balance-stability-oil-markets.

7   Economist Intelligence Unit, 'Strategic US–Saudi Alliance Under Pressure', 1 November 2022, https://www.eiu.com/n/strategic-us-saudi-alliance-under-pressure/.

8   Quoted in Graeme Wood, 'Absolute Power', *Atlantic*, April 2022, https://www.theatlantic.com/magazine/archive/2022/04/mohammed-bin-salman-saudi-arabia-palace-interview/622822/.

9   See Martin Chulov and Michael Safi, 'Jordan Scrambles to Affirm Its Custodianship of Al-Aqsa Mosque', *Guardian*, 26 November 2020, https://www.theguardian.com/world/2020/nov/26/jordan-scrambles-affirm-custodianship-al-aqsa-mosque.

10 Ministry of Foreign Affairs of the People's Republic of China, 'Xi Jinping Speaks with Saudi Arabia's Crown Prince Mohammed bin Salman on the Phone', 15 April 2022, https://www.fmprc.gov.cn/eng/zxxx_662805/202204/t20220416_10668788.html.

11 See IISS, 'The Defence Policy and Economics of the Middle East and North Africa', IISS Riyadh Defense Forum 2022, 5 March 2022, https://www.iiss.org/blogs/research-paper/2022/05/the-defence-policy-and-economics-of-the-middle-east-and-north-africa.

Copyright © 2022 The International Institute for Strategic Studies

Indo-Pacific Dilemmas: The Like-minded and the Non-aligned

James Crabtree

In October, the Biden administration finally released its National Security Strategy. President Joe Biden's team had initially aimed to place the Indo-Pacific – in particular, the challenge of managing China – at the strategy's heart. Russia's invasion of Ukraine had prompted an arduous rewrite, producing a compromise document that attempted to balance US commitments in the Indo-Pacific and Europe. Overall, the document established two global priorities: pushing back powers, like China and Russia, that 'layer authoritarian governance with a revisionist foreign policy'; and solving 'challenges that cross borders', from climate and terrorism to food insecurity, pandemics and inflation.[1]

The strategy outlines three ways to meet these challenges. The first two involve building up the US economy and investing in its military. The third focuses on the seemingly innocuous idea of partnership. The United States wants 'to build the strongest possible coalition of nations to enhance [its] collective influence' and places 'a premium on growing the connective tissue – on technology, trade and security – between [its] democratic allies and partners in the Indo-Pacific and Europe' because 'they are mutually reinforcing and the fates of the two regions are intertwined'.[2]

This partnership rubric reflects the reality that no nation alone can fix the kind of transnational challenges the Biden team identifies. But in the security domain, it also implicitly concedes an American limitation – namely, that the

James Crabtree is Executive Director of IISS–Asia.

Survival | vol. 64 no. 6 | December 2022–January 2023 | pp. 23–30   https://doi.org/10.1080/00396338.2022.2150423

US also cannot handle its authoritarian rivals without help. In Europe, the NATO Alliance remains key to its approach to Russia. But no comparable alliance exists in the Indo-Pacific. Instead, the US intends to manage China's rise by trying to forge a new balancing coalition of 'like-minded' partners – in particular, by pushing for closer US integration with Australia, India and Japan through the Quad – and by developing deeper ties with other nations that view themselves as broadly non-aligned in Southeast Asia, the Western Pacific, and South and Central Asia.[3] Closer ties to the US and its partners, Washington hopes, will stop such countries from drifting towards China. But to create these deeper relationships, the non-aligned group also needs reassurance that attempts by the like-minded partners to integrate capabilities and fashion a new regional balance of power will not tip the Indo-Pacific towards conflict.[4]

The American challenge

For the US and its partners, this creates a dilemma, given that these twin objectives of like-minded integration and regional reassurance are often in tension. It is not yet clear how Chinese President Xi Jinping will shape China's foreign policy during his third term. But on the evidence from his first two, China will keep pressing for revisions to the regional order. To counter this, the like-minded grouping – which also includes several European nations, Canada, New Zealand and South Korea – will continue to try to build a stronger balancing coalition. These steps are likely to alarm non-aligned partners like Indonesia, Malaysia and Vietnam, whose leaders are nervous about conflict between the US and China. Addressing this dilemma is now a core security challenge for the US and its regional partners.

Integration among like-minded allies and partners has accelerated rapidly under Biden. In a July 2021 speech to the IISS in Singapore entitled 'The Imperative of Partnership', US Secretary of Defense Lloyd J. Austin III outlined Washington's new theory of 'integrated deterrence'.[5] For decades, the US relied on a hub-and-spoke system of alliances enlisting nations such as Australia, Japan and South Korea. But Jake Sullivan, the US national security advisor, now envisions a 'latticework of alliances and partnerships' involving deeper, overlapping ties.[6] This includes 'mini-lateral' partnerships, of which the Quad is the most prominent example, anchoring the United States' regional strategy. AUKUS, a submarine and technology deal signed in September 2021 among Australia, the United Kingdom and the US, is another. Elsewhere, a host of new bilateral agreements are springing up. Australia and Japan established a security pact in October, following a defence deal earlier in the year.[7] Deeper bilateral security ties are developing between Australia and India, and between India and Japan. There are also thickening links between Asian and European nations, including a likely defence pact between Japan and the UK.[8]

Like-minded nations are also seeking deeper ties with more tentative Southeast Asian countries, however. In part, this trend reflects a more multipolar region. A larger number of Indo-Pacific nations are economically significant than was the case a generation ago. But it is the perceived geopolitical compulsion to blunt rising Chinese influence that amplifies Western nations' motivation to secure their cooperation and potential allegiance. As a result, smaller regional players can suddenly take on outsize significance, as when the Solomon Islands became a focal point of Sino-US competition this year.[9]

Regional calculations

Efforts to build deeper regional partnerships within the like-minded group are now contributing to intensified regional anxieties about Sino-US relations. In his address to the 2019 Shangri-La Dialogue, Singaporean Prime Minister Lee Hsien Loong noted that the region did not want to choose between the two superpowers, but rather required a new modus vivendi under which China recognised the United States' enduring regional role and the US acknowledged that China's increasing heft warranted greater Chinese influence in regional affairs. 'The bottom line', he argued, 'is that the US and China need to work together, and with other countries too, to bring the global system up to date, and to not upend the system.'[10] But a more recent speech took a darker and more fatalistic tone. 'We can expect more political contestation in the Asia-Pacific', Lee suggested in August. 'We must get real, and we must get ourselves prepared psychologically.'[11]

Threat perceptions rose further across the Indo-Pacific in the aftermath of Russia's invasion of Ukraine, with Japanese Prime Minister Kishida Fumio warning in his address to the IISS Shangri-La Dialogue that 'Ukraine today could be East Asia tomorrow'.[12] As a result, regional leaders have become more nervous about initiatives undertaken by the US and its partners that risk antagonising China. Consider US Speaker of the House Nancy Pelosi's visit to Taiwan in August 2022. Australian Foreign Minister Penny Wong described China's military response as 'disproportionate and destabilising'.[13] But Southeast Asian observers tended to blame the US, viewing the visit as provocative and unconducive to regional stability.[14] They saw China's response as predictable and to some degree understandable, illuminating the different yardsticks those in the region often use to judge China and the United States. This reaction partly underscores Southeast Asia's long-term strategy of hedging between major powers. But it also reveals a paradoxical approach to the sub-region's future security. Few Southeast Asian nations relish sustained Chinese hegemony. Many also feel threatened by Chinese behaviour – for instance, with respect to its claims in the South China Sea – and in private most welcome a balancing role for the US and its partners. In public, however, they are wary of supporting specific balancing measures and unwilling to criticise Chinese behaviour.

Put another way, non-aligned Asian nations tend to support the aim of a balanced region in the long term but are typically unwilling to support steps that might achieve that aim in the short term. Such caution is frustrating to the US and its partners, but it is also understandable. Any decision to support like-minded activities designed to contain China carries clear short-term risks of a rebuke and possibly punishment from Beijing.

More broadly, the prospect of military confrontation between the US and China is leading Indo-Pacific nations to look hard at their core security interests. Could a future Sino-US crisis produce naval confrontations in Indonesia's archipelagic sea lanes? What would happen to the approximately 200,000 overseas Filipino workers in Taiwan if China made a military move on it? Might Western powers find themselves so distracted by Taiwan that they would cease to support Vietnam's claims in the South China Sea? Set against these short-term risks, the long-term benefits of a balanced region are vague and uncertain. This discrepancy helps explain regional responses to developments like AUKUS, which Indonesia and Malaysia openly criticised as risking nuclear proliferation. Defence establishments in the Philippines and Singapore were more sympathetic, but neither publicly supported the move.

Reassuring regional partners

Australian Deputy Prime Minister and Defence Minister Richard Marles has prescribed 'reassuring statecraft' to help resolve the like-minded dilemma.[15] The required reassurance can come in various forms. Firstly, like-minded nations might suggest they are seeking to build genuine long-term economic and security partnerships rather than projecting ties with nations in Southeast Asia and other regions primarily through the prism of great-power competition. Secondly, they could emphasise a common vision for the region, as Wong recently did in describing an 'order framed by a strategic equilibrium where countries are not forced to choose but can make their own sovereign choices, including about their alignments and partnerships'.[16] Finally, the like-minded group can simply emphasise that measures to balance China will be undertaken responsibly, avoiding needless provocation and mindful of regional risks. Here Biden's meeting with Xi during the G20 summit in Indonesia in November 2022 is likely to prove constructive. Although the in-person bilateral contact did little to address the structural challenges facing Sino-US relations, it did at least strike a civil and pragmatic tone, and help reduce regional anxiety.

Another important dimension of reassurance is the West's, and especially the United States', ability to assuage Asian doubts about its staying power. On this score, regional responses to lower-profile European forays have been telling. France, Germany and the UK, as well as the European Union, have signalled plans for deeper diplomatic and military engagement in the region. Though broadly welcoming, regional powers worry that European nations might both antagonise China and further complicate an already intricate regional security picture, while also questioning the durability of any European commitment, which they suspect could fade for lack of attention, resources or political will.

As for America's stamina, Victor Cha has noted that Asian nations often feel competing and contradictory fears of entrapment and abandonment with respect to their relationship with the United States. That is, they dread not only being drawn into great-power conflict but also being forgotten if Washington eventually decides that the costs of deep regional engagement aren't worth the benefits and gradually withdraws from the region.[17] Such worries are not idle or unreasonable. It is plausible that the United States could get distracted from Asia, if not by events in Ukraine then by domestic political dysfunction. It is also far from a foregone conclusion that the current inchoate like-minded coalition can ultimately balance China's rising power.

Yet, as China continues to challenge elements of the existing order, like-minded countries remain likely to balance more energetically, in part to re-establish deterrence. Beijing will view this as escalatory, and other regional capitals may be tempted to echo that sentiment, as some did after China's condemnation of Pelosi's visit to Taiwan. Strategic reassurance therefore remains essential to avoid such a negative diplomatic spiral, and in turn to achieve long-term integration while sustaining regional support.

*   *   *

The dilemma between like-minded integration and non-aligned reassurance has already spurred debate about the purpose of the Quad. Originally styled the Quadrilateral Security Dialogue, the grouping at times appears to focus explicitly on coordinating security and acting as a counterweight to China. But its leaders also often characterise it as a provider of regional public goods, such as vaccines or maritime security, to reassure regional partners that the Quad is not the germ of the 'Indo-Pacific NATO' that China claims it to be.[18] In Southeast Asia, the Quad is already viewed with suspicion for undermining the Association of Southeast Asian Nations' traditional centrality with respect to regional security. At the same time, there is scepticism about whether the four nations are sufficiently united and cohesive to achieve a new regional balance vis-à-vis China.

Given these differing and often cross-cutting perceptions, like-minded nations will need to develop sophisticated approaches to managing their long-term regional partnerships. This means understanding how security initiatives like the Quad and AUKUS look from the region itself, and the risks they are perceived to create. It also means realising that visions of a future regional order in Canberra or Tokyo are unlikely to be warmly embraced in Hanoi or Jakarta. Regular engagement and presence are also part of the package; Wong has pledged to visit every nation in Southeast Asia and the Pacific. In addition, building trust and confidence over the long term is likely to require substantial material investment, as exemplified by Japan. No matter how deft national policies and like-minded coordination are, tension between integration and reassurance will inevitably endure.

Notes

1   White House, 'National Security Strategy', 12 October 2022, pp. 6, 8, https://www.whitehouse.gov/wp-content/uploads/2022/10/Biden-Harris-Administrations-National-Security-Strategy-10.2022.pdf.

2   *Ibid.*, p. 11.

3   See White House, 'Indo-Pacific Strategy of the United States', February 2022, https://www.whitehouse.gov/wp-content/uploads/2022/02/U.S.-Indo-Pacific-Strategy.pdf.

4   The Obama administration, albeit haltingly and controversially, considered providing what James Steinberg, deputy secretary of state during Barack Obama's first term, and Michael O'Hanlon called 'strategic reassurance' to China in order to encourage US–China cooperation. See Robert Kagan and Dan Blumenthal, 'China's Zero-sum Game', *Washington Post*, 10 November 2009, https://www.washingtonpost.com/wp-dyn/content/article/2009/11/09/AR2009110902793.html; Evan Osnos, 'Strategic Reassurance', *New Yorker*, 6 October 2009, https://www.newyorker.com/news/evan-osnos/strategic-reassurance; and James Steinberg and Michael E. O'Hanlon, *Strategic Reassurance and Resolve: U.S.–China Relations in the Twenty-first Century* (Princeton, NJ: Princeton University Press, 2015). Now, with US–China relations more fraught, strategic reassurance is instead needed to bolster those inclined to confront China.

5   US Department of Defense, 'Transcript: Secretary of Defense Lloyd J. Austin III Participates in Fullerton Lecture Series in Singapore', 27 July 2021, https://www.defense.gov/News/Transcripts/Transcript/Article/2711025/secretary-of-defense-lloyd-j-austin-iii-participates-in-fullerton-lecture-serie/. See also White House, 'National Security Strategy', p. 22.

6   Jake Sullivan, '2021 Lowy Lecture', Lowy Institute, 11 November 2021, https://www.lowyinstitute.org/publications/2021-lowy-lecture-jake-sullivan.

7   See Australian Government, Department of Foreign Affairs and Trade, 'Australia–Japan Joint Declaration on Security Cooperation', 22 October 2022, https://www.dfat.gov.

au/countries/japan/australia-japan-joint-declaration-security-cooperation.

8   See Kana Inagaki and Demetri Sevastopulo, 'Japan to Sign Military Pact With UK as Allies Eye China Threat', *Financial Times*, 5 November 2022, https://www.ft.com/content/6ea15304-551b-4161-af6c-38cccf56d40d.

9   See Euan Graham, 'Assessing the Solomon Islands' New Security Agreement With China', IISS Analysis, 5 May 2022, https://www.iiss.org/blogs/analysis/2022/05/china-solomon-islands.

10 Prime Minister's Office Singapore, 'PM Lee Hsien Loong at the IISS Shangri-La Dialogue 2019', 31 May 2019, https://www.pmo.gov.sg/Newsroom/PM-Lee-Hsien-Loong-at-the-IISS-Shangri-La-Dialogue-2019.

11 Prime Minister's Office Singapore, 'National Day Message 2022', 8 August 2022, https://www.pmo.gov.sg/Newsroom/National-Day-Message-2022.

12 '"Ukraine Today Could Be East Asia Tomorrow": Japan PM Warns', France 24, 10 June 2022, https://www.france24.com/en/live-news/20220610-ukraine-today-could-be-east-asia-tomorrow-japan-pm-warns.

13 See Penny Wong, 'Cross-strait Tensions', Minister for Foreign Affairs, Australia, 5 August 2022, https://www.foreignminister.gov.au/minister/penny-wong/media-release/cross-strait-tensions.

14 See Su-Lin Tan, 'Ex-diplomat Says There Are "More Intelligent Ways"

for the U.S. to Support Taiwan than to Visit', CNBC, 5 August 2022, https://www.cnbc.com/2022/08/06/speaker-pelosis-taiwan-visit-made-things-worse-ex-singapore-diplomat.html.

15 Richard Marles, 'Address: IISS 19th Shangri-La Dialogue, Singapore', Australian Government, Defence, 11 June 2022, https://www.minister.defence.gov.au/speeches/2022-06-11/address-iiss-19th-shangri-la-dialogue-singapore.

16 Penny Wong, 'Special Lecture to the International Institute for Strategic Studies – A Shared Future: Australia, ASEAN and Southeast Asia', Minister for Foreign Affairs, Australia, 6 July 2022, https://www.foreignminister.gov.au/minister/penny-wong/speech/special-lecture-international-institute-strategic-studies-shared-future-australia-asean-and-southeast-asia.

17 See Victor D. Cha, 'Abandonment, Entrapment, and Neoclassical Realism in Asia: The United States, Japan, and Korea', *International Studies Quarterly*, vol. 44, no. 2, June 2000, pp. 261–91.

18 See Ananth Krishnan, 'China's Foreign Minister Says U.S. Using Quad to Build "Indo-Pacific NATO"', *Hindu*, 13 October 2020, https://www.the-hindu.com/news/international/china-fm-calls-us-indo-pacific-strategy-a-huge-security-risk/article32844084.ece.

Copyright © 2022 The International Institute for Strategic Studies

America's Defence of Its Partners in the Middle East

Bilal Y. Saab

Under what conditions is the United States likely or unlikely to intervene militarily on behalf of a close partner with which it may have defence arrangements short of a formal alliance? This is an increasingly relevant question for the United States as it engages in strategic competition with China and Russia for regional partners, as well as for resources and broader influence.

In the United States' present strategy too, security partnerships are regarded as its 'most important strategic asset'.[1] Partners and allies are considered force multipliers that allow the United States to reduce its international security burdens, project power and safeguard its security, diplomatic and economic interests worldwide. Yet US resources and political bandwidth are finite, and Washington cannot be the guardian of all of them.

The main factors American presidents typically consider before committing military resources to protect a partner include perceived US national interests, US domestic politics, the nature of the attack itself, the military capabilities of the aggressor and the possibility of escalating or open-ended conflict with that aggressor. If the US stakes are perceived to be high, the American president is politically strong at home, the attack is devastating, the adversary is not armed with weapons of mass destruction or intercontinental ballistic missiles that can reach the US homeland, and the risk of an uncontrollable conflict with that aggressor is small, it is more likely that the United States would punish the aggressor to deter another

Bilal Y. Saab is Senior Fellow and Director of the Defense and Security Program at the Middle East Institute. He is the author of *Rebuilding Arab Defense: US Security Cooperation in the Middle East* (Lynne Rienner, 2022).

Survival | vol. 64 no. 6 | December 2022–January 2023 | pp. 31–39   https://doi.org/10.1080/00396338.2022.2150425

attack. More often than not, however, only some of these conditions arise. In that case, a president is compelled to contemplate trade-offs.

An additional factor, which has gained prominence in recent years in US strategic thinking, is the ability and willingness of the partner to conduct joint and combined operations with the United States and possibly others in a coalition. The availability of a capable partner so inclined would make an intervention less costly and burdensome to the US and thus increase its chances of success.

US national interests

Does defending a US partner against external aggression constitute a national interest? The short answer is that it depends. Typically, the national interest is defined in terms of the state's physical security, freedom and independence, the integrity of its institutions and the preservation of its values. But sometimes presidents perceive a military attack against a US partner as an assault on its national interest. Saddam Hussein's invasion and occupation of Kuwait in 1990 is a case in point. Six months later, the United States launched a major military campaign, its biggest since Vietnam, to restore the status quo ante. A little over a month after that, American soldiers liberated Kuwait and achieved a complete military victory, forever changing Iraq's future.

The only formal ally the United States had then or has now in the Middle East is Turkey, a NATO member. But Washington deployed 700,000 troops and went to war on behalf of a small, non-allied state because it perceived that the stakes of allowing Saddam to gobble up Kuwait and dominate the oil-rich Persian Gulf were too high. He would have been able to exert substantial control over the region's considerable energy resources, on which the US economy relied heavily at the time.

Contrast those circumstances with Iran's September 2019 attack against Saudi Arabia's oil facilities from its own territory using 25 drones and cruise missiles. Never in the troubled history of Saudi–Iranian relations had the Iranians assaulted the Saudis in such a direct, brazen and destructive fashion. Saudi Arabia remained an important regional partner. Yet the United States chose not to respond to Iran's belligerence, casting doubt on the viability of the 1980 Carter Doctrine, which proclaimed the United

States' intention to use its military resources to defend its interests in the Middle East if necessary.

In 2019 the United States was, and still is, much less dependent on Middle Eastern oil due to its own energy revolution and significant increases in production, which made it a net exporter in 2020 and 2021. But the US recognised that major supply disruptions from the region can still inflict pain on its economy; Iran's attack on Saudi Aramco represented the single-largest disruption of daily oil supply in history. Furthermore, the Trump administration had developed a close relationship with Saudi Crown Prince Muhammad bin Salman (MbS), Saudi Arabia's de facto leader. The United States diplomatically and militarily supported Saudi Arabia's war against the Houthis in Yemen and refrained from punishing the Kingdom for order-ing the assassination of the US-based Saudi journalist Jamal Khashoggi in Turkey in October 2018.[2] But Washington still opted not to intervene militar-ily in support of Riyadh or even entertain a limited punitive strike because it didn't consider vital national interests to be at risk.

US domestic politics

Presidents who can mobilise public opinion, manage relations with Capitol Hill, form large and diverse political coalitions, advance their political agendas with little resistance from the opposing party, govern effectively and generate high approval ratings can be described as politically strong. This quality generally gives the president as commander-in-chief greater flexibility in foreign policy, as well as the latitude to take risks in defend-ing US interests abroad, including deploying military resources to defend a partner under attack.

George H.W. Bush wasn't necessarily a strong president – he failed to win a second term – but he wasn't a weak one either. Presidential historian Stephen Knott has commented that 'Bush came into the presidency as one of the most qualified candidates to assume the office'.[3] He had extensive expe-rience in politics, knew how to work the bureaucracy and shrewdly made public-policy deals with a Congress controlled by Democratic opponents. In foreign policy, his preferred arena, Bush ably led the United States through a period of historic geopolitical transition out of the Cold War, in part by orchestrating an extraordinarily efficient and dominating military victory in the Gulf War with wide domestic and international support.

When Iran hit Saudi Arabia in 2019, Donald Trump had promised the American people that he would end the 'endless wars' in the Middle East. In theory, that meant he wasn't prepared to start a new one against Iran to prevent another attack or avenge the Saudis. But Trump was anything but predictable. Shortly after the attack, perhaps thinking of his closeness with MbS, he declared that the United States was 'locked and loaded' and 'waiting to hear' from the Saudis.[4] Notwithstanding the bluster, Trump held fire. This decision probably turned on his political position at home. His multiple legislative failures, his inability to engineer the federal government to implement many of his policies, his alienation of his national-security principals, domestic criticism of his acquiescence to Khashoggi's murder and his polarising style could have made it difficult for him to secure Congress's authorisation for, and even his own generals' full cooperation on, large-scale military action against Iran.[5]

The attack and the aggressor

The severity or lethality of an attack against a US partner can significantly influence US decision-making regarding intervention. The more severe or lethal the attack, the greater the chances that the United States would intervene militarily to punish the aggressor and restore US extended deterrence. When a US partner, especially a close and long-standing one, is viciously attacked, political pressure is likely to build from congressional supporters and sympathetic media to come to its defence. From a strategic standpoint, the United States' failure to mount a military response could lead the targeted partner to seriously question and possibly even terminate the security relationship. Other US regional partners might feel less confident about their security arrangements with the United States and seek to diversify their international defence ties. America's reputation as a dependable security partner, as well as the credibility of its extended deterrence, could be undermined.

Had Saddam not invaded and occupied Kuwait in 1990, in violation of a core international norm that the United States felt bound to protect, the US response might have been less forceful. Conversely, had Iranian Supreme Leader Ayatollah Sayyid Ali Khamenei instructed the Islamic Revolutionary Guard Corps to team up with Iran-aligned Iraqi militias to conduct a ground incursion into Saudi Arabia or bombed its royal palaces instead of just using stand-off weapons against oil facilities in 2019, Trump might have ordered airstrikes against Iran. Clearly, there is greater US tolerance for a one-off, limited strike against a partner than a full-on military invasion or a strategic attack that leads to decapitation or heavy civilian casualties.

The military capabilities of the state that attacks the US partner also matter a great deal in the politics of US intervention. If the aggressor possesses strategic military capabilities, such as weapons of mass destruction and ballistic missiles that can hit the US homeland and imperil forward-deployed US troops and assets, it's more likely that Washington will avoid getting entangled in a costly war with that aggressor. To take an obvious example, the United States has sought to avoid a direct military confrontation with Russia over Ukraine for fear of escalation that could result in the use of nuclear weapons and a world war.

If the attacker has weak retaliatory capabilities that can't significantly harm the United States at home or abroad, however, Washington would tend to have fewer qualms about intervening in defence of its partner. In 1990, the United States launched *Operation Desert Storm* against Iraq knowing that Saddam was a vastly inferior opponent. The Bush administration assessed that overwhelming US power would deter Iraq from using chemical weapons and that the costs of US intervention would therefore be tolerable – as in fact they were, at 219 US military fatalities.

Assessing Iran is more complicated. For now, it has neither nuclear weapons nor intercontinental ballistic missiles, and US military power vastly outstrips Iran's. However, as every American president since Jimmy Carter has implicitly understood, while it would be easy to start a conflict with the Islamic Republic, it could be very difficult to end it owing to Iran's acute enmity and implacable resolve. When the US militarily supported its anti-Iran allies in the Lebanese civil war in the early 1980s and Saddam's Iraq in the 1980–88 Iran–Iraq War, Iran mounted retaliation through asymmetric means, including catastrophic terrorist attacks in Beirut and the kidnapping and murder of American soldiers, diplomats and civilians, and by confronting the US Navy at sea. If Trump had ordered retaliation against Iran in 2019, it might well have fought back using ballistic missiles, armed drones, cyber warfare and international terrorism.

The partner

The military capabilities of the partner in question also matter. When Russia began military operations against Ukraine in February 2022, the United States was unsure about the Ukrainians' ability or will to fight. US officials suspected that they would fold and that the Russian military would perform competently and overrun Kyiv in a matter of weeks, if not days.[6] These assumptions were clearly wrong. Several months later, the Ukrainians, though having suffered heavy casualties, held the military edge in the war and were inflicting serious costs on their opponent. The Ukrainians' will to resist crucially determined America's, and more broadly the West's, decision to provide them with military assistance.

When the United States finds itself in a situation where it is contemplating intervention on the side of an attacked partner, it should want to know before firing a single shot whether that partner can and wants to fight. Ideally, the partner would not just provide access, basing and financial compensation to the United States, as Kuwait did in 1990–91, but actually contribute forces should a collective decision be made to conduct operations against the aggressor.

For Washington, accurately assessing a partner's military effectiveness can be hard, especially if it hasn't fought for a long time. Gauging its willingness to fight is even harder.

If Kuwait were attacked again today, would its self-defence capabilities be better than they were in 1990, when Saddam's military quickly crushed the country's armed forces? On paper, they are. Kuwaitis are generally competent with some high-end, US-purchased equipment. The Kuwaiti Air Force has relatively skilled pilots and modern equipment, and has recently doubled in size and capabilities due to new acquisitions. The Kuwaiti Navy is very small and in need of repair, better maintenance and recapitalisation. But its sailors are proficient. That navy has assumed command roles on five occasions in US Naval Forces Central Command's Combined Task Force 152 since 2010. The Kuwaitis have invested heavily in the Udairi Range Complex to provide premier training for their armed forces on ground manoeuvre and ground gunnery.

Neither the Kuwaitis nor the Americans, however, fully know the Kuwaiti military's strengths and weaknesses because it hasn't gone to battle for more than three decades and doesn't 'task-organise' its forces in ways designed to accomplish particular missions. Deficiencies in human capital, command structures and defence-resource management strongly hint that it may be less than reliable as a war-fighting partner. Like almost all other Arab partners of the United States, Kuwait does not invest sufficiently in what the US military calls 'Phase Zero' – that is, activities meant to favourably shape the combat environment through better training, readiness and management – instead relying almost exclusively on the US.[7]

Saudi Arabia is in a better position than Kuwait. Firstly, it has been at war for the past seven years against the Houthis in Yemen, so Washington knows what capabilities it has and doesn't have. Some are strong (air and missile defence), some are weak or mixed (naval and aerial operations), and some are poor (ground operations). Secondly, Saudi Arabia is 121 times larger than Kuwait, fielding one of the best-funded and -equipped armed forces in the world. Thirdly, since 2018, Saudi Arabia has been undergoing a process of defence transformation, learning from scratch how to generate effective and sustainable combat power, though that process is not without significant challenges and is far from complete.

*   *   *

No single factor relating to US intervention on an attacked partner's side is decisive. The potential harm to US national interests should be the primary basis for a US decision to use force abroad. But sometimes domestic politics dominates the president's calculus. In addition, some factors are interdependent. For example, if the attack against the partner is not devastating, or if the aggressor doesn't pose a formidable military challenge to the United States, a domestically weak president may feel more inclined to defend the partner because the chances of a failed US intervention, producing high political costs at home, would be smaller.

In a situation presenting a reasonable but not airtight case for US intervention, the partner's ability and willingness to fight effectively alongside the United States could tip the balance towards intervention. It would also have to be clear that the partner would be unlikely to be able to resist the aggressor without US help. At the same time, a partner's robust ability to defend itself is the ultimate prize of US security cooperation.[8] Nowhere is it more important than in the Middle East. As Washington prioritises the Indo-Pacific and Europe, US military forces will draw down in the Middle East and be less able to intervene there promptly. To maintain strong regional deterrence, therefore, it is critical that security arrangements between the United States and its Arab partners be reconfigured to ensure that they can confront regional threats, Iran's in particular, without *immediate* American assistance.

Many of America's partners are unable to enhance their defence structures and military preparedness on their own. They need US help and advice. As the United States' experiences in Afghanistan and Iraq have painfully shown, more US weapons, joint training and combined exercises alone will not turn America's partners into more competent coalition fighters. What partners need most is US assistance in creating a sustainable and effective joint force through sound investments in defence management and institutional capacity-building.[9]

Notes

[1] White House, 'National Security Strategy', October 2022, p. 11, https://www.whitehouse.gov/wp-content/uploads/2022/10/Biden-Harris-Administrations-National-Security-Strategy-10.2022.pdf. See also US Department of Defense, 'National Defense Strategy of the United States of America', October 2022, pp. 14–16, https://media.defense.gov/2022/Oct/27/2003103845/-1/-1/1/2022-NATIONAL-DEFENSE-STRATEGY-NPR-MDR.PDF.

[2] See, for example, Steven Simon, 'The Arabian Prince', *Survival*, vol. 61, no. 1, February–March 2019, pp. 75–84.

[3] Stephen Knott, 'George H.W. Bush: Impact and Legacy', Miller Center, University of Virginia, https://millercenter.org/president/bush/impact-and-legacy.

[4] Quoted in, for example, Eric Schmitt, Farnaz Fassihi and David D.

Kirkpatrick, 'Saudi Oil Attack Photos Implicate Iran, U.S. Says; Trump Hints at Military Action', *New York Times*, 15 September 2019, https://www.nytimes.com/2019/09/15/world/middleeast/iran-us-saudi-arabia-attack.html.

5   While Trump later ordered the targeted killing of Iranian General Qasem Soleimani, the operation did not require congressional authorisation, surprised several of Trump's senior advisers and was highly controversial.

6   See, for example, Joshua Yaffa, 'Arming Ukraine', *New Yorker*, 24 October 2022, https://www.newyorker.com/magazine/2022/10/24/inside-the-us-effort-to-arm-ukraine.

7   The exception may be the United Arab Emirates, which has raised its military game with purpose and determination. See David B. Roberts, 'Lifting the Protection Curse: The Rise of New Military Powers in the Middle East', *Survival*, vol. 63, no. 2, April–May 2021, pp. 139–54.

8   See Bilal Y. Saab, 'Enabling US Security Cooperation', *Survival*, vol. 63, no. 4, August–September 2021, pp. 89–99.

9   A downside risk for the United States is that more militarily capable Middle Eastern partners will perforce be harder for the US to restrain. But that may be the result in any event. See Roberts, 'Lifting the Protection Curse'.

Copyright © 2022 The International Institute for Strategic Studies

Noteworthy

Ukraine: trial and triumph

'We're already villains for the Western world. So let's scare them rather than be a laughing stock. Ukraine must be plunged into the Dark Ages. Bridges, dams, railways, power stations and other such infrastructure objects must be destroyed.'

Vladimir Soloviev, a prominent state-television commentator in Russia, calls for the destruction of Ukraine's infrastructure in early October 2022.[1]

'Go ahead with the pullout of troops and take all measures to ensure safe transfer of troops, weapons and equipment to the other bank of the Dnipro River.'

Russian Defence Minister Sergei Shoigu orders the withdrawal of Russian forces from the city of Kherson and surrounding areas in southern Ukraine on 9 November.[2]

'Vladimir Putin said Russia would be here for ever. In the end they left in five minutes and ran away like goats.'

Serhii Melnikov, a resident of Mylove village in the Kherson region of Ukraine, comments on the withdrawal of Russian soldiers from the area.[3]

'If there won't be any upcoming successes with major towns captured and no advancement during the winter offensive, the series of military setbacks would accumulate a much greater internal discontent than sanctions.'

Boris Rozhin, a Russian military analyst, comments on the Russian withdrawal.[4]

'It's evidence of the fact that they have some real problems, the Russian military.'

US President Joe Biden.[5]

A hijab too far

'They have to explain for what crime, for what reason did they do this?'

Mahsa Amini's mother demands an explanation for her daughter's death on 16 September 2022 after she was detained by morality police for an alleged violation of Iran's mandatory-hijab law.[6]

'Amini's death must lead to modification of the hijab law. And religious people like me should only trust in God and hope that women will choose the hijab themselves.'

An Iranian woman named Fatemeh, a self-described supporter of the Islamic Republic, tells the Financial Times *that she believes Iran's laws on female dress should be scrapped.[7]*

'Your daughter is like my own daughter, and I feel that this incident happened to one of my loved ones.'

Iranian President Ebrahim Raisi tells Amini's family on 18 September that he has ordered an investigation into her death.[8]

'On the night of 21 September alone, shootings by security forces left at least 19 people dead, including at least three children. Amnesty International has reviewed

Survival | vol. 64 no. 6 | December 2022–January 2023 | pp. 40–42   https://doi.org/10.1080/00396338.2022.2150426

photos and videos showing deceased victims with horrifying wounds in their heads, chests and stomachs.'

Amnesty International reports on the use of violent means by the Iranian authorities to stop protests that erupted in the wake of Amini's death.[9]

Strait poker

'Taiwan is China's Taiwan. Resolving the Taiwan question is a matter for the Chinese, a matter that must be resolved by the Chinese. We will continue to strive for peaceful reunification with the greatest sincerity and the utmost effort, but we will never promise to renounce the use of force, and we reserve the option of taking all measures necessary. This is directed solely at interference by outside forces and the few separatists seeking "Taiwan independence" and their separatist activities; it is by no means targeted at our Taiwan compatriots.

The wheels of history are rolling on toward China's reunification and the rejuvenation of the Chinese nation. Complete reunification of our country must be realized, and it can, without doubt, be realized!'

Chinese President Xi Jinping delivers his report to the 20th National Congress of the Communist Party of China on 16 October 2022.[10]

'Instead of sticking with the status quo that was established in a positive way, [Beijing has made] a fundamental decision that the status quo was no longer acceptable and that Beijing was determined to pursue reunification on a much faster timeline.

And if peaceful means didn't work, then it would employ coercive means – and possibly, if coercive means don't work, maybe forceful means – to achieve its objectives. And that is what is profoundly disrupting the status quo and creating tremendous tensions.'

US Secretary of State Antony Blinken speaks at Stanford University on 17 October.[11]

'I absolutely believe [there] need not be a new Cold War … I've met many times with Xi Jinping, and we were candid and clear with one another across the board. And I do not think there's any imminent attempt on the part of China to invade Taiwan.'

US President Joe Biden speaks at a press conference in Bali following a meeting with President Xi on 14 November.[12]

Lula's return

'On this historic October 30th, the majority of the Brazilian people made it clear that they want more democracy, not less. They want more social inclusion and opportunities for all, not less. They want there to be more respect and understanding among Brazilians, not less. In short, they want more freedom, equality, and fraternity in our country, not less.
[…]

Let's fight for zero deforestation of the Amazon. Brazil and the planet need a living Amazon … For this reason, we will resume monitoring and surveillance of the Amazon, and combat any and all illegal activity – whether it be mining, logging or illegal agriculture … We are not interested in a war for the environment, but we are ready to defend it from any threat.'

Luis Inácio Lula da Silva claims victory in Brazil's presidential election on 30 October 2022.[13]

'I am as upset and sad as you, but we have to keep our heads straight. It hurts everyone having these highways closed. I appeal to you: clear the roads, protest another way, in other places – that is very welcome, it's part of our democracy.'

Jair Bolsonaro, Lula da Silva's opponent in the election, asks his supporters to end road blockades set up in protest against his defeat.[14]

Old flame?

'Giorgia Meloni doesn't want to drop the symbol because it's the identity she can't escape from; it's her youth.'

Professor of Political Science Gianluca Passarelli offers an explanation for Italian Prime Minister Giorgia Meloni's acceptance of her Brothers of Italy party's use of the tricolour-flame logo, which is associated with Benito Mussolini, following the party's electoral success in September 2022.[15]

An insurgent president

'We have left no doubt – none – that Donald Trump led an effort to upend American democracy that directly resulted in the violence of January 6. He tried to take away the voice of the American people in choosing their president and replace the will of the voters with his will to remain in power. He is the one person at the center of the story of what happened on January 6. So we want to hear from him.'

Representative Bennie Thompson, chair of the congressional committee investigating the riot on Capitol Hill in Washington on 6 January 2021, comments on a unanimous vote on 13 October 2022 to subpoena former president Donald Trump.[16]

Sources

1 Max Seddon and Christopher Miller, 'Crimean Bridge Explosion Leaves Russian Supply Lines Exposed', *Financial Times*, 9 October 2022, https://www.ft.com/content/453d8aff-b8f2-42a3-919b-10a327475dfb.

2 Marc Santora et al., 'Russia Orders Retreat From Kherson, a Serious Reversal in the Ukraine War', *New York Times*, 9 November 2022, https://www.nytimes.com/2022/11/09/world/europe/ukraine-russia-kherson-retreat.html.

3 Luke Harding, "They Ran Away Like Goats": Villagers Celebrate Liberation in Kherson Region', *Guardian*, 12 November 2022, https://www.theguardian.com/world/2022/nov/12/they-ran-away-like-goats-villagers-celebrate-liberation-in-kherson-region.

4 Santora et al., 'Russia Orders Retreat From Kherson, a Serious Reversal in the Ukraine War'.

5 *Ibid.*

6 Farnaz Fassihi, 'In Iran, Woman's Death After Arrest by the Morality Police Triggers Outrage', *New York Times*, 16 September 2022, https://www.nytimes.com/2022/09/16/world/middleeast/iran-death-woman-protests.html.

7 Najmeh Bozorgmehr, 'Iran's Conservative Women Join Backlash Over Enforcement of Hijab Rule', *Financial Times*, 23 September 2022, https://www.ft.com/content/dd2bbbb2-c909-4fa2-a1bc-ab41c98d9e2f.

8 Cora Engelbrecht and Farnaz Fassihi, 'Protests Intensify in Iran Over Woman Who Died in Custody', *New York Times*, 21 September 2022, https://www.nytimes.com/2022/09/21/world/middleeast/iran-protests-mahsa-amini.html?searchResultPosition=7.

9 Amnesty International, 'Iran: World Must Take Meaningful Action Against Bloody Crackdown as Death Toll Rises', 23 September 2022, https://www.amnesty.org/en/latest/news/2022/09/iran-world-must-take-meaningful-action-against-bloody-crackdown-as-death-toll-rises/.

10 'Transcript: President Xi Jinping's Report to China's 2022 Party Congress', Nikkei Asia, 18 October 2022, https://asia.nikkei.com/Politics/China-s-party-congress/Transcript-President-Xi-Jinping-s-report-to-China-s-2022-party-congress.

11 US Department of State, 'A Conversation on the Evolution and Importance of Technology, Diplomacy, and National Security with 66th Secretary of State Condoleezza Rice', Stanford University, 17 October 2022, https://www.state.gov/secretary-antony-j-blinken-at-a-conversation-on-the-evolution-and-importance-of-technology-diplomacy-and-national-security-with-66th-secretary-of-state-condoleezza-rice/.

12 White House, 'Remarks by President Biden in a Press Conference', 14 November 2022, https://www.whitehouse.gov/briefing-room/speeches-remarks/2022/11/14/remarks-by-president-biden-in-a-press-conference-bali-indonesia/.

13 Progressive International, 'Brazil Has a Way Forward: Read Lula da Silva's Victory Speech', 31 October 2022, https://progressive.international/wire/2022-10-31-brazil-has-a-way-forward/en.

14 Michael Pooler, 'Jair Bolsonaro Urges Supporters to End Roadblock Protests', *Financial Times*, 3 November 2022, https://www.ft.com/content/67f523df-31ea-4a49-8893-297bf7094bfd.

15 Mark Lowen, 'Giorgia Meloni: Far-right Leader Poised to Run Italy', BBC, 26 September 2022, https://www.bbc.co.uk/news/world-europe-62659183.

16 David Smith, 'Capitol Attack Panel Votes to Subpoena Trump – "the Central Cause of January 6"', *Guardian*, 13 October 2022, https://www.theguardian.com/us-news/2022/oct/13/january-6-hearing-trump-state-of-mind-capitol-attack.

Copyright © 2022 The International Institute for Strategic Studies

The Maritime Logic of the Melian Dialogue: Deterrence in the Western Pacific

James J. Wirtz

About midway through Thucydides' account of the Peloponnesian War, the 'Melian Dialogue' tells the story of a thinly disguised ultimatum delivered by an Athenian naval expedition to the inhabitants of the island of Melos.[1] Students often encounter it as an illustration of the practice of realpolitik in the anarchy that can characterise international affairs. If one examines the story from a maritime perspective, however, it actually foreshadows a turn of events that might confront the US Navy during a maritime crisis in the Western Pacific, with implications for American foreign policy in general and for US naval strategists in particular as they contemplate deterrence strategies.

Resistance is futile

The Melian Dialogue revolves around the Athenian demand that the inhabitants of Melos abandon their alliance with Sparta and throw in their lot with Athens. This may sound routine, but there are dimensions of this message that are not apparent to the modern reader, notably that becoming part of the Athenian empire would entail jettisoning a 700-year tradition of Melian independence.[2] What the Athenians are suggesting is not participatory membership in a NATO-like organisation, but instead something closer to

James J. Wirtz is a Professor at the Naval Postgraduate School in Monterey, California. The opinions expressed here are those of the author and do not reflect the position of any government, government agency or commercial firm.

Survival | vol. 64 no. 6 | December 2022–January 2023 | pp. 43–56   https://doi.org/10.1080/00396338.2022.2143083

assimilation by the Borg from *Star Trek*.[3] It is no coincidence that the under-lying message behind the Athenian ultimatum – 'resistance is futile' – is also a favourite message of the Borg.

Because the Athenians are Greeks and not Borg, and because Thucydides is not simply recording a debate but is instead using the dialogue to illus-trate the fundamental points in contention, the discussion on Melos covers a range of philosophical, strategic and political issues.[4] Everything from the relationship between morality and power, to expectations of justice and fair play in world affairs, to the political perceptions of third parties, to compet-ing appeals to heaven are entertained by the Athenians, who make a sincere effort to help the Melians see their situation for what it is. The Athenians plead with the Melians not to base their decision on what *might* happen in the future or on the actions of an absent and unreliable Spartan ally, but instead to recognise their predicament and act constructively on the obser-vation that in an anarchic world, the strong do what they can and the weak suffer what they must.

The Melians do in fact recognise their weakness and make a counter offer: neutrality. They argue that because they cannot make any difference in the contest between Athens and Sparta, their insignificance makes their failure to take sides no more consequential to the struggle than their active participation in the war. Leave us alone on Melos, plead the islanders, and you won't have to worry about Spartans around here anymore. For that matter, you won't be hearing much from us either. In a reply that has been condemned as gratuitous, excessive and politically counterproductive ever since, the Athenians reject what appears to be a reasonable offer of neutral-ity on the grounds that leaving such a weak polity to its own devices would be interpreted by other members of the Athenian collective as a sign that the empire might in fact be slipping.[5] The Athenians note that it is the weak-ness of Melos itself that dictates its assimilation; it would be impossible to explain to friend and foe alike why little Melos was allowed to have its way.

The maritime logic of the Melian Dialogue
Even with much hindsight, the failure of the Athenians to take the deal, along with their rather myopic determination to turn every foreign

encounter into an opportunity to demonstrate ruthlessness, still appears extreme. For instance, prudent strategists generally shy away from launching unnecessary campaigns because things can go unexpectedly badly in war – the Athenians discovered this lesson when a token force left to besiege Melos was slaughtered by the islanders in an act that sealed the Melians' fate. Additionally, forces frittered away in revenge attacks are not available for more strategically important engagements.[6] Thucydides himself, however, is probably to blame for the incongruity of the failed deal. Originally, the dialogue might have been intended as the literal turning point in his unfinished *History of the Peloponnesian War* – Thucydides was using the dialogue to illustrate the logic that drove the Athenians to launch their disastrous invasion of Sicily.[7] Melos is where the fortunes of war began to turn against the Athenians, or at least it is the point in Thucydides' history where he brings to light the ideas and rules of thumb that led the Athenians to exceed the 'culminating point of victory', to use a term of modern origin to explain an ancient turn of events in Sicily. Nevertheless, a simpler maritime explanation can account for the course of events on Melos – that is, the strategic imperatives that drove the Athenian expedition to demand Melian submission.

When one considers the Melian Dialogue from a maritime perspective, a strategically significant justification emerges for the Athenian decision to deliver an ultimatum to the Melians. The *island* of Melos was important to the maritime strategy adopted by Athens in its war with Sparta. Much like Iceland's contribution to NATO during the Cold War (Iceland has no military), gaining access to Melos was strategically significant, not its potential contribution of combat power to the military balance. Melos offered two very important resources of value to Athens: its location and its protected port.

The Peloponnesian War is traditionally depicted as a conflict between Sparta, a land power, and Athens, a sea power. The Athenians repeatedly used their navy and what might today be called 'naval infantry' to raid Spartan territory, harass Spartan allies, interdict trade and attack Spartan units which found themselves isolated on their island garrisons. As John Nash notes, this aggressive expeditionary strategy had a profound effect on Sparta:

The Spartans split their forces and stationed them throughout the most threatened areas of the Peloponnese, and took the unusual step of raising a force of cavalry and archers to act as a mobile reserve. Thucydides describes the Spartans as on the defensive, fearing internal revolution, afraid of another disaster ... The cause of this anxiety and outright fear was constant, unimpeded Athenian raiding along the Peloponnesian seaboard. This scourge was made possible by a strong Athenian navy that could land a force of troops in hostile territory, protect them from enemy naval intervention, and bring them off again to safety or keep them supplied and protected so they could cause even greater damage.[8]

To undertake this maritime campaign against a land power, Athens needed bases among the relatively dense archipelago that populates the Aegean Sea. Indeed, as Figure 1 illustrates, Melos, located at the southernmost tip of the string of islands running south from Athens, was in an especially important location. Melos stood nearest to the intersection of the Aegean and Mediterranean seas and the Sea of Crete, allowing the Athenian navy operating from Melos to monitor this intersection among important sea lines of communication. Melos was not just an insignificant polity whose weakness made it a notable political symbol; it was an important base whose geographic importance greatly outweighed its political or military significance. From a maritime perspective, Melos could not be neutral, because neutrality would prevent Athens from using the island to prosecute its naval campaign against Sparta. Instead of focusing on this maritime explanation for their ultimatum, the Athenians chose to highlight the weakness of the Melians as an obvious reason for capitulation. Melian weakness probably offered a face-saving justification for the decision to capitulate to a demand that was in fact not as tactically, operationally and strategically unimportant as the Athenians seemed to suggest. Indeed, the fact that the Athenians downplayed the importance of Melos fits in with their overall objectives. There was no reason to encourage the Melians to hold out by drawing attention to the fact that their island was of great geopolitical significance, an outpost that Sparta might have to attempt to rescue from an approaching Athenian armada.

Figure 1. **Melos in relation to Athens and Sparta**

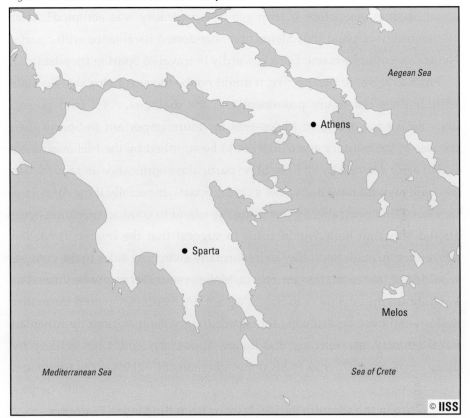

The fact that the seafaring Athenians rejected the Melian plea for neutrality is thus no more surprising than the fact that the idea of neutrality
appealed to the inhabitants of Melos. The Melians could do little to influence the great-power competition of their day and clearly wanted to avoid
becoming the site of a destructive battle between Athens and Sparta. Leave
us out of it, and we will stay out if it, was the offer Melos made to Athens.
Athens responded that, unfortunately, Melos could not be left to its own
devices. From a maritime perspective, a simple explanation thus exists for
the Athenian and Melian positions voiced in the dialogue. The Melians were
happy to opt out of the conflict and sit out the war on their island, while
the Athenians were interested in retaining access to Melos to facilitate their
maritime operations. What seems to be missing from Thucydides' narrative, however, is any indication of the Spartan attitude about the Melian

offer of neutrality. For that matter, why were the Melians unconcerned about Spartan vengeance if their offer of neutrality was accepted? After all, neutrality implied that Melos had abandoned its alliance with Sparta. Neutrality could be framed as a cowardly betrayal of Spartan friendship.

From a maritime perspective, it might not be too surprising that Sparta's attitude does not figure prominently in the dialogue. As a land power, denying Athens access to Melos was far more important to Sparta than the loss of the military assets that could be supplied by the Melians, assets which were deemed by all to be of no particular significance. In fact, Melian neutrality would have been a net gain for Sparta, especially if the Athenians honoured that neutrality by not using the island to conduct maritime operations. Although logic would seem to suggest that the loss of its Melian ally, either through neutrality or by formally switching sides in the contest, would have been a net loss for Sparta, Melian neutrality might be viewed as a significant improvement in Sparta's position. Neutrality would mean that Melos would not be available for expeditionary campaigning by Athenian naval infantry, an outcome that Sparta apparently could not achieve by using its own naval forces to keep the Athenians off Melos in the first place.

Deterrence in the Western Pacific: lessons from the Melian Dialogue

Much has changed since the delivery of the Athenian ultimatum on Melos, but navies still benefit from the availability of ports, air bases and maintenance facilities in relatively close proximity to operating areas.[9] Indeed, as Bernard Brodie noted during the Second World War, naval strategy is initially motivated by the need to secure the bases required to conduct operations against the land targets or the sea lines of communication important to the opponent.[10] Island bases not only serve as stepping stones that allow fleets to break up long voyages into operationally manageable segments, but bases located near the coastlines of potential opponents help naval forces deny access to sea lines of communication, conduct close blockades or influence the battle ashore.

This principle of maritime strategy is apparent in today's Indo-Pacific, where the greatest enemy encountered by the US Navy is distance. More than 11,000 kilometres of ocean separate the west coast of the United States from the Asian mainland, and ships must traverse this vast expanse before they can patrol around the First Island Chain comprising Japan, the Ryukyu Islands, Taiwan and the Philippine archipelago. From a historical and practical perspective, the United States has worked to extend its influence to this chain, if not to the shores of the Asian mainland itself, to achieve its primary strategic objectives in the Pacific.[11] Lose control of the First Island Chain, and control of the Second Island Chain (from the Kurils to the Marianas and including the US territory of Guam) becomes problematic. For instance, the US island-hopping campaign against the Japanese in the Second World War depended on the capture of bases on these islands that were critical for the movement of American forces across the Pacific. In the words of a recent RAND report, the Second Island Chain is 'tantamount to a power-projection superhighway running through the heart of the North Pacific into Asia, connecting U.S. military forces in Hawaii to those in theater, particularly to forward-operating positions on the U.S. territory of Guam'.[12] Because traffic on this 'superhighway' can flow in both directions, a prudent naval strategy would seek to defend the barrier, and the important allies and friends, that constitute the First Island Chain.

Allies become crucial in this distance game, especially those that are most exposed at the periphery of the US maritime presence in the Western Pacific. Allies can provide invaluable port facilities that can help reduce the length of logistical pipelines. They can also shape de facto force ratios by allowing elements of the US Fleet to be forward based closer to their intended operating areas, although care must be taken not to move major portions of the fleet within range of an opponent's opening salvo. Nevertheless, as Jakub Grygiel and A. Wess Mitchell note, 'Washington often seems to think of great-power rivalries as dyadic affairs, with the other states as dispensable accessories rather than as the strategic prizes'.[13] Allies are in fact the strategic enabler of the US naval presence in the Western Pacific and can contribute in such areas as anti-submarine warfare, ballistic-missile defence and even long-range land-based anti-ship missiles to deny opposing fleets freedom to manoeuvre.[14]

There is also reason to believe that the maritime logic inherent in the Melian Dialogue has not been lost upon today's strategists as they contemplate deterrence in the Western Pacific. Members of the 'offshore-control school', for example, have suggested a maritime strategy to deploy land-based anti-ship missiles or aircraft to interdict various choke points and channels surrounding the First Island Chain, cutting off Beijing from global commerce and essentially bottling up the Chinese fleet along the littorals of the Asian mainland.[15] Andrew Krepinevich has also suggested that the US Army should develop coastal artillery units, equipped with modern mobile launchers and anti-ship cruise missiles, and deploy them on the archipelago in the Western Pacific to hold People's Liberation Army targets at risk in the South China Sea.[16] The US Marine Corps is moving quickly to develop concepts and doctrine to enable operations in and along the First Island Chain. The marines' 'Stand-in Forces' concept describes an effort to deploy small, lethal and low-signature forces to win the reconnaissance battle in contested areas of the maritime domain, especially along the littorals of the First Island Chain.[17] The marines have also developed an Expeditionary Advanced Base Operations (EABO) concept in which small contingents of marines would be deployed at various positions along the First Island Chain to make offshore control a reality by using shore-based fires to hold surface and air targets at risk.[18] The marines are working hard to implement this concept – they are replacing 14 towed artillery howitzers with self-propelled rocket artillery and anti-ship missile batteries that are better suited to EABO.[19]

Missing from these emerging strategic concepts is the idea that airports and harbour facilities located on the First Island Chain are so strategically significant that Beijing might move at the outset of hostilities, or even during the lead-up to hostilities, to deny US forces access to the logistical infrastructure needed to conduct operations in the Western Pacific. One could imagine a *coup de main* intended to seize control of ports or airfields so that they could be used by the People's Liberation Army. US forces and allies would then have to devote resources to recapturing these facilities or else create alternative logistical nodes and supply lines. It is easy to imagine how the loss of critical facilities could upset planned operations and the flow of forces into the theatre. Given even less consideration is the possibility that denying access to these logistical facilities might be a political priority for

Beijing in the run-up to potential military action. It would not be surprising if the diplomatic and media message delivered to the inhabitants of the First Island Chain would be simple and straight to the point: stay out of it, and we will leave you out of it.

All of this suggests that the idea of 'neutrality' might again emerge during a crisis, when land powers attempt to interfere with the naval strategies of their maritime opponents. Beijing might suggest neutrality as a way for 'militarily insignificant' island nations to sidestep a brewing conflict by denying use of their air bases and ports to all comers. Indeed, those suggesting neutrality might even propose helping to defend that neutrality, offering to occupy or police facilities to prevent them from being used in military operations. Neutrality would be justified publicly as a gesture to reduce tensions and facilitate negotiations, complicating the political position of those championing the need for strong alliances to deter aggression. Nevertheless, much as the Athenians rejected Melian neutrality out of hand, maritime strategists would be hard-pressed to accept the emergence of a 'non-aligned movement' during a crisis because it would undermine the very basis of a maritime deterrence strategy in the Western Pacific. Because the incentives to restrict US access to forward-operating bases are so clear-cut, strategists need to anticipate the emergence of all sorts of ideas related to limiting the ability of US naval units to use port and air facilities in the Western Pacific. A newfound interest in neutrality during a crisis tops the list of these ideas.

The Melian Dialogue revisited

Scholars have searched *History of the Peloponnesian War* for insights into rising great-power competition in the Western Pacific. Graham Allison used the term 'Thucydides Trap' to describe the increased risk of war that is produced by a shifting balance of power.[20] Much like Spartan fears of a rising Athens prompted the Peloponnesian War, Allison suggests that the fear produced by a growth in Chinese power will eventually lead to conflict. James Holmes and Toshi Yoshihara also have drawn the link between Melos and Taiwan in the sense that both serve as a beacon of independence, and both constitute important island bases. Beijing, like Athens, sees island independence as a beacon of hope to politically repressed minorities else-where.[21] It is that political symbolism that drives China's policy towards Taiwan, according to Holmes and Yoshihara.

Nevertheless, there is a maritime logic that drives the Melian Dialogue, a logic that was given short shrift by Thucydides in the course of his effort to address loftier philosophical issues concerning the use of force in world politics. In a contest between a continental and a maritime power, the conti-nental power will be interested in denying island bases to its opponent, but almost by definition will lack the maritime capability to control the ports and airfields of concern. Under these circumstances, neutrality, a political solution to this military problem, will quickly come to mind as a win–win proposition. The island nation can avoid becoming embroiled in a war over issues of less than existential importance with forces that will do little to alter the war's outcome, thereby avoiding the deadly consequences of becoming a battleground in a great-power conflict. The continental power would benefit by denying forward-operating bases to a maritime oppo-nent, forcing it to relocate repair facilities and to reroute the logistical flows needed to backstop its deterrent threats. The fact that neutrality needs to apply to all those involved in the conflict works to the direct disadvantage of the maritime power, whose strategy requires forward bases. 'Opting out' of a crisis will be depicted as a step for peace despite the fact that it weakens the maritime power's deterrent threats, made to preserve the status quo. Allowing the United States to use island bases will be described by the con-tinental power as a step towards war, while denying access will be depicted as a vote for peace.

The Athenians never lied in their dialogue with the Melians, but they also never fully revealed the strategic logic that drove them to take action against an island that lacked military resources. In a sense, the Athenians used the language of a land power to explain the (in)significance of Melos – the island's lack of military capabilities made it barely a nuisance. Its loca-tion, however, gave the Melians an asset of the utmost strategic significance in maritime affairs.

One wonders how this dialogue might play out during a future crisis, and what action might be taken pre-emptively to preserve access to ports and airfields that are necessary to maritime operations in the Western Pacific. In any case, now is the time to address the maritime dimensions of the Melian Dialogue with America's allies in the Pacific. Without their commitment, deterrent threats will appear hollow and hampered by a politically vulnerable logistical infrastructure. Regardless of how the health of alliances are judged in Washington, opponents can come to see them as an Achilles heel that could be undermined in a crisis. Bolstering alliances in peacetime strengthens deterrence because it reduces opponents' hopes that political setbacks can be used to foreclose strategic options and undermine the military capabilities of maritime powers.

Acknowledgements

This research is supported by funding from the Naval Postgraduate School, Naval Research Program (PE 0605853N/2098). NRP Project ID: NPS-FY21-N177-8.

Notes

1   See Thucydides, *History of the Peloponnesian War* (New York: Penguin, 1972).

2   As Felix Martin Wassermann explains, 'Like tragic heroes [the Melians] have the choice only between evils: whether to sacrifice their physical existence by saying no to the Athenian proposal, or their moral existence by saying yes, and the only decision they can make without betraying their character, is the one which inescapably leads to [their] fate'. Felix Martin Wassermann, 'The Melian Dialogue', *Transactions and Proceedings of the American Philological Association*, vol. 78, 1947, p. 28.

3   The Borg collective appeared as a nemesis of Star Fleet in a 1989 episode of *Star Trek: The Next Generation*. The Borg 'is made up of millions of drones, hybrids of machine and organic creatures, limbs replaced with mechanical prostheses, and eyes enhanced by technology. Their individuality has been lost to the Collective, a hive mind which speaks as one voice through all members', writes Judith Clemens-Smucker in '*Star Trek: Voyager* – The Monstrousness of Humans in "Scorpion, Parts 1 & 2"', *Interdisciplinary Literary Studies*, vol. 23, no. 3, September 2021, p. 321.

4   As David Welch notes, Thucydides was not simply retelling history. He was 'directing his audience's attention to transhistorical truths'. David A. Welch, 'Why International Relations Theorists Should Stop Reading Thucydides', *Review of International Studies*, vol. 29, no. 3, July 2003, p. 303. On how the dialogues in *History of the Peloponnesian War* were constructed to do more than report events, see

Molly Wancewicz, 'Thucydides on Strength and Justice in the Melian and Mytilenian Debates', *Armstrong Undergraduate Journal of History*, vol. 9, no. 1, 2019, pp. 116–17, https://doi.org/10.20429/aujh.2019.090109.

5   Richard Ned Lebow and Robert Kelly offer the following observation about the Athenian position: 'Raw force can impose its will at any given moment, but few hegemons have the military and economic capability to repress their subjects indefinitely … Allies and subjects must believe that hegemony also benefits them.' Richard Ned Lebow and Robert Kelly, 'Thucydides and Hegemony: Athens and the United States', *Review of International Studies*, vol. 27, no. 4, 2001, p. 601.

6   In June 1944, the movement of the 2nd SS Panzer Division towards Normandy was slowed when it conducted repeated reprisals against French civilians along the way. See Max Hastings, *Das Reich: The March of the Second SS Panzer Division Through France* (New York: Henry Holt, 1982).

7   See Wassermann, 'The Melian Dialogue', p. 36.

8   John Nash, 'Sea Power in the Peloponnesian War', *Naval War College Review*, vol. 71, no. 1, Winter 2018, pp. 128–9.

9   Some of the material in this section is taken from James J. Wirtz, Jeffrey E. Kline and James A. Russell, 'A Maritime Conversation with America', *Orbis*, vol. 66, no. 2, Spring 2022, pp. 166–83.

10   See Bernard Brodie, *A Layman's Guide to Naval Strategy* (Princeton, NJ: Princeton University Press, 1943).

11   Michael Green provides a succinct description of these objectives: 'For over two centuries, the national interest of the United States has been identified by key leaders as ensuring that the Pacific Ocean remains a conduit for American ideas and goods to flow westward, and not for threats to flow eastward towards the homeland'. See Michael J. Green, *By More than Providence: Grand Strategy and American Power in the Asia Pacific Since 1783* (New York: Columbia University Press, 2017), p. 5.

12   Derek Grossman et al., *America's Pacific Island Allies: The Freely Associated States and Chinese Influence* (Santa Monica, CA: RAND, 2019), p. 1.

13   Jakub J. Grygiel and A. Wess Mitchell, *The Unquiet Frontier: Rising Rivals, Vulnerable Allies and the Crisis of American Power* (Princeton, NJ: Princeton University Press, 2016), p. 16.

14   See Donald Abenheim et al., 'American Sea Power in the Contemporary Security Environment', *Comparative Strategy*, vol. 37, no. 5, 2018, p. 400.

15   See T.X. Hammes, 'Offshore Control: A Proposed Strategy for an Unlikely Conflict', *Strategic Forum*, no. 278, June 2012, https://ndupress.ndu.edu/Portals/68/Documents/stratforum/SF-278.pdf.

16   Andrew F. Krepinevich, Jr, 'How to Deter China: The Case for the Archipelagic Defense', *Foreign Affairs*, vol. 94, no. 2, March/April 2015, pp. 78–86.

17   US Marine Corps, 'A Concept for Stand-in Forces', December 2021, https://www.hqmc.marines.mil/Portals/142/Users/183/35/4535/211201_A%20Concept%20for%20Stand-In%20

Forces.pdf?ver=MFOzu2hs_
IWHZlsOAkfZsQ%3D%3D.

18 US Marine Corps, 'Expeditionary
Advanced Base Operations (EABO)
Handbook: Considerations for Force
Development and Employment,
Version 1.1', 1 June 2018, https://mca-
marines.org/wp-content/uploads/
Expeditionary-Advanced-Base-
Operations-EABO-handbook-1.1.pdf.

19 US Marine Corps, 'Force Design
2030: Annual Update', April 2021,

https://www.marines.mil/Portals/1/
Docs/2021%20Force%20Design%20
Annual%20Update.pdf.

20 Graham Allison, 'The
Thucydides Trap', *Foreign
Policy*, 9 June 2017, https://
foreignpolicy.com/2017/06/09/
the-thucydides-trap/.

21 James R. Holmes and Toshi Yoshihara,
'Taiwan: Melos or Pylos?', *Naval War
College Review*, vol. 58, no. 3, Summer
2005, p. 5.

Copyright © 2022 The International Institute for Strategic Studies

The Economic Consequences of Xi Jinping

George Magnus

The footage from the 20th National Congress of the Chinese Communist Party (CCP) showing Hu Jintao, the party's ageing former general secretary, being unceremoniously removed from his chair next to Xi Jinping's and escorted out of the hall will survive as the abiding memory of the event. Whatever the circumstances may have been, no one mistook the messaging about Xi's dominant political status for the foreseeable future. Hu's removal from the meeting may not have conveyed something we did not already know, but the symbolism is important. Over the last decade, Xi has given China's politics and economy a new, ideologically Leninist direction, and added a nationalist bite to the country's international relations and foreign policy. These shifts are designed to propel China towards the party's ultimate goal, which is to triumph in the struggle against liberal capitalism and become the dominant world power by the middle of the century.

It is important to note that China's growing economic heft has been the platform on which the CCP has based its legitimacy at home and sought to project power abroad. The centralisation of power and Xi's political philosophy have come to dominate the party's rhetoric and narratives, and have had real and observable effects on policy. However, whereas most observers were once in thrall to China's economic resilience and dynamism, concern

George Magnus is a research associate at Oxford University's China Centre and at SOAS in London, and is the author of *Red Flags: Why Xi's China Is in Jeopardy* (Yale University Press, 2018). He is a former Chief Economist at UBS (1997–2016).

Survival | vol. 64 no. 6 | December 2022–January 2023 | pp. 57–76   https://doi.org/10.1080/00396338.2022.2150427

has begun to emerge about China's mounting economic travails, the country's increasingly hostile external environment, the bust in its real-estate sector and high levels of income inequality. The consequences of an apparently worsening and more unstable economic outlook are unlikely to be trivial. The coming decade, therefore, promises to be of considerable significance for China's economic prospects, and for those of Xi Jinping himself.

The 20th National Congress

The 20th National Congress was largely characterised by continuity and consolidation. Little of substance was aired that wasn't known or hadn't been said before. Still, the meeting served a purpose in formally clarifying themes, priorities and beliefs that have gathered pace in Xi's China over the last five to ten years. In some respects, it may even have gone further than expected. Xi broke a long-standing precedent at this quinquennial event by seeming to downplay the economy while giving new emphasis to national security and what he sees as China's external strategic challenges and opportunities. His opening address was peppered with references to 'national security', 'military' situations and preparedness, 'strategy' and 'struggle'. On the domestic front, while still portraying China as being under threat, he reminded the party of the importance of becoming self-reliant in science and technology, of protecting the security and resilience of China's supply chains, and of the need for the country to sanction-proof its economy.

A shift in emphasis towards more political strategies and goals was also evident in the decision to replace, over the next few months, the entire economic-, financial- and regulatory-policy elite, ostensibly for age-related reasons or because they have fallen out of favour. Replacements for outgoing officials will be chosen from among the new members appointed to the CCP Central Committee, and to China's top decision-making body, the Politburo Standing Committee, who were selected for their loyalty to Xi, rather than for their experience and technocratic expertise.

It is debatable whether these changes will make much difference, given that the outgoing officials were also obliged to toe the party line as established by Xi. However, it is possible that policymaking will become even more mechanical and unquestioning, and that poor decisions will be implemented more easily. The changes may well increase the likelihood of policy mistakes and poor judgement.

A slowing economy

China's economic slowdown has been widely acknowledged, but it would be a mistake to attribute this solely to 'zero-COVID' polices and short-term problems that are easily fixable. By the 2010s, the country's GDP growth had halved compared with the 2000s to around 5–6%, and it is now on track to halve again in the 2020s to about 2–3%.[1] This deceleration is, to some extent, only natural, since no country can keep growing at double-digit rates in perpetuity. More pedestrian growth, in and of itself, is not necessarily a bad outcome for an economy already measured officially – though probably not accurately – at about \$17 trillion.[2] Lower growth could be relatively benign and sustainable if China were to change tack and rebalance its economy towards consumption; income support and stronger provision of public goods and services; private enterprise and initiative; higher educational attainment; high-quality job creation and so on. Yet it could also turn out to be more troublesome and unstable if the country continues to focus on state-centric industrial policies, non-productive and debt-financed investment in infrastructure and real estate, and a heavily politicised regulatory and governance regime. It remains to be seen whether and how China's politicians will embrace the kind of political reforms required to move economic and commercial power to households and private firms. The supporting evidence is inauspicious.

The immediate problem for policymakers is that growth has faltered in 2022 in part because of the bust in China's property market and the consequences of Beijing's zero-COVID policies, which look set to continue into 2023. These are just two of an array of growth-sapping problems that have emerged from an economic-development model that has been exhibiting signs of stress and resource misallocation since the 2007–08 financial crisis. This model now needs a makeover.

China's economy has become overly dependent on debt, but the country's ability to absorb debt productively and service it has deteriorated sharply. Property is just the most obvious manifestation of a problem that runs through state enterprises and local governments too. Even Chinese households now have liabilities – principally mortgages – that are higher in relation to their income than in the United States.[3]

In addition, census data shows that China's working-age population started to decline in 2012, and that the country's total population may soon peak before entering a period of decline.[4] The speed at which the Chinese population is ageing is extraordinary, making China the fastest-ageing country on the planet.[5] China's demographic problems extend to important shortcomings in what economists call the 'stock of human capital' that go beyond a straightforward decline in the labour force. As explained later, measures of educational attainment of the Chinese workforce are relatively low, and the ratio of low-pay, low-skill jobs to higher-paying and higher-skill ones has been moving decisively in favour of the former.

A further problem, one that China has identified as significant yet has so far failed to tackle, is chronically and persistently high levels of income inequality. This applies both to disparities between income groups and to those between China's regions. Such inequalities are important because there is no country with Chinese levels of income inequality that has successfully become a rich, developed nation, and left unaddressed, such inequalities will weigh on China's economic performance and potential.

Some provinces, such as those in the northeast and west, are trapped in a sort of negative feedback loop in which the outward migration of labour and poor economic capacity are inextricably linked. Hardship and poverty still prevail in rural China, where half the population still lives, and are also present in urban areas. Xi's 2021 notable revival of the slogan 'Common Prosperity' is apparently intended as China's answer to the problem of inequality.

China's economic problems are being accentuated by changes in its governance system, which has become more statist and politicised. In the last two years, China has introduced a blizzard of regulations aimed principally at the private sector, including not just firms in the technology, internet, finance and data sectors, but also those engaged in private tutoring, logistics, the gig economy and so-called 'frivolous' activities, such as gaming and live-streaming. The regulatory clampdown joined other initiatives that seek to widen the role of party committees in all firms employing three or more party members; to encourage private firms and entrepreneurs to fulfil social and moral goals set by political leaders; and to bring about what the government calls the 'orderly expansion of capital' – in effect, the official approval of investment. The authorities have also brought in new laws affecting anti-trust, cyber security, data privacy and national security.

These developments have been unfolding in the midst of a parallel, unprecedented recalibration of industrial policy, in which the primacy of state enterprises is being strengthened in order to mobilise domestic investment, especially at the cutting edge of technology and science. This new industrial policy emphasises key sectors, such as semiconductors and artificial intelligence (AI), in which China aims to realise self-sufficiency. It also calls for self-reliance in all matters pertaining to national security, and for military–civil fusion, which requires that all civilian-based technology initiatives and developments be shared with military institutions.[6]

Decoupling and disengagement

Until recently, foreign firms in China had shown no inclination to reconsider their presence in the country. For decades, they displayed a willingness to accommodate the idiosyncrasies of the CCP, but this now appears to be changing. There is growing anxiety about China's governance system, and zero-COVID policies have unquestionably interfered with the conduct of business in China, not least by affecting transfers of personnel into and out of the country. Feistier geopolitical relations have also undermined businesses, forcing them to contend with 'entity lists' and blacklists that limit or prohibit trade with certain firms;[7] export controls; market-access restrictions; sanctions related to human rights in Xinjiang and Hong Kong; and secondary-sanctions risks in relation to Russia. Companies are increasingly having to make choices about whose rules to follow, and whose to flout.

While most foreign firms are reluctant to give up revenue streams and future earnings from China's market, a rising number are reported to have been affected by, or become involved in, decoupling, and are admitting to doubts about their future activities in China. The European Union Chamber of Commerce, for example, which represents more than 1,700 firms in China, has formally stated that China's government has allowed ideology to trump the economy, and pointed out that roughly a quarter of its members are looking at future investment outside China.[8] A recent survey by the American Chamber of Commerce in Shanghai stated that a record 52% of its members' parent companies had become less confident in China, while just over a third had already redirected investment to other countries.[9]

This disengagement from China represents a reversal of the globalisation that defined the period starting in the 1990s and lasting until the financial crisis in 2008. Decoupling will raise costs, complicate supply chains, and make business activities more complex and inefficient. These effects might be more apparent in China than in any other major economy because openness and integration were the handmaidens of China's 'inevitable rise' to prominence in the global economic system. To the extent that disengagement frays or severs China's global commercial bonds, the country's economic prospects will doubtless suffer.

Decoupling will make business more complex

As things stand, decoupling remains variable – not every supply chain, sector or product is affected. It is most apparent, however, in areas that impinge on national security, technology, data services, storage and transfer, aerospace, and applications in which the Chinese government has declared military–civil fusion to be a national goal. In such areas there are already different systems of data governance, extensive data-localisation requirements and barriers to the transfer of data. In technology systems, firewalls are being erected directly through market access, negative lists and national-security measures, and indirectly through the application of party- and state-determined standards and licensing requirements.

In the US, firms have to contend with a whole-of-government infrastructure of restraint directed not just at the Chinese state, but also at Chinese firms and individuals. Japan has been encouraging its own companies to move their operations back home, while other developed nations in Europe and Asia are taking a tougher view on Chinese trade, technology and investment. China, for its part, is just as keen to de-Americanise its supply chains as the US is to de-Sinify its own. Beijing is equally determined to 'sanction-proof' its economy and financial system in the wake of the sanctions regime imposed on Russia.

The most extraordinary form of decoupling, one with far-reaching consequences, came into effect in mid-October 2022, when the US Department
of Commerce imposed new regulations designed not merely to sanction one
or two firms, but, in effect, to decapitate much of China's more advanced
semiconductor industry. The new regime does not affect less sophisticated, consumer-sector chip applications, but does take a whole-of-industry
approach to the advanced integrated-circuit ecosystem to address what the
White House sees as a whole-of-government problem in China. The regulations target high-end applications and functions involving the supply
of inputs, tools, production and fabrication equipment, software, and the
activities of Americans working in or for Chinese enterprises in the sector.
In addition to provisions for export controls for about a dozen different
types of products and parts used in semiconductor production that were not
previously subject to such controls, there are new regulations that apply specifically to China, which other restraints did not, at least by name. US firms
can no longer supply Chinese firms with advanced chip-making equipment
unless they first obtain a licence. The new rules are also designed to prevent
the supply of designated semiconductor-production items and transactions
for specific end uses, such as supercomputers, AI, and semiconductor development and production. Moreover, US citizens and green-card holders are
banned from working on certain technologies for Chinese companies and
other entities, and from providing support and know-how to them.

The US government is clearly no longer willing to stand by while its
principal adversary and competitor uses state-centric acquisition and procurement policies to access sophisticated technologies, whether US-made
or foreign-made with US inputs. Washington is particularly concerned
about technologies that have so-called 'force-multiplier' properties, such as
machine learning and climate modelling, which have commercial uses but
which can also be used in advanced military applications or to suppress
human rights.

The Chinese government is expected to retaliate, and will certainly try to
circumvent US restrictions, for instance by exploiting any gaps that may be
created should American partners not formally sign up to the regulations.
Yet it seems very likely that China will find it much harder to achieve its

goal of global technology leadership given that the semiconductor industry is mostly dependent on the US and countries aligned with it, including Taiwan, for chip design, tools and fabrication. As things stand, China remains highly dependent on imported chips, which account for about 80% of local demand.[10]

China will doubtless redouble its efforts to realise self-reliance in this sphere, as in other key industrial and technology sectors. While it remains true that China regards global trade, finance, technology and exchanges of people as important, there are unmistakeable signs of disengagement. Not for the first time, China is, according to one observer, walling itself off, with the CCP separating its people from the influence of the outside world through the creation of physical, political and economic barriers.[11] The ultimate goal is to secure the unchallenged rule of the CCP.

Real-estate bust

Housing bubbles can be wonderful, for a time. They can make people feel wealthy, encourage the use of property as collateral for bigger loans, fuel consumption and generally lift economic spirits – until, that is, they go bust. The bursting of housing bubbles usually has worse effects than other kinds of bubbles given that homes are widely owned, leverage for households is usually higher than for other borrowers, and banks and leverage institutions are invariably heavily involved. The consequences stretch to wealth effects, unemployment, consumption and investment intentions in the real economy, as well as to illiquidity, opacity and network effects in the financial system.

Although there have been cyclical slowdowns in Chinese real estate in the past – usually coinciding with times of crisis, such as the Tiananmen crisis in 1989, the Asian crisis in the late 1990s and the financial crisis of 2008–09 – there has never been a bust, as such, since China's housing market was transformed in the 1990s from a housing welfare system into a proper market. The central government in Beijing, local governments, property developers, banks and households have never been on the hook for as much as they are now that the real-estate market appears finally to have keeled over.

The consequences are likely to be profound and last for some time. China's property market, estimated to be worth about \$55trn, has played a key role in sustaining economic growth and in driving global commodity prices.[12] According to the economist Ken Rogoff and co-author Yuanchen Yang, China's real-estate market – encompassing investment, housing services, and commodities and goods that go into building new homes – accounts for about 29% of GDP, a substantially higher proportion than in any other country.[13] Even if this measurement is somewhat high, the ballpark range of 22–25% still tells us a lot about how important the sector is.

China's housing market first began to sputter when Evergrande, the world's biggest property-company borrower, started to have difficulties in 2021. It wasn't alone, and the problems in the development sector resulted in double-digit declines in construction volumes and sales.[14] The contraction in activity, and especially in home prices, has been particularly severe in cities designated 'Tier 3' and 'Tier 4' in the widely used, if unofficial, ranking of metropolitan areas in China. These cities may be less well known than 'Tier 1' cities such as Beijing and Shanghai, but they account for 78% of China's housing stock, 66% of its urban population, 60% of GDP, and more than 80–90% of construction enterprises and new road construction.[15]

China's real-estate market is notable, moreover, for the way in which people typically buy homes according to a so-called 'pre-sale' model. Under this scheme, which accounted for about 90% of home sales in 2021,[16] developers sell uncompleted housing units to households that take out full mortgages, even though they may not take possession of the homes for months. Until recently this model worked for homeowners, and certainly for developers, which received payments on uncompleted properties with which to begin construction on yet more properties. However, this model requires continuously rising property prices, high levels of confidence among participants, and commercially sound banks and development companies. All of these were disrupted in the wake of the government's decision in 2020 to tighten housing-market restrictions and impose stronger balance-sheet constraints on developers. These changes in turn precipitated the failure of highly indebted and illiquid property-development firms.

In a rare act of civil disobedience, several hundred thousand homeowners began a mortgage boycott in July 2022, anxious they would never take delivery of their homes. It has been estimated that there are roughly 800,000 unfinished housing units in China.[17] It has also been reported that many homeowners have lost confidence in the real-estate market,[18] and that there has been a surge in the number of homeowners selling financial assets in order to pre-pay their mortgages.[19]

Faced with this crisis, the government has tried to protect the interests of the middle class, whose wealth may be eroded by falling property prices, job losses and even foreclosures. It has relaxed restrictions on home ownership, lowered down payments and offered new subsidies to both would-be purchasers and developers. The latter have also been offered additional liquidity and generous loan-rollover terms, while central and local governments have been trying to use asset sales (for example, of parking lots, mining rights, and even schools and hospitals), construction funds, state-owned enterprises and their own stretched budgets to shore up construction and the completion of new homes.

Whether these measures will work over time is debatable. It is clear that the debt-driven model for developers is now broken. China's demographics are unfavourable, with a declining population leading to lower rates of household formation and a fall in the cohort of 25–34-year-old first-time home purchasers.[20] More to the point, the problems in China's real-estate market are the outcome of decades of poor policymaking, in which the market was allowed, even encouraged, to over-expand and over-extend. These problems will not be easily corrected. A long period of readjustment seems likely, in which the role of property in the economy will shrink, the burden of liabilities will be reduced, and losses will be allocated among participants.

The government will probably seek to shield households from significant losses for political reasons, so it will fall to banks and local governments to pick up the tab. The CCP will be wary, however, of the contagion effects that could arise should banks report deposit flight and funding difficulties because of a loss of confidence. The authorities may be especially sensitive to this now that they seem to be more tolerant of defaults and losses among developers, companies and asset markets. Local governments, therefore, are liable to take the biggest hit, even though few are in a good position to do so. They are typically the agents that deliver economic growth and ensure that growth targets are met. They spend on infrastructure, housing and other projects to meet any shortfall, but generally without regard for commercial viability and need. They also account for the lion's share of industrial, social-welfare and housing expenditure, as well as, more recently, funding expensive mass-testing programmes related to zero-COVID policies. Yet they account for a relatively small share of revenues, and are reliant on land sales for about a third of their income. Land-sale revenues, of course, are now under pressure from the downturn in property and real-estate prices.[21] Local governments and borrowing agencies have debts that account for about 50% of GDP, and many are experiencing severe cash-flow and debt-servicing difficulties.[22]

The political problem for Beijing is that if financially stressed local governments are not able to raise new revenues from taxes and fees, they will either fall further into debt, or have to cut back on the provision of public goods and services at a politically inconvenient time. Ultimately, Beijing may have to bail out local governments by assuming what are, in effect, its contingent liabilities. Yet it will be reluctant to do so because this would add a charge to its own balance sheet, possibly hurting its own credit rating and impairing its own spending programmes, including defence.

Common Prosperity and income inequality

The 20th National Congress made clear that while security has elbowed aside economic growth in the party's order of priorities, the economy is by no means an afterthought. Xi made copious references to Common Prosperity at the meeting, a campaign slogan urging both the party and citizens to embrace efforts to reduce wealth and income disparities, and realise both material and spiritual prosperity. Less clear is how the party will transform Common Prosperity from a slogan into actual solutions.

In the early iterations of the campaign in 2021, the party emphasised its intention to introduce a nationwide property tax, a proposal that has surfaced more than once over the years, but which appears to have been jettisoned again. Common Prosperity has also been associated with the blizzard of regulations introduced in 2020–21, as well as with measures to 'encourage' firms to make what can only be described as coercive donations to party causes. Since then, the government has softened its rhetoric and lowered the intensity of its regulatory clampdown, not least because the valuations of targeted companies were crushed in the stock market. Yet a major switch in emphasis seems unlikely.

Indeed, the 20th National Congress appeared not to signal any change in thinking or direction that might address the faltering economy. At the Congress, Xi said:

> We need to improve the distribution system, adhere to the distribution of labour as the main body, the coexistence of a variety of distribution methods, adhere to 'work more and get paid more', encourage getting rich through hard work, promote fair opportunities, increase the income of low-income earners, expand the middle-income group, regulate the order of income distribution, regulate the wealth-accumulation mechanism.[23]

Much could be read into these words, but then again they may convey little more than the 'regulation' of income distribution and wealth accumulation. (This was certainly the message received by Chinese financial markets.) There was a worrying familiarity to Xi's words, in that such language has been used before but has rarely led anywhere specific. There were no hints of a mechanism of redistribution between richer and poorer people, or between richer and poorer regions. Redistribution is, in fact, the key to resolving the problem of inequality. Beijing would need to make a regressive tax system progressive; create a more inclusive and generous social-welfare system; and consider using the sale of state assets to influence income and wealth distribution, and to empower households and the private sector.

All this becomes clear when considering the scale of income inequality in China, which is not only high today, but has remained persistently high over time.[24] China's Gini coefficient – a measure of income inequality where 0 denotes perfect equality and 1 maximal inequality – has been assigned by the World Bank at 0.38 for 2019,[25] comparable to the US but higher than the United Kingdom, continental Europe and Japan.[26] Other estimates, however, suggest that this might be a significant underestimate. The China Family Panel Survey, for example, has assigned a Gini coefficient of 0.54–0.55.[27] This would make China one of the most unequal societies on earth. We can also glimpse the disparities between income groups by looking at the distribution between high and low earners. The top 20% of income earners, for example, receive about 46% of income, a figure that has remained virtually unchanged over the last decade or so, while the bottom 40% receive a bit over 13%.[28]

Tackling income inequality in China is, in important ways, more complicated than doing so in other countries. It may be relatively easy to change the tax code, but it is much harder to address inequality when the causes are systemic, as they are in China. This is because, firstly, Chinese consumption, and the income that drives it, accounts for a low share of the economy. Total final consumption, which includes the state sector, accounts for 55% of the national economy, a figure that is low compared with China's peer group as defined by income per head. It is also no higher than it was in 2004. Private consumption accounts for only 38% of the economy. The reason this level is so low is that the labour share of national income is low – only about 55%, compared with 70–80% in many developed economies.[29] Much of this discrepancy is attributable to social transfers to households, which are about 8–9% of GDP in China, but 15–20% in the US and EU.[30]

China's welfare system is fairly threadbare and still immature. The reasons for this are partly historical and partly related to cost. The break-up of older 'iron rice bowl' and 'cradle to grave' care systems, patterns of mass migration from the countryside to cities where most migrants still lack access to free public goods and services, and the one-child policy all contrived to leave China with a social-welfare vacuum and contractual arrangements between employers and employees that in many cases have not been properly enforced. Furthermore, the local governments, which administer welfare funds and benefits, are, as mentioned, financially hard-pressed and in a poor position to take on the responsibilities of more comprehensive welfare spending.

Of course, the central government doesn't want the responsibility either, though in the end, the obligations of local governments, from townships all the way up to provinces, are ultimately contingent liabilities of the state. Beijing may prefer to keep local governments on a leash and exercise control via the transfers it makes, but if the financial fragility of local governments persists, Beijing may eventually have to throw them a lifeline, even at a cost to its own balance sheet, credit rating and spending capacity, or via concessions to dispose of state assets. These options will entail the spending of political capital and, quite possibly, friction. Indeed, the struggle between China's central and local governments over the allocation of revenues and the distribution of expenditure responsibilities is likely to become increasingly important in the years ahead.

A second reason why tackling income equality will be difficult in China is that it isn't only a question of distribution between the state and private sectors, or between richer and poorer individuals. A more durable and fundamental approach is to equip more people to lead better lives, and in this regard China has also fallen behind. When it was still a poor country, it needed workers that were numerate, literate and disciplined. Now that it has a $17trn economy and an income per head in its more prosperous regions approaching that of, say, Portugal, it needs workers with much higher educational attainment who are endowed with the skills needed for a digital and information-driven lifestyle. Considering that Chinese workers are even now losing jobs to places like Bangladesh, Cambodia and Vietnam on costs grounds; to India and perhaps other places as technology firms diversify away from China; and to the country's own robotics and AI industries, it is clear that China will need to upgrade the skills and education its citizens receive so that they can work and compete effectively.

According to Scott Rozelle and Natalie Hell, one of China's main development problems is its low level of educational attainment. About 30% of workers had high-school qualifications or better in 2015, compared to 78% in developed nations, and only about 15% had tertiary qualifications, compared to 35% in wealthy countries.[31] Based on China's 2020 census, these numbers have improved somewhat to roughly 37% and 17% respectively.[32]

Government programmes seem to be having some effect in turning out younger Chinese who not only have better schooling than their parents, but are more digitally savvy too. This may be a generational phenomenon, rather than a quick fix, but it should make a difference over time provided that the requisite improvements are made to school and university curriculums, the teaching profession and the provision of suitable jobs.[33]

There is an urgency about all this because the labour market in China is already exhibiting trends that should worry policymakers. The number of skilled, higher-paying manufacturing and construction jobs is declining, while the number of informal, labour-intensive, lower-skill and lower-pay jobs has been rising. In 2020, for example, it is estimated that about 60% of Chinese workers in urban areas were employed in the informal sector, where low skills and pay prevail, compared with 40% in 2015.[34] In countries with comparable levels of development, such as Brazil and Chile, the share of informal-sector jobs tends to be appreciably lower, in the region of 35–40%.[35]

*　　*　　*

Until relatively recently, most people were fairly optimistic about China's economy, but a darker consensus has now emerged about the country's economic prospects and the ability of the CCP to manage them. China's long-running investment-intensive development model is no longer working, except to accentuate the misallocation of capital, rising debt and the risk of financial instability. Change is certainly needed, but it is not safe to assume that the government will shift its focus away from politics and ideology to new efforts to boost entrepreneurship, openness, rebalancing and productivity. China's economic growth, therefore, can be expected to slow. It remains to be seen what the consequences of this slowdown will be, both for the CCP at home, and in its relations with other countries.

Based on the government's behaviour and rhetoric over the last 12 months, it seems inclined to pursue a muddling-through strategy. Beijing still seems drawn to aspects of its faltering development model, but it has not launched any large-scale stimulus programmes to help the economy, nor does it want to bail out entities and individuals that might take on egregious risks, or to fund the capitalistic misadventures of banks, speculators, property developers or companies. Indeed, the authorities seem more willing than before to tolerate financial mishaps, defaults and losses. Anything else would not be compatible with Common Prosperity, or Xi Jinping's ideology.

Yet Xi's ideological imprint and personal power, bolstered by the wholesale replacement by loyalists of the party's technocratic elite, makes pedestrian economic growth and financial instability that much more likely. China's shifting political priorities, the country's mounting economic headwinds and the absence of a viable alternative development model, combined with a more politicised approach to business and regulation in which the government's role as backstop to private markets is withdrawn, are likely to trigger behavioural changes that undermine financial confidence. This may well disrupt China's ability to project economic power, build military capacity, develop its Belt and Road Initiative or carry out diplomacy under the Global Security Initiative.

As China struggles with severe distributional questions about who will pay for the property bust, the unwinding of debt or income inequality, and wrestles with how to build a new, politically acceptable development model, the consequences of the country's more troubled outlook will extend far beyond its borders. They will resonate for the many beneficiaries of China's economic upsurge, including commodity producers and those countries that have made China their top export destination, or relied on Chinese finance capital for infrastructure and other goods. Many of these countries have preferred not to take a side in the burgeoning geopolitical struggle between China and the liberal-capitalist economies, but they may soon find that diplomatic promiscuity is no longer an option.

Notes

1   See IMF, 'World Economic Outlook Database', October 2022, https://www.imf.org/en/Publications/WEO/weo-database/2022/October.

2   World Bank, 'GDP (Current US$) – China', https://data.worldbank.org/indicator/NY.GDP.MKTP.CD?locations=CN.

3   Nicholas Borst, 'How Strong Is China's Household Balance Sheet?', Seafarer, Prevailing Winds blog, March 2022, https://www.seafarerfunds.com/prevailing-winds/chinas-household-balance-sheet/.

4   Yvaine Ye, 'When Will China's Population Peak? It Depends Who You Ask', *Nature*, 25 August 2022.

5   George Magnus, 'China's Age-old Problem', 9 February 2019, https://georgemagnus.com/chinas-age-old-problem/.

6   See US Department of State, 'The Chinese Communist Party's Military–Civil Fusion Policy', https://2017-2021.state.gov/military-civil-fusion/index.html.

7   The US Department of Commerce Entity List, which names 'certain foreign persons – including businesses, research institutions, government and private organizations, individuals, and other types of legal persons – that are subject to specific license requirements for the export, reexport and/or transfer (in-country) of specified items', now has about 530 Chinese firms, four times as many as in 2018. See US Department of Commerce, Bureau of Industry and Security, 'Entity List', https://www.bis.doc.gov/index.php/policy-guidance/lists-of-parties-of-concern/entity-list.

8   European Union Chamber of Commerce in China, 'Business Confidence Survey 2022', 22 June 2002, pp. 10–11.

9   American Chamber of Commerce in Shanghai, 'AmCham Shanghai Releases 2022 China Business Report', 28 October 2022.

10   Nigel Inkster, Emily S. Weinstein and John Lee, 'Ask the Experts: Is China's Semiconductor Strategy Working?', LSE blog, 1 September 2022, https://blogs.lse.ac.uk/cff/2022/09/01/is-chinas-semiconductor-strategy-working/.

11   Bill Hayton, 'China Has Given Up on the West', UnHerd, 14 October 2022, https://unherd.com/2022/10/china-has-given-up-on-the-west/.

12   'Measuring the Universe's Most Important Sector', *The Economist*, 26 November 2021.

13   Kenneth S. Rogoff and Yuanchen Yang, 'Peak China Housing', National Bureau of Economic Research, Working Paper 27697, August 2020.

14   See Martin Farrer, 'A Ponzi Scheme by Any Other Name: The Bursting of China's Property Bubble', *Guardian*, 25 September 2022.

15   Kenneth S. Rogoff and Yuanchen Yang, 'A Tale of Tier 3 Cities', IMF, Working Paper No. 2022/196, 30 September 2022.

16   'Fresh Woe for China's Property Sector: Mortgage Boycotts', *The Economist*, 21 July 2022.

17   Alicia Garcia Herrero et al., 'What to Expect from the Bursting of China's Real Estate Bubble? Lessons from Japan', Natixis, 1 September 2022, https://research.natixis.com/Site/en/economics/publication/cTu7VEnNhm5kS_Wpqlmlpg%3D%3D.

18   Goldman Sachs, 'Why Some Homebuyers in China Are Boycotting Their Mortgage Payments', 15 August 2022, https://www.goldmansachs.com/insights/

pages/why-some-homebuyers-in-china-are-boycotting-their-mortgage-payments.html.

19 'Chinese Rush to Repay Mortgages Gains Momentum in Abrupt U-turn', Bloomberg, 14 September 2022, https://bloom.bg/3CokeBG.

20 Population data for China is available from the United Nations Department of Economic and Social Affairs at https://population.un.org/wpp/.

21 See Guo Yingzhe, 'China's Plunging Land Sales Threaten Local Government Coffers', Caixin Global, 5 July 2022, https://www.caixinglobal.com/2022-07-05/chinas-plunging-land-sales-threaten-local-government-coffers-101908587.html.

22 Massachusetts Institute of Technology Center for Finance and Policy, 'Policy Brief: China's Growing Local Government Debt Levels', January 2016, p. 4.

23 Iris Zhao, 'Fear Xi Jinping Flaunting "Collective Prosperity" in CCP Congress Speech, Signalling Further Winding Back of Economic Reforms', ABC News, 17 October 2022, https://www.abc.net.au/news/2022-10-18/xi-jinping-ccp-congress-speech-economy/101543966.

24 Sonali Jain-Chandra et al., 'Inequality in China: Trends, Drivers and Policy Remedies', IMF, 5 June 2018, https://www.imf.org/en/Publications/WP/Issues/2018/06/05/Inequality-in-China-Trends-Drivers-and-Policy-Remedies-45878.

25 'Income Inequality: Gini Coefficient, 2000 to 2019', Our World in Data, https://ourworldindata.org/grapher/economic-inequality-gini-index?tab=chart&time=2000..latest&country=CHN~USA~GBR~FRA~DEU~JPN.

26 Organisation for Economic Co-operation and Development, 'Income Inequality', 2022, https://data.oecd.org/inequality/income-inequality.htm.

27 Sho Komatsu and Aya Suzuki, 'The Impact of Different Levels of Income Inequality on Subjective Well-being in China: A Panel Data Analysis', Chinese Economy, July 2022, https://doi.org/10.1080/10971475.2022.2096809.

28 Ilaria Mazzocco, 'How Inequality Is Undermining China's Prosperity', Center for Strategic and International Studies, 26 May 2022, https://www.csis.org/features/how-inequality-undermining-chinas-prosperity.

29 Michael Pettis, 'Will China's Common Prosperity Upgrade Dual Circulation?', Carnegie Endowment for International Peace, 15 October 2021, https://carnegieendowment.org/chinafinancialmarkets/85571.

30 Organisation for Economic Co-operation and Development, 'Social Benefits to Households', https://data.oecd.org/socialexp/social-benefits-to-households.htm.

31 Scott Rozelle and Natalie Hell, Invisible China (Chicago, IL: University of Chicago Press, 2020), p. 5.

32 'China Is Improving Its Human Capital. Gradually', The Economist, 30 June 2022.

33 See Mazzocco, 'How Inequality Is Undermining China's Prosperity'.

34 Scott Rozelle and Matthew Boswell, 'Complicating China's Rise: Rural Underemployment', Washington Quarterly, vol. 44, no. 2, 2021,

https://doi.org/10.1080/01636
60X.2021.1932097.

35 Georgios Petropoulos and
Sybrand Brekelmans, 'Artificial
Intelligence's Great Impact on
Low and Middle-skilled Jobs',
Bruegal blog, 29 June 2020, https://
www.bruegel.org/blog-post/
artificial-intelligences-great-impact-
low-and-middle-skilled-jobs.

Copyright © 2022 The International Institute for Strategic Studies

Vietnam's Strategic Adjustments and US Policy

Bich Tran

Vietnam has become an important space for Sino-US competition. The country's location is strategic. It has access to major shipping routes in the South China Sea via its long coastline and shares a lengthy land border with China. Vietnam is China's biggest trading partner in Southeast Asia and provides sea access to several landlocked Chinese provinces. Since the pronouncement in 2012 of an American rebalance to Asia, Vietnam has become a focal point of American efforts to counter China's assertiveness in the South China Sea and the Mekong region.[1] Several high-ranking officials in the Biden administration, including Secretary of Defense Lloyd J. Austin III and Vice President Kamala Harris, have recently visited Hanoi to strengthen bilateral ties. US allies, including Australia, the United Kingdom and other European countries, are also seeking deeper ties.

Vietnam, however, remains haunted by the Vietnam War, during which it experienced first-hand the detrimental impact of Cold War great-power competition. In the 1950s, the US supported non-communist South Vietnam with military equipment, financial aid and military advisers. Active combat units started arriving in Vietnam in 1965, and by 1969 more than 500,000 US military personnel were deployed there. US forces used the full array of their conventional firepower to inflict catastrophic losses on communist

Bich Tran is a PhD candidate at the University of Antwerp, an adjunct fellow at the Center for Strategic and International Studies, and a former IISS Visiting Fellow.

Survival | vol. 64 no. 6 | December 2022–January 2023 | pp. 77–90   https://doi.org/10.1080/00396338.2022.2150428

North Vietnam, which was supported by the Soviet Union, until the war ended in 1975. In light of that experience, Hanoi is understandably reluctant to choose between Beijing and Washington.

At present, Vietnam is hedging between China and the United States, and it remains unlikely that it will become a robust partner of the US against China. But a more nuanced understanding of what Vietnam really cares about will allow the development of more mutually beneficial forms of diplomatic and security links between Hanoi and Washington.

A grand strategy

The concept of grand strategy tends to be reserved for great powers because only they have sufficient institutional and material resources to deliberately shape the course of history.[2] But whenever a state tries to align foreign-policy goals with finite national resources, it is developing a grand strategy.[3] Indeed, a small, relatively poor country may be more likely to develop such a blueprint to ensure its survival. Its focus may be regional rather than global, and its approach reactive rather than assertive, involving shifts in alliance commitments, foreign aid, military deployments and expenditures, and diplomatic initiatives. Although Vietnam has never claimed that it had a grand strategy, it has announced what it calls a 'foreign policy' to reconcile its external goals with the extent of its resources. In effect, therefore, it has sought to develop its own grand strategy.[4]

The Communist Party of Vietnam (CPV) dominates the country's foreign policy. Article 4 of Vietnam's 1992 constitution designates the CPV as the leading element of the state and society, dictating all aspects of its foreign affairs. The Politburo is the highest-ranking organ of the CPV and decides most of the important foreign-policy issues, though it may table certain issues with the Central Committee for discussion and voting to increase the legitimacy of its positions.[5]

From the Central Committee's political reports, it is clear that the main objectives of Vietnam's foreign affairs since the Doi Moi (renovation) policy that began in 1986 have been 'maintaining peace', 'constructing the nation' and 'defending the homeland'. In pursuit of these goals, Vietnam has maintained a foreign policy of 'independence, autonomy, openness, multilateralisation, and diversification of international relations' since the 8th National Congress of the Communist Party of Vietnam in 1996.[6] This constitutes Vietnam's grand strategy. It has been reiterated in every political report since then, but Vietnam has modified the implementation of the strategy three times.

Change in threat perceptions

Vietnam's first strategic adjustment, in 2003, was to soften communist ideology in determining the country's international friends and foes. For over a decade, Vietnam had considered China a de facto ally that would protect socialism, and the United States an arch-enemy that had led imperialist forces against communist regimes around the world. As the US invasion of Iraq unfolded, however, Vietnamese leaders assessed that a small state could not effectively challenge American power. At the same time, China was increasingly challenging Vietnam's maritime rights in the South China Sea. Accordingly, in 2003, the CPV issued Resolution No. 8 on 'Strategy to Protect the Homeland in the New Situation', which adopted the twin concepts of 'partners of cooperation' and 'objects of struggle'.[7] In effect, Vietnam was acknowledging that China was not a pure friend, and the US was not a mere enemy. While cooperating in some areas, in others Vietnam and China inevitably clashed. The strategic adjustment also opened the way for Vietnam to cooperate with the US in certain areas despite their differences.

Hanoi wished to continue strong cooperation with Beijing on the ideological and economic fronts. China in 1950 was the first country to recognise North Vietnam. After China's border war with Vietnam in 1979, triggered by Vietnam's Soviet-supported invasion of Cambodia to dislodge the genocidal Khmer Rouge regime, shared ideology was a critical catalyst for restoring normal relations in 1991. China and Vietnam are two of only five remaining communist regimes in the world (the others are Cuba, Laos and North Korea), and Vietnam has counted on China to uphold communist rule.[8] Furthermore, since China joined the World Trade Organization in 2001, it has become a globally important manufacturing powerhouse. Vietnam, like other Southeast Asian countries, sees enormous opportunities for doing business with the Chinese. As a result, China has been Vietnam's largest trading partner since 2004.

China's coercive maritime activities, however, threaten Vietnam's interests in the South China Sea, which is richly endowed with natural resources and encompasses major sea lanes. The two countries are involved in a bilateral territorial dispute over the Paracel Islands and a multilateral one over the Spratly Islands (the other claimants being Brunei, Malaysia, the Philippines and Taiwan). The Chinese government used force against Vietnam in disputed waters in 1974 and 1988, killing dozens of Vietnamese.[9] Since the mid-2000s, Beijing has become increasingly aggressive, claiming almost the entire area by way of its 'nine-dash line', intensifying its administration of disputed areas and interfering with other claimants' economic activities in their exclusive economic zones (EEZs). Furthermore, China has intruded in Vietnam's waters, converted rocks and reefs into artificial islands and militarised them. Another main challenge is Vietnam's heavy dependence on China for capital and intermediate goods, which puts Vietnam's entire production chain at risk. A major disruption in Chinese supplies would seriously damage the Vietnamese economy.

Vietnam's need to hedge against China has led to qualified cooperation with the United States, which has military capabilities superior to China's in addition to being one of Vietnam's leading trade partners.[10] After the Vietnam War, bilateral cooperation on war-legacy issues, such as recovering the remains of American soldiers, built a new foundation for the relationship and played an important role in the re-establishment of diplomatic relations.[11] Washington has repeatedly assured Hanoi that it respects Vietnam's political system. Vietnamese leaders suspect that US support for pro-democracy dissidents and endorsement of higher human-rights standards betray a preference for regime change.[12] Even so, while Vietnam places its strategic partnership with China at the highest level, Vietnam and the United States are expected to upgrade their relationship to a strategic partnership in 2023, when they celebrate the 10th anniversary of the current comprehensive partnership.

The main objective of Vietnamese–American partnerships is to advance shared interests and tackle mutual challenges rather than to counter a particular country or group. They are relatively loose, non-binding and multidimensional in nature. Accordingly, Vietnam can gain benefits, such as economic or security assistance, without undue risk of entrapment or loss of autonomy.

Diplomatic engagement with China has helped to ease tensions in the South China Sea. There has not been any major incident since 2020. Close party-to-party ties have proven essential in preserving cordial relations after incidents in disputed waters. In 2014, for example, China's deployment of an oil rig in Vietnam's EEZ sparked violent anti-China riots in some Vietnamese provinces, resulting in the deaths of several Chinese nationals. Hanoi sent Politburo member Le Hong Anh to Beijing as a special envoy to ease tensions and restore bilateral ties, with positive results.

Close trade and investment relations with China and the United States have played an essential role in Vietnam's economic development. Since 2009, Washington has also worked with Hanoi through the Lower Mekong Initiative, which was renamed the Mekong–U.S. Partnership in 2020, to promote sustainable economic growth, enhance connectivity and respond to transnational challenges in the region.

From a continental to a maritime nation

Effecting Hanoi's second strategic adjustment, the 10th National Congress in 2006 declared the aim of turning Vietnam into a robust regional marine economy. The plan involved building a system of seaports, maritime-transport capabilities, oil and gas exploitation and processing plants, marine-product processing factories and sea services.[13] Vietnam also started investing in military-modernisation programmes, prioritising the navy and air force in response to Beijing's increasingly assertive claims in the South China Sea. Vietnam's 2019 defence White Paper put a stamp on Vietnam's strategic shift by identifying it as a 'maritime nation'.[14] Vietnam's new orientation has also been evident in closer defence cooperation with maritime nations, notably India, Japan and the United States.

From 2006 to 2010, Vietnam doubled its defence spending despite the negative impact of the 2008 global financial crisis.[15] During this period, the country procured two coastal-defence systems, five surface-to-air missile systems, 200 surface-to-air missiles, 200 anti-ship missiles, 200 guided rockets, 200 guided bombs, 160 torpedoes, six patrol craft, six submarines and 20 fighter/ground-attack aircraft.[16] Notably, following China's submission of a *note verbale* to the United Nations incorporating a map with the nine-dash line in May 2009, Vietnam inked a $2 billion contract with Russia to acquire six *Kilo*-class submarines.

In 2007, India and Vietnam established a strategic partnership involving regular defence dialogue, training, exercises, navy and coastguard ship visits, capacity-building and think-tank exchanges. In September 2016, India and Vietnam agreed to upgrade their relationship to a comprehensive strategic partnership. Furthermore, India granted $600 million in defence credits to Vietnam to assist the latter in modernising its defence forces. With long experience in operating Russian *Kilo*-class submarines, India has trained hundreds of Vietnamese sailors in comprehensive underwater-combat operations.[17]

Hanoi established a strategic partnership with Tokyo in 2009, and in 2011 the two sides agreed a Memorandum on Bilateral Defense Cooperation and Exchanges. In 2014, they elevated their relationship to an 'extensive strategic partnership', their joint statement stressing the importance of freedom of navigation and overflight in the South China Sea and calling upon relevant parties to practise self-restraint.[18] As part of their cooperation on maritime security, Japan has provided Vietnam with seven used and six new patrol vessels, as well as maritime-safety equipment. In 2020, Hanoi agreed to buy six coastguard patrol boats worth $348.2m from Tokyo, to be delivered in 2025, under a loan from the Japan International Cooperation Agency.[19]

Amid rising tensions in the South China Sea, the United States has assisted Vietnam in improving its maritime law-enforcement capabilities by way of the US Cooperative Threat Reduction programme, Foreign Military Financing programme and the Maritime Security Initiative. During the fourth annual Defense Policy Dialogue in October 2013, Washington and Hanoi agreed on bilateral coastguard cooperation, paving the way for the US Coast Guard to provide formal training to the Vietnam Coast Guard. Between 2017 and 2019, the United States delivered 18 new Metal Shark patrol boats to Vietnam. The United States has also transferred two *Hamilton*-class cutters, the largest such American vessels until they were replaced by *Legend*-class cutters in 2008, to Vietnam in 2017 and 2020. Other

US security assistance includes *ScanEagle* uninhabited aerial vehicles and T-6 trainer aircraft.[20]

The shift to a maritime orientation has helped Vietnam better safeguard its economic and security interests in the South China Sea, as well as diversify its external relations so as to reduce its dependence on any power. The commissioning of six *Kilo*-class submarines, equipped with 3M14E *Klub*-S land-attack cruise missiles and 3M54E1/E *Klub*-S long-range anti-ship missiles, has boosted Vietnam's maritime-combat capability significantly, as the country had been operating only two ageing Korean *Yugo*-class submarines.[21] Although Hanoi's military capability is, of course, far behind that of Beijing, Vietnam's limited anti-access/area-denial capability could still complicate Chinese operations. In an armed confrontation with China, Vietnamese forces should now be able to respond quickly and impose costs on the Chinese. At the same time, diversified defence cooperation with Japan, India and others has helped Vietnam avoid overdependence on the United States.

Enhancing national status
By enhancing its status in the international community, Vietnam has aimed to develop greater independence and autonomy, and to attenuate the effects of great-power competition. Galvanised by its successful term as a non-permanent member of the UN Security Council (UNSC) from 2008 to 2009 and chairmanship of the Association of Southeast Asian Nations (ASEAN) in 2010, Vietnam explicitly announced the additional foreign-policy goal of raising its international status at the 11th National Congress in 2011.

On the economic front, Vietnam has concluded multiple free-trade agreements (FTAs) to reduce its dependence on any power – in particular, China. Of the 15 FTAs it has struck, two – the Comprehensive and Progressive Agreement for Trans-Pacific Partnership (CPTPP) and the European Union–Vietnam Free Trade Agreement (EVFTA) – are especially noteworthy in their breadth and ambition. While traditional FTAs emphasise tariff elimination, the CPTPP and EVFTA also include provisions on environment, labour, intellectual property, state-owned companies and sustainable development.

Hosting the Asia-Pacific Economic Cooperation (APEC) summit in 2017 – defining themes, setting priorities and harmonising cooperation agendas – enabled Vietnam to elevate its position in several ways. Firstly, it raised the country's international profile. During the APEC summit week, Chinese President Xi Jinping, US president Donald Trump, Chilean president Michelle Bachelet and Canadian Prime Minister Justin Trudeau paid official visits to Hanoi. Secondly, it demonstrated Vietnam's diplomatic skills. Lastly, Vietnam's preparations and convening power were impressive. The choice of the coastal city of Da Nang for the event showcased Vietnam as a beautiful, peaceful, dynamic and hospitable country.

In February 2019, Vietnam emerged as a peacebuilder, playing a mediation role in hosting the second round of nuclear talks between Trump and North Korean leader Kim Jong-un. Hanoi was selected as the summit venue because it is one of the few capitals to enjoy decent relations with both Pyongyang and Washington. Beyond that, Vietnam has been mooted as a model for an economically reformed and diplomatically normalised North Korea.[22] Although the summit did not bear fruit in terms of substantive arms control, Vietnamese leaders embraced the event as an opportunity to advertise their country on the world stage and reinforce the CPV's legitimacy.

In 2020, at the beginning of the global COVID-19 pandemic, Vietnam demonstrated proactive leadership as chair of ASEAN in coordinating the responses of member states and external partners. It held teleconferences for member states to share information about their situations and the implementation of control measures. Then it chaired two sessions of ASEAN foreign ministers to discuss ways to strengthen collaboration. Vietnam also organised the Special ASEAN Summit to help member states remain united and act decisively in response to the pandemic. A COVID-19 ASEAN Response Fund and regional reserves of medical supplies were created. Vietnam also used its tenure as ASEAN chair to advance the organisation's pandemic-response cooperation with other countries and organisations, including China, the European Union, Japan, South Korea and the United States.

Serving again as a non-permanent member of the UNSC for the 2020–21 term further enhanced Hanoi's prestige. Vietnam assumed the UNSC presidency in January 2020 and again in April 2021, thus enjoying the authority to influence the monthly programme and organise council events on topics of interest. During its term, Vietnam proposed two resolutions that were approved by the UNSC: one on protecting essential infrastructure in armed conflict – among the few resolutions supported by all 15 members – and a second on reappointing the prosecutor and reviewing the two-year operation of the International Residual Mechanism for Criminal Tribunals.

Notwithstanding these bright spots, the Vietnamese government's attitude toward Russia's invasion of Ukraine has damaged its reputation. In March 2022, Vietnam abstained from voting on two UN General Assembly resolutions, one condemning the invasion and another concerning the humanitarian consequences of Russia's aggression. In April, Vietnam voted against a resolution on suspending Russia from the UN Human Rights Council. In October, Vietnam abstained from condemning Russia's illegal annexation of four Ukrainian territories – Donetsk, Kherson, Luhansk and Zaporizhzhia. While it was perhaps understandable that Vietnam was loath to antagonise its largest arms supplier – more than 80% of Vietnam's military equipment has come from the Soviet Union or Russia – these decisions, broadly in line with China's, posed new problems for its relations with the West.

*   *   *

Over the last several decades, Vietnam has broken out of diplomatic isolation and economic stagnation to become an engaged member of the international community, one of the fastest-growing economies in the world and a favourable international-security partner. But Hanoi faces an interconnected set of economic, political and security challenges to more deftly manage its relations with China and the United States in an era of great-power competition increasingly centred on Asia.

By understanding Vietnam's grand strategy and strategic adjustments, the United States and other democratic countries could take steps to build closer ties with Vietnam and encourage greater convergence. Although Vietnam is unlikely to move dramatically closer to the West, its evolved elevation of national interest over ideology should permit deeper cooperation. Vietnam's new maritime orientation, for instance, suggests that the US and other democratic partners should prioritise areas like maritime law-enforcement capability, offshore energy and seaborne trade for cooperative initiatives. Given that Vietnam wants to keep burnishing its credentials as an international player, other actors could find limited opportunities to encourage it to improve its human-rights record, perhaps by emphasising the economic and reputational benefits of doing so and downplaying ideological differences that raise the spectre of regime change.

New areas of cooperation between the United States and Vietnam could include intelligence-sharing and arms acquisition. The two countries are reportedly in the final stage of negotiating a General Security of Military Information Agreement, which would set the legal framework for classified-information-sharing and facilitate Vietnam's acquisition of sophisticated US-made defence items.[23] This could also assist Vietnam in its efforts to diversify its arms suppliers away from Russia. Nevertheless, there are limits to US–Vietnam relations. Hanoi's 'four-no' policy of no military alliances, no siding with one country against another, no foreign military bases and no use of force or threat to use force will complicate American efforts to bolster security ties with Vietnam for the purpose of countering Chinese coercion in the South China Sea and the broader Asia-Pacific region.

A more searching and flexible approach to Vietnam, if successful, could provide lessons for the US and like-minded countries for better engagement with other less-than-democratic Southeast Asian nations that are reflexively sensitive to foreign interference and are currently sorting out their own responses to great-power competition.

The United States should downplay talk of 'democracy versus autocracy'. Despite being a key strategic partner of the US, Singapore was not invited to the United States' December 2021 Summit for Democracy, even though the invitees did include questionable choices such as Brazil and Pakistan. Accordingly, some Southeast Asians criticised the event as divisive and counterproductive.[24] The Biden administration might also change its primary terms of reference from defending against authoritarianism and promoting human rights to advancing security, prosperity and human development. Promoting human rights in multilateral settings could reduce suspicions in Southeast Asian capitals about Washington's intention to target any country in particular.

Given China's size, power and proximity, it will always be a significant factor in Southeast Asian countries' relations with the United States. Certainly, they are concerned about Beijing's ambitions in the South China Sea and the environmental costs of Chinese dams along the Mekong River.[25] But China is the region's biggest trading partner, its largest source of tourists and its second-largest investor.[26] This means that Southeast Asian states are loath to choose between the two great powers in the region and unwilling to join initiatives that are openly aimed at containing China. Fully appreciating this reality would enable the United States and like-minded countries to deal with Southeast Asian countries more effectively.

Acknowledgements

This research was made possible by an IISS Visiting Fellowship under the Southeast Asian Young Leaders' Programme (SEAYLP). The author would like to express her gratitude to Aaron Connelly, James Crabtree, Euan Graham, Tim Huxley, Lynn Kuok and others for their encouragement and support.

Notes

1   See White House, 'National Security Strategy of the United States of America', 18 December 2017, https://trumpwhitehouse.archives.gov/wp-content/uploads/2017/12/NSS-Final-12-18-2017-0905.pdf.

2   See, for instance, John Lewis Gaddis, *On Grand Strategy* (New York: Penguin, 2018).

3   See Colin Dueck, 'Ideas and Alternatives in American Grand Strategy, 2000–2004', *Review of International Studies*, vol. 30, no. 4, October 2004, pp. 511–35.

4   See Thierry Balzacq, Peter Dombrowski and Simon Reich, 'Introduction: Comparing Grand Strategies in the Modern World', in Thierry Balzacq, Peter Dombrowski and Simon Reich (eds), *Comparative Grand Strategy: A Framework and Cases* (Oxford: Oxford University Press, 2019), pp. 1–22.

5   See Le Hong Hiep, 'Introduction: The Making of Vietnam's Foreign Policy Under Doi Moi', in Le Hong Hiep and Anton Tsvetov (eds), *Vietnam's Foreign Policy Under Doi Moi* (Singapore: ISEAS–Yusof Ishak Institute, 2018), pp. 3–22.

6   Seventh Central Committee, 'Báo cáo Chính trị của Ban Chấp hành Trung ương Đảng khóa VII tại Đại hội đại biểu toàn quốc lần thứ VIII của Đảng' [Political report of the 7th Party Central Committee presented at the 8th National Party Congress], 1996, http://tulieuvankien.dangcongsan.vn/ban-chap-hanh-trung-uong-dang/dai-hoi-dang/lan-thu-viii/bao-cao-chinh-tri-cua-ban-chap-hanh-trung-uong-dang-khoa-vii-tai-dai-hoi-

dai-bieu-toan-quoc-lan-thu-viii-cua-dang-1549.

7   Carlyle Thayer, 'Vietnam's Strategy of "Cooperating and Struggling" with China Over Maritime Disputes in the South China Sea', *Journal of Asian Security and International Affairs*, vol. 3, no. 2, August 2016, p. 210.

8   See Do Thanh Hai, 'Vietnam: Riding the Chinese Tide', *Pacific Review*, vol. 31, no. 2, March 2018, pp. 205–20.

9   See 'Vietnam Marks 40th Anniversary of China's Invasion of Paracel Islands', *South China Morning Post*, 19 January 2014, http://www.scmp.com/news/asia/article/1409007/vietnam-marks-40th-anniversary-chinas-invasion-paracel-islands; and 'Protest in Vietnam Marks Anniversary of Clash with China at Spratly Islands', *South China Morning Post*, 15 March 2013, http://www.scmp.com/news/asia/article/1190804/protest-vietnam-marks-anniversary-clash-china-spratly-islands.

10 See, for example, Evelyn Goh, 'Meeting the China Challenge: The U.S. in Southeast Asian Regional Security Strategies', East–West Center, 2005; and Le Hong Hiep, 'Vietnam's Hedging Strategy Against China Since Normalization', *Contemporary Southeast Asia*, vol. 35, no. 3, December 2013, pp. 333–68.

11 See Murray Hiebert, Phuong Nguyen and Gregory Poling, 'A New Era in U.S.–Vietnam Relations: Deepening Ties Two Decades After Normalization', Center for Strategic and International Studies, June 2014, https://csis-website-prod.s3.amazonaws.com/s3fs-public/legacy_files/files/publication/140609_Hiebert_USVietnamRelations_Web.pdf.

12 See Nguyen Ngoc Hoi, 'A New Mask of "Peaceful Evolution"', *National Defence Journal*, 26 April 2017, http://tapchiqptd.vn/en/events-and-comments/a-new-mask-of-peaceful-evolution/10056.html. Apparent American statements of political tolerance include White House, 'Joint Statement by President Barack Obama of the United States of America and President Truong Tan Sang of the Socialist Republic of Vietnam', 25 July 2013, https://obamawhitehouse.archives.gov/the-press-office/2013/07/25/joint-statement-president-barack-obama-united-states-america-and-preside; and White House, 'Joint Statement for Enhancing the Comprehensive Partnership Between the United States of America and the Socialist Republic of Vietnam', 31 May 2017, https://trumpwhitehouse.archives.gov/briefings-statements/joint-statement-enhancing-comprehensive-partnership-united-states-america-socialist-republic-vietnam/.

13 See Ninth Central Committee, 'Báo cáo chính trị của Ban Chấp hành Trung ương Đảng khoá IX tại Đại hội đại biểu toàn quốc lần thứ X của Đảng' [Political report of the 9th Party Central Committee presented at the 10th National Party Congress], 2006, http://tulieuvankien.dangcongsan.vn/ban-chap-hanh-trung-uong-dang/dai-hoi-dang/lan-thu-x/bao-cao-chinh-tri-cua-ban-chap-hanh-trung-uong-dang-khoa-ix-tai-dai-hoi-dai-bieu-toan-quoc-lan-thu-x-cua-dang-1537.

14 Vietnamese Ministry of Defence, *Vietnam National Defence* (Hanoi: Phu

Thinh Printing and Services Limited Company, 2019), p. 31.

15 World Bank, 'Military Expenditure (Current USD) – Vietnam', https://data.worldbank.org/indicator/MS.MIL.XPND.CD?locations=VN.

16 Stockholm International Peace Research Institute, 'Arms Transfers Database', https://www.sipri.org/databases/armstransfers.

17 Indian Ministry of External Affairs, 'Joint Statement on the Occasion of the State Visit of the General Secretary of the Communist Party of Vietnam to India', 20 November 2013, https://mea.gov.in/bilateral-documents.htm?dtl/22510/joint+statement+on+the+occasion+of+the+state+visit+of+the+general+secretary+of+the+communist+party+of+vietnam+to+india.

18 See Ministry of Foreign Affairs of Japan, 'Japan–Viet Nam Joint Statement on the Establishment of the Extensive Strategic Partnership for Peace and Prosperity in Asia', 18 March 2014, https://www.mofa.go.jp/files/000031617.pdf.

19 See Khanh Vu, 'Vietnam Agrees $348 Million Japan Loan to Build Six Patrol Vessels: Media', Reuters, 28 July 2020, https://www.reuters.com/article/us-vietnam-japan-defence-idUSKCN24T1J5.

20 US Department of Defense, 'Indo-Pacific Strategy Report: Preparedness, Partnerships, and Promoting a Networked Region', 1 June 2019, https://media.defense.gov/2019/Jul/01/2002152311/-1/-1/1/DEPARTMENT-OF-DEFENSE-INDO-PACIFIC-STRATEGY-REPORT-2019.PDF.

21 See 'Asia', in International Institute for Strategic Studies, *The Military Balance 2022* (Abingdon: Routledge for the IISS, 2022), pp. 220–317.

22 See Le Hong Hiep, 'The Vietnam Model for North Korea', *Asia Times*, 27 February 2019, https://asiatimes.com/2019/02/the-vietnam-model-for-north-korea/.

23 See Jeffrey Ordaniel, 'The United States and Viet Nam: Charting the Next 25 Years in Bilateral Security Relations', Pacific Forum International, September 2021, https://pacforum.org/wp-content/uploads/2021/09/US-Vietnam-Issues-and-Insights-2021.pdf.

24 See, for example, Justin Ong, 'Singapore Left Out of Summit Because US Doesn't See It as a Democracy: Tommy Koh', *Straits Times*, 9 December 2021, https://www.straitstimes.com/singapore/politics/spore-left-out-of-democracy-summit-because-us-doesnt-see-it-as-one-tommy-koh.

25 See Murray Hiebert, *Under Beijing's Shadow: Southeast Asia's China Challenge* (Lanham, MD: Rowman & Littlefield, 2020), pp. 5–6.

26 See Sebastian Strangio, *In the Dragon's Shadow: Southeast Asia in the Chinese Century* (New Haven, CT: Yale University Press, 2020), pp. 23–4.

Copyright © 2022 The International Institute for Strategic Studies

Russia's War Against Ukraine: Military Scenarios and Outcomes

Michael Jonsson and Johan Norberg

Nine months into a campaign in Ukraine that Moscow assumed would be a cakewalk, the Russian Armed Forces are in dire straits. Following a summer of massive Russian artillery barrages and grinding attritional warfare, during which Ukrainian forces suffered major losses and slowly retreated, the momentum shifted. Ukrainian offensives began in early September, and Ukrainian forces routed Russian forces east of Kharkiv, Ukraine's second city, threatening Russian supply lines and imposing substantial losses of materiel and personnel.[1] Meanwhile, Ukrainian artillery strikes on logistics arteries gradually made the position of Russian troops in Kherson, west of the Dnipro River, untenable.[2] Exhausted and demoralised after taxing offensives, with individual units suffering devastating casualty rates and hobbled by dubious logistics as well as few if any rotations, they were forced to retreat in early November. Long-range artillery systems provided by Western governments to Ukraine have exacted a steady toll on Russian supply chains, ammunition dumps and artillery batteries. Against improved air defences and the radar-seeking missiles supplied to Ukraine, Russian air dominance – already uneven and of limited utility – also declined. Overall, Russian forces suffered some of their worst setbacks since the early stages of *Operation Barbarossa* in the

Michael Jonsson is head of the Defence Policy Studies programme at the Swedish Defence Research Agency. **Johan Norberg** is Deputy Research Director and analyst of Russian military affairs at the same agency. The authors are solely responsible for the content of this article, which does not necessarily reflect the views of the Swedish Defence Research Agency or the Swedish government.

Survival | vol. 64 no. 6 | December 2022–January 2023 | pp. 91–122   https://doi.org/10.1080/00396338.2022.2150429

Second World War.[3] This time, of course, US material support benefitted Ukraine rather than Russia.[4]

Faced with possible defeat, Russian President Vladimir Putin had escalated by announcing, on 21 September, a mobilisation of up to 300,000 Russian men and, nine days later, the pseudo-annexation of four Ukrainian regions – Luhansk, Donetsk, Kherson and Zaporizhzhia – following sham referendums.[5] Kyiv responded promptly by announcing its application for NATO membership. Given that both sides have upped the ante since Russia invaded Ukraine last February, a negotiated outcome still seems unlikely as long as Putin remains in power and either side retains hope of achieving battlefield advances, unless outside actors force Kyiv's hand.[6]

It is tempting to infer that Ukraine is on a firm trajectory towards outright victory over Russia despite its forces' numerical superiority. But it is too soon to be certain. Barring regime change or major collapse, the sheer scale and intensity of fighting, the large area involved (the Russian-occupied territories alone are still approximately equal to Belgium, the Netherlands and Switzerland combined), the vital interests in play and international involvement on both sides gravitate towards a more drawn-out and ambiguous conflict. The war has also repeatedly confounded analysts, with predictions made during any one phase quickly overtaken by events.[7] Accordingly, we explore three possible military outcomes over approximately the next year: an outright Ukrainian victory restoring its 1991 borders; Russian victory, including a puppet regime in Kyiv; or a drawn-out war of attrition. Throughout, we endeavour to resist the urge to extrapolate from a day-by-day analysis of the war, which risks myopia and wishful thinking, and instead review military operational functions to determine what conditions need to be fulfilled for each party to fulfil its maximal war aims. While dramatic events could intervene, our analysis suggests that the war could become more drawn-out than many hope or anticipate, and that both combatants are now preparing for this contingency.

Two other possible outcomes – Russia's escalation to nuclear use and NATO's direct involvement in combat – are unlikely but cannot be ruled out, even though the United States has done its utmost to preclude them. Nuclear use remains unlikely for several compelling reasons. In particular, it would have limited battlefield efficacy, risk affecting friendly troops and populations, squander what little international support Russia still retains, probably not break the Ukrainians' will to resist, and almost inevitably produce a devastating NATO response, even if it remains conventional.[8] If Russia nonetheless crosses the line, we would obviously be entering *terra incognita*. The fact that a course of action would be ill-advised, however, is no guarantee that Putin will not attempt it, particularly with his political future on the line. In that event, for NATO to yield to nuclear extortion would invite reprisals from Russia and possibly other rogue states, and risk spiralling proliferation, leaving NATO no realistic option but to respond forcefully.[9] Vertical and horizontal escalation remain conceivable, and the latter would not necessarily exclude the former, but both appear unlikely.

The war so far

As Russian troops crossed Ukrainian borders, their principal aim was to decapitate Ukraine, in the hope that capturing Kyiv, or at least forcing the government to flee, would quickly unravel the defence of the country.[10] The CIA and almost all Western analysts, ourselves included, expected Russia to capture Kyiv in a week or two.[11] Ironically, Russia's Federal Security Service (FSB), as well as the CIA, underestimated both the Ukrainian will to fight and the devastating impact that corruption had had on Russian combat power.[12]

The first phase of the conflict, from late February to mid-April, went disastrously for the Russian Armed Forces. Russian units attacked on multiple axes with little combat support or well-coordinated joint operations. Even elite Russian units suffered major casualties, largely due to inappropriate deployments of forces; in particular, there was insufficient infantry to protect advancing main battle tanks.[13] This phase could easily have ended differently. The Ukrainians' fierce resistance, against the odds, at times tipped the scales, as did their clever tactics.[14] Russian forces advanced in southern Ukraine, met stiff resistance along the previous line of contact in Luhansk and Donetsk, engaged in intense urban-combat operations in both Kharkiv and Mariupol, and, after initially establishing a bridgehead on the outskirts of Kyiv, were soundly routed.[15] Recognising its error, Russia withdrew its forces from northern Ukraine in late March, consolidating them in eastern and southern Ukraine. Having failed to take Kyiv, Russia still tripled the territory under its control compared to before the war, including a crucial land bridge to Crimea.[16]

During the second phase of the war, from late April to mid-August, Russian forces engaged in a withering war of attrition, relying on a reported ten-to-one advantage in indirect fires – primarily artillery – and waves of attacks to incrementally advance in Donbas.[17] Ukraine threw quickly mobilised units into intense battles, especially in urban centres, slowing down the rate of Russian advances and exacting high costs. But Ukrainian forces also suffered significant casualties, especially from Russian artillery barrages.[18] In the Black Sea, Ukraine used two long-range anti-ship missiles to sink the Russian cruiser *Moskva*, the flagship of the Russian Black Sea Fleet, in mid-April.[19] In the south, despite dogged Ukrainian resistance, Russian troops eventually took control of the Azovstal steel plant in Mariupol after two months of brutal siege warfare.[20]

In the skies over Ukraine, however, the Russian Aerospace Forces (VKS) did not establish air superiority, despite initially holding a clear quantitative and qualitative advantage.[21] Having failed to take out enough Ukrainian mobile surface-to-air-missile (SAM) systems early, and proving unable to provide effective close air support to Russian ground forces, the VKS largely resorted to operating at stand-off ranges, high altitudes or at night, which made their targeting weak and their overall performance underwhelming.[22] Both at sea and in the air, a form of mutual area denial developed, with SAMs and anti-ship missiles holding enemy platforms at risk and at bay. Both VKS and Ukrainian fighter aircraft have continued to operate, but cautiously and at great risk. The Russian Black Sea Fleet now stays well offshore or in port, and largely out of the fight, an expected amphibious assault on Odessa having never materialised.[23] By mid-August, the Russian offensive had slowly ground to a halt, and combat intensity had decreased.[24]

In the third phase, from late August to late September, the Armed Forces of Ukraine (AFU) began their long-awaited counter-offensive. Newly received Western artillery systems, such as the American High Mobility Artillery Rocket System (HIMARS) and M270s provided by the United Kingdom and

Germany, but also modern French, German, Polish and Slovak howitzers, struck high-value targets such as ammunition dumps, bridges and railways crucial to Russian logistics.[25] No single weapons system will decide the outcome of the war, even if several have auditioned for the role.[26] Rocket artillery with precision munitions has proven very useful, however, and Russia has been unable to counter it effectively.[27] In August, the US also acknowledged providing high-speed, anti-radiation missiles (HARM) that were quickly integrated into legacy Ukrainian fighter aircraft. Taking out, or holding at risk, Russia's already vulnerable SAMs further eroded the VKS's tenuous effectiveness, and facilitated Ukrainian ground operations.[28]

Furthermore, precision strikes reduced the potential for Russian forces to advance and set the scene for Ukrainian manoeuvre warfare. Having telegraphed a Kherson offensive for months, Ukraine instead launched operations in both the southern and the eastern directions. While the AFU met strong resistance in the south, they overran Russian lines around Kharkiv, defended primarily by lightly equipped Rosgvardia (national guard) and pro-Russian

No single weapons system will decide the war

separatist units.[29] Circumventing minor pockets of resistance, the AFU quickly took Izium, imposing withering losses on Russian troops who were shambolically retreating to escape envelopment. The liberation of the city of Lyman in Kharkiv oblast the day after Putin declared annexations clearly humiliated the Kremlin and rattled the Russian elite.[30] Meanwhile, some of Russia's best remaining units were still in southern Ukraine, west of the Dnipro River, where their positions were increasingly precarious. But while military commanders recommended retreat, Putin declined, presumably determined not to lose more annexed territory.[31] Simultaneously, Russian troops kept up a high-cost, low-benefit offensive against a small city in Donetsk, led by the Wagner Group, an infamous Russian private military corporation.[32] Its owner, Yevgeny Prigozhin, was apparently jockeying for increased prominence in Ukraine, and perhaps also in Russia itself.[33] The Ukrainian advances demonstrated the AFU's capacity for offensive operations, and more broadly the feasibility of a Ukrainian victory and the indispensability of further Western material support. A chorus of Western voices arguing that Kyiv should negotiate quieted, at least temporarily.

The fourth stage of the war began on 21 September, as Putin announced the mobilisation of up to 300,000 men, some of whom were unceremoniously sent to the front with little training and poor equipment. What difference these troops can make militarily, beyond pushing up casualty and defection counts, is an open question.[34] But in general, mobilisation, which the Kremlin had long postponed, was necessary, as Russian forces had already absorbed losses that would have broken most European armies.[35] The precise number of casualties is practically impossible to verify, but even conservative estimates suggest that more than half of the soldiers comprising the original invading force had, by early November, been killed or seriously wounded.[36] Ukrainian commander-in-chief General Valerii Zaluzhny's claim that Ukrainian forces had 'destroyed the professional Russian army; it is time to end the amateur one' is illustrative, if somewhat hyperbolic.[37] Photographic evidence indicates that Russia as of early November had lost at least 1,400 main battle tanks and the equivalent of more than 40 battalion tactical groups, more than could be fielded by France, Germany, Italy, Spain and the UK combined.[38] But while dented and demoralised, Russian forces in Ukraine are not defeated.[39]

During the first month of mobilisation, Russia pushed the newly mobilised soldiers to replenish depleted units.[40] According to the Kremlin, mobilisation was concluded by the end of October, with some 82,000 troops having been deployed to the front, half of them in combat units. The remaining 218,000 troops were supposedly in training.[41] While analysts pointed out the callous use of Russian troops as cannon fodder and their dubious prospects for success, Russia appeared to have few other military options.[42] For now, Russia need not win, but simply needs to avoid losing by making Ukrainian advances slower and costlier.[43] Russian losses were unusually high in October, but some reports also indicated that Russian lines had grown denser.[44] At the same time, there is abundant anecdotal evidence of Russian contract as well as mobilised soldiers being demoralised, so the swift deployment of poorly prepared troops to the front will probably push up defection rates.[45] The scale and trajectory of the phenomenon is difficult to gauge with precision, however. As Ukraine encouraged Russian soldiers to defect, Russia implemented increasingly brutal methods to dissuade them.[46]

A key unknown in any assessment of the balance of forces is Ukrainian fatalities and the condition of AFU units. This opacity is a by-product of Ukraine's strategic-communication strategy and operational-security efforts.[47] Although Ukraine has demonstrated its determination to continue fighting, its capabilities for doing so are not unlimited, as the AFU too has sustained substantial losses, especially in the Donbas over the summer, and probably in the Kherson offensive.[48]

Functions in a military operation

To understand why Ukraine has outperformed expectations, but also why all sides are now bracing for a longer war, we apply an analytical framework adopted from prior analysis of Russian military capability. Grossly simplified, there are five basic functions in a military operation.[49] While far from all-encompassing, they provide a basic framework for analysing battlefield outcomes. The first is command, control and communications (C3), which coordinate all forces' actions into a coherent fighting effort. Secondly, manoeuvre involves taking and holding territory – a key task, for example, of infantry and airborne as well as tank units. The third function is fire support, which includes artillery, surface-to-surface missiles, SAMs, anti-tank systems, attack helicopters and ground-attack aircraft, and arguably sabotage and diversionary units, to facilitate manoeuvre. Fourthly, mobility calls for transport units, movement control and engineers to ensure that forces can reach and move within the area of operations. Finally, sustainability enables a force to keep fighting once initial supplies are exhausted. For brevity, we emphasise the first three, with a less granular analysis of mobility and sustainability. We also discuss intangibles, such as morale, which, though difficult to measure before the fact, the war has demonstrated can have decisive effects on the battlefield.[50]

As winter approaches, both sides are bracing for a longer war than most had anticipated. In Russian culture and literature, 'General Frost' is a metaphor signifying the presumed Russian advantage over poorly prepared foreign invaders – such as those under Charles XII, Napoleon Bonaparte or Nazi Germany – who crumbled under Russia's harsh winter. But General Frost has at times struck Russian and Soviet forces too – for instance, during the Winter War in Finland – and now Russia is the poorly prepared invader. Both armies know how to operate in freezing conditions, so winter will not necessarily stop war fighting, although harsher conditions make functioning harder for man and machine alike. The problem for Russian forces in Ukraine, and to a lesser extent the AFU, concerns equipment and preparations. Russian logistics will struggle to equip and sustain potentially hundreds of thousands of reservists.[51] At the same time, the Kremlin is clearly attempting to enlist General Frost by aggravating the impact of the cold winter months on Ukrainian civilians. With 45% of Ukraine's power-generation capacity already offline, further Russian strikes on Ukrainian energy infrastructure transparently aim to cause a heating crisis.[52] In parallel, Moscow wants to leverage spiking energy prices to try to exploit the continent's energy dependence and high fuel prices to undermine popular support for the Ukrainian war effort and induce European leaders to back off.[53] While public opinion varies significantly among countries, as of mid-November Moscow's bet on the weather was not paying great dividends. Attacks targeting energy infrastructure across Europe have so far proven hard to attribute, but the US provided advance warning of the Nord Stream-pipeline attack.[54] Both sides, however, are now preparing for a drawn-out war. The Kremlin is putting parts of its economy on a war footing, and the US has established a separate command to coordinate its support effort with partner countries.[55] The Ukrainian military leadership is now planning for war well into 2023, preparing to turn winter warfare to its advantage and, if possible, further reinforce their successes in Kherson oblast.[56]

Ukrainian victory: borders of 1991

An outright Ukrainian victory is now a distinct possibility, as Ukrainian officials have been arguing for months.[57] More detached scholars have also increasingly recognised the possibility of a Ukrainian victory, potentially coinciding with regime instability in Russia.[58] For Ukraine, the maximalist version of victory, on which Kyiv has insisted, would entail a complete return to the borders of 1991, reversing not only Russia's gains since February (approximately 70,000 square kilometres) but also areas under de facto occupation since 2014 in Donetsk, Luhansk and Crimea (some 40,000 km²).[59] Entertaining such an eventuality is a dramatic shift from prevalent expectations at the outset of the war, or even during the summer, when Russian forces seemed to be wearing down Ukrainian defences.[60] That a Ukrainian military victory is even thinkable absent regime change in Russia is partly a consequence of its largely failed military reforms.[61] But it is equally a product of the AFU's successful ones. Effective military modernisation has turned it from an ill-prepared military in 2014 into an effective fighting force in 2022.[62]

Firstly, Ukrainian C3 has apparently afforded Ukraine an advantage at the strategic, operational and tactical levels. Ukrainian President Volodymyr Zelenskyy reportedly entrusts operational-level military affairs to General Zaluzhny and his general staff.[63] In contrast, Putin's reported dabbling in tactical-level decisions has complicated the tasks of field commanders. He has insisted on pursuing futile missions, procrastinated on crucial decisions such as mobilisation and sought to divert blame.[64] Successive Russian generals have been fired.[65] It is not clear that the appointment of General Sergei Surovikin in early October as head of Russian forces in Ukraine can make any decisive difference given the dysfunctional system he inherited.[66] Further down the chain of command, Ukrainian generals have effectively adopted mission command, delegating lower-level tactical decisions to junior officers in the field, while Russian decision-making remains notoriously centralised and slow.[67] The key Russian weakness, however, has been poor decision-making on the strategic level, in the Kremlin. Although local initiative can be vital tactically, Lawrence Freedman has concluded that the Russia–Ukraine war 'is foremost a case study in a failure of supreme command'.[68]

Secondly, the quality of the intelligence, surveillance, target acquisition and reconnaissance received by Ukraine has proven key to its military successes.[69] The operational effect of precision-guided munitions is only as good as the intelligence guiding them. This less visible aspect of the war includes internet access provided partly through Starlink, real-time intelligence shared by Western partners and technical innovations.[70] That said,

C3 is still challenging for Ukrainian forces, particularly National Guard and Territorial Defence troops.[71] While Russia may not be able to decisively improve its C3, Ukrainian communications could be jeopardised by Russian electronic warfare and the disputes over who should fund the continued operation of Starlink.[72]

Thirdly, prior to the war it was widely assumed that Russia held the advantage in manoeuvre warfare, partly due to greater numbers of mechanised and airborne units, and partly because Russian air superiority would presumably degrade Ukrainian manoeuvre. But due to Russia's initial attempt at blitzkrieg, during which several of its most elite mechanised and airborne units were badly damaged, and the inability of the VKS to provide close air support to its ground troops, the tables turned.[73] Ukraine's autumn offensives in Kharkiv and Kherson demonstrated that the AFU could carry out offensive actions despite a shortage of main battle tanks, armoured personnel carriers and infantry fighting vehicles.[74] To repeat these successes at acceptable risk and cost against denser lines, however, the AFU would benefit greatly from modern Western tanks.[75] Ukrainian authorities requested 500 main battle tanks in June. While Poland gave Ukraine 250 T-72 tanks in the spring and Germany backfilled countries that had provided older armour, Berlin has denied requests by the Spanish government to donate German *Leopard* tanks and Rheinmetall, their manufacturer, to export them to Ukraine.[76] With more than 2,000 *Leopard* tanks in operation in 13 European armies, there is at least some potential for a joint effort to stand up sizeable tank units.[77] But such units are dependent on a large logistics tail, and reaching full operational capability can be time-consuming.[78]

The AFU would benefit from modern tanks

In terms of indirect fires, Western partners have gradually decreased Russia's ten-to-one artillery advantage by supplying not only HIMARS and high-end self-propelled howitzers, but also the much more numerous M777 and other towed howitzers. While Ukrainian troops have effectively adapted to Western artillery more quickly than many expected, the broad variety of platforms is bound to complicate logistics and maintenance. But while Russia retains a clear numerical artillery advantage, precision munitions and real-time intelligence arguably afford Ukraine a qualitative edge.[79] Russian electronic-warfare capabilities and air defences may have diminished the impact of Ukraine's Turkish-made *Bayraktar* drones, which were crucially effective in the early stages of the war.[80] But while Russia retains the advantage in long-range precision-guided munitions, their inventories are dwindling. Major-General Kyrylo Budanov, head of Ukraine's Military Intelligence Directorate (GRU), claimed in late October that Russia had expended most of its cruise-missile arsenal, retaining only 13% of its pre-war *Iskander*, 43% of its *Kaliber*, and 45% of its Kh-101 and Kh-555 pre-war stockpiles. Its ability to replace them under Western sanctions is questionable.[81]

In mobility and sustainability, Ukraine enjoys the advantage of faster transportation routes, enabling it to shift troops along the stretched-out front more swiftly than Russia. This was deftly exploited in the Kharkiv offensive, and could be critical again as units are freed up or arrive fresh from training. The Ukrainians' strikes on the Kerch Bridge, and on bridges over the Dnipro River, have strained Russia's logistics and placed some of its troops in a precarious situation, contributing to the Russian withdrawal from Kherson.[82]

Lastly, the pure scale and intensity of the fighting is turning the war into a competition of durability and industrial capacity. Ukrainian officials have long been clear that continued Western support is necessary for Ukrainian victory. While Russia is evidently experiencing some significant logistics and sustainment challenges, Ukraine's Western supporters may face shortages in platforms – including artillery, artillery munitions and various missiles – that they can provide to Ukraine, beyond what has already been sent.[83] Massive expenditures of ammunition are straining both sides' inventories and production capacities. For instance, the annual US peacetime production of 155-millimetre shells, 80,000, is reportedly only enough for two weeks of fighting for the AFU. Similarly, Ukraine used 300 *Javelin* anti-tank weapons in the first week of the war – one-seventh of the United States' standard annual production of 2,100.[84]

Similar problems constrain Russian forces. One example is ammunition for artillery, which Russians often call the 'god of war'. Massed artillery barrages are still at the heart of Russian ground forces' operations. In early September, media outlets quoted US intelligence sources as saying that Russia sought to buy artillery ammunition from North Korea.[85] In late October, a Ukrainian commentator pointed out that Russian forces were using 122-mm artillery rounds produced in 2022, suggesting that older ammunition was running out. He also noted that mainly older towed artillery pieces were emerging from Russian inventories, implying slower and more vulnerable Russian artillery support going forward.[86] Russia's god of war faces very human limitations, and may be suffering from exhaustion. Clearly, neither side believed a war of this scale would arise or prepared properly for it, as reflected by Russia's procurement of Iranian loitering munitions and Ukraine's privately funded supplies of drones, vehicles and other equipment.

Russian forces found out the hard way that seizing even parts of Ukraine might look easy on a map but is an immense military undertaking in the real world. The same goes for a Ukrainian effort to evict them and restore the 1991 borders. While Ukrainian troops have recovered some 45,000 km² since March, Russia still controlled some 105,000 km² as of mid-November.[87] To complete the job of ousting Russian forces from Ukrainian territory with offensive ground forces, Ukraine may need Western main battle tanks and the time to stand up cohesive units.

Russian victory: a puppet regime in Kyiv

In July 2021, Putin published an article about the unity of the Russian and Ukrainian peoples, which suggests that Russia's original goal was decisive political control over Ukraine, perhaps in the guise of a pro-Russian puppet regime in Kyiv.[88] As of October 2022, with Russian military operations faltering, this appeared implausible, so the Kremlin moved the goal posts. The initial rhetoric of effecting the de-Nazification and demilitarisation of Ukraine was gradually replaced by that of waging a proxy war with NATO, augmented by eccentric bluster about societies having to succumb to satanic Western dictatorship.[89] This has little to do with actual military achievements. The annexation on 30 September 2022 of four oblasts in southeast Ukraine was a political measure conducted with great fanfare, but without the proper military foundation of full control over the territories and their borders. The combined vagueness of policy goals and the fluidity of the situation on the ground could have enabled Moscow to declare 'mission accomplished' and withdraw its forces. But Putin needs more tangible results to avoid appearing weak to the Russian public and elites. Historically, they are not kind to rulers who lose wars, such as Tsar Nicholas II after the First World War and the Soviet Union after the war in Afghanistan.[90] Mobilisation has further raised the stakes, possibly making the war existential for the Putin regime. That move, and placing the Russian economy on a war footing, signal that Moscow is in it for the long haul, and willing to take its chances, although Russia's November retreat from the western side of the Dnipro makes the long-term goal ever more distant.

The prospects for decisive Russian military victory are contingent on having at least three unknowns all turning out in its favour. The first is the state and durability of the AFU as a whole and of its individual units. The Ukrainian general staff has ensured tight operational security throughout the war, probably to ensure integrity of operations, retain high morale and maximise Western support. The AFU may be weaker, however, than its battlefield success in autumn 2022 suggests. Owing to Kyiv's effective strategic communication – including frequent combat footage – Ukraine has been winning the information war.[91] But there is less solid data about the objective status of the AFU, which likely has also taken substantial casualties.

The second unknown is the steadfastness of Western military support to Ukraine, in terms of both will and capability. Russia is working to undermine Western unity, hoping to aggravate existing challenges and betting that Western public support will flag with skyrocketing energy prices over the winter. Whereas the US, the UK and Russia's European neighbours have been strongly supportive of Ukraine, the relative reserve of Germany and France – critical by virtue of their size and military-industrial capacity – is causing some internal friction.[92] Russia will seek to exploit this friction, along with pockets of isolationism among Donald Trump-aligned members of the US Congress; however, opportunities to do so may be diminished given the underwhelming performance of the Republican Party in the US midterm elections.

The effectiveness of Russia's mobilisation, which had a rocky start, is the third unknown. To make a difference in the war, mobilised reservists have to translate into enhanced offensive capabilities, and the reservists need time for individual training and to build unit cohesion. The bigger the unit or formation, the longer it takes to train. Yet Russia's military constantly needs reinforcements. Its dilemma is whether to use them now, as replacements, with less effect, or later, in cohesive units, with greater effect. Russia's defence industry may have to choose between producing new items of modern equipment and overhauling old equipment in its inventory for decades. More broadly, having failed to overwhelm Ukraine using its best troops and equipment and with the advantage of strategic initiative, succeeding with reluctant or outright unwilling reservists and ageing equipment while on the defensive is a dubious proposition.[93] Yet Russia has few other conventional military options left.

Russia's qualitative edge is slipping

The Russian expression, *ne umeniem, a chislom*, meaning 'not with skills, but with numbers', appears to characterise the mobilisation effort. By Russia's own accounts, as of early November it had deployed some 80,000 newly mobilised troops to front-line units, with 220,000 in training. While anecdotal evidence of unhappy reservists abounds, this may not be representative: successful Russian mobilisation efforts could get less media attention, which skews the Western understanding of the process. If Russian numbers are reliable – a big if – the military is allocating one-third of mobilised soldiers to the front and two-thirds to force generation for future use. The latter number roughly equals Russia's initial invasion force and would constitute a second echelon of forces in the war. While Sergei Shoigu, the Russian minister of defence, claimed that subsequently only volunteers and contract soldiers would be recruited, new rounds of mobilisation could well continue throughout 2023 because, if nothing else, the daily toll of Russian casualties could require it. For October alone, the Ukrainian Ministry of Defence reported that an estimated 11,000 Russian soldiers had been killed, which would imply approximately 40,000 total casualties, including the severely wounded.[94] Russia's qualitative edge is slipping. Equipment now being pulled from storage may be from the 1960s. Examples include T-62 main battle tanks.[95] There is speculation that even Second World War-vintage Russian artillery pieces may come into play.[96] Russia's putatively modernised army is thus becoming more old-fashioned by the day in personnel, kit and doctrine. It has few options other than a resort to quantity.

In addition to needing all three unknowns to redound to its benefit, Russia must address operational problems. Nine months of war has revealed Russian shortfalls in all five operational functions. Concerning C3, apparent challenges have arisen involving inter-service and combined-arms coordination, as well as unit-level leadership and unit morale. These could bar success no matter how many mobilised reservists or new units go to the front. As for manoeuvre, the war has degraded most of Russia's best-trained and -equipped units, thus undercutting the potential for offensive operations.

Russia's initial numerical advantage in fire support was most pronounced with respect to artillery.[97] But it also prevailed in SAMs, surface-to-surface missiles and anti-tank weapons, as well as attack helicopters and other aircraft. Yet this nominal superiority did not enable Russian forces to prevail in the first nine months of the war. The reasons include poor individual targeting and the daunting number of possible targets the scale of the war entails. Russia chose to expend an abundance of artillery rounds and missiles on cities, such as Mariupol, terrorising civilians. Similarly, after the attacks on the Kerch Bridge on 8 October, Russia used precision munitions to launch punitive strikes on Ukrainian cities. The Kremlin may have political motivations for taking such measures, but they consume precious assets to little military avail. Furthermore, Ukrainian air defences had downed at least 63 Russian aircraft and 57 helicopters by late October.[98] This diminished Russia's ability to support ground manoeuvres.

If the AFU is weaker than current appearances suggest, if Western military support dries up, and if Russia's mobilisation generates more capable and motivated soldiers and units than not in the coming year – again, three big ifs – Russian forces could conceivably start to retake the initiative. But, as the Kherson offensive has shown, Ukraine has retained the initiative, and Russia's task is at best long-term and uphill. Even in a best-case scenario for Russia, it would require many months, if not several years, to grind down the AFU. Having exhausted substantially qualitative assets, Russia is hoping that quantity will enable it to overwhelm the combined resources of Ukrainian soldiers and Western equipment. From Moscow's evolved perspective, it is not about who has the most modern tank, but who has the last tank standing. Such a mindset suggests not a sharp, clear-cut victory but a war of attrition.

Last tank standing: reverting to a war of attrition

It is possible that the Russian mobilisation will generate sufficient combat power to stop Ukraine's autumn offensive, but not enough to break Ukrainian troops. Neither side may be able to muster sufficient offensive capability to win or be willing to negotiate. Fighting could ebb and flow without producing decisive action or a sustained trend favouring either side, leaving front lines relatively static. Accordingly, an indefinite war of attrition at lower intensity is quite plausible.[99] Ironically, Russia gambled on achieving a Crimea 2.0, but ended up with Donbas 2.0, but on a larger scale and against a much stronger home team.

While attrition warfare can be intense and ghastly, it can be conducted more deliberately than dynamic operations.[100] Compared to the war thus far, reversion to attrition would constitute an operational pause, in theory enabling both sides to plan future operations and bring more resources to the area of operations, as well as rotate and organise front-line units with high losses, repair damaged equipment, call up reserves and regroup forces for coming operations.

A war of attrition could reduce pressure on C3, but only slightly. Both sides see command posts as high-value targets and will likely continue to prioritise them. Although information about systemic effects on the AFU is limited, in June Russia claimed to have hit a Ukrainian command centre and killed some 50 officers.[101] The BBC, which has continuously tracked Russian officer losses, noted in October that 17% of recorded Russian casualties were officers.[102] Of almost 1,300 killed, 340 had the rank of major or above, thus constituting commanding officers of battalions or larger units, or staff officers in brigade headquarters and higher up.[103] Senior officers take decades to train and often offer valuable wisdom from experience. These losses were serious, as they were in units composed primarily of contract soldiers, who bore the brunt of the fighting early on. An attritional war may provide more time to reinforce command posts, reconstitute communication systems and plan operations, which would decrease the likelihood of poor performance. The established shortage of experienced Russian officers, however, will probably inhibit Russian efforts to train new units and lead them in operations.

A war of attrition would imply that both sides lacked the resources and the will to employ manoeuvre at an operational level, although combat reconnaissance and smaller tactical-level offensive actions could be feasible. Both sides would probably try to re-establish manoeuvre capability by increasing the amount of available motor-rifle and tank units, since improving offensive capabilities is key to achieving each side's war aims, particularly given that neither side can transport sizeable units by air or sea.[104]

The war thus far has put immense strain on fire support, with inventories on both sides already reaching dangerously low levels. In theory, an attritional phase could enable both sides to stock up and plan for either prolonged attrition or resumed dynamic operations. But assuming tactical-level mobile operations slow down, as they would, fire support would be the main way to inflict harm on the enemy. Accordingly, substantial pressure on this capability would continue.

Although attrition may reduce the role of mobility at the tactical level, it may increase it on operational and strategic levels. For example, while fewer offensive operations would temporarily reduce the need for mobile bridges and mine-clearing, a force build-up and a redisposition of forces would require robust strategic- and operational-level mobility to bring forces to the area of operations. For both sides, this would require railway echelons, as well as long-haul road transports to move ground forces. For Ukraine, many vital supplies from the US come across the Atlantic by plane or ship. With the Black Sea cordoned off for Russian military sealift, rail and road transport are key for moving Russian units to Ukraine. Thus, in a war of attrition, using fire support to target enemy transport infrastructure, such as the Kerch Bridge or Russian railways, may be preferable to pounding fortified enemy front-line positions.

Finally, a war of attrition by nature hinges on how sustainability evolves. Both sides have major challenges in producing new resources for the war and deploying them to the area of operations. Even if it is betting on a drawn-out war, though, Russia's ability to sustain it may be in doubt, as the departure from Russia of up to 700,000 Russian men of military age since the start of the mobilisation illustrates.[105] If casualties mount and new waves of mobilisation loom, this exodus might grow further. Russia controls many of its own supplies, but the combination of sanctions and brain drain will hamper the production of high-end equipment such as modern aircraft and precision-guided munitions. In turn, Ukraine depends on the West for these assets, and neither Western resources, especially military equipment and ammunition, nor Western political will may last forever.[106] The shooting war in Ukraine is gradually morphing into a competition of will and production capabilities between Russia and the West.

A drawn-out war?

In the first phase of the war, Russia bet on manoeuvre to take Ukrainian territory, but poor logistics and C3 doomed the effort. The emphasis then shifted to Russia banking on massive fire support to grind down the AFU, but Ukrainian morale and Western intelligence, artillery and precision-guided munitions prevented a decisive win. Ukraine's autumn offensive gained ground using crafty manoeuvres, but slowed down due to limitations in sustainment. Russian mobilisation measures indicate that Moscow's latest, and possibly last, bet is on sustainability: it will simply persevere in what is at bottom a contest of wills against Ukraine and its Western supporters. Especially insofar as winter is coming, both sides appear to have shelved immediate designs on a swift, decisive victory, and instead seem to be bracing for a drawn-out war.

To prevail in a war of this scale and scope requires sustainable joint and combined ground operations in which all five functions are working in close coordination. Among the five, only manoeuvre – the ability to take and hold terrain – will enable a decisive military victory. Generous and multifaceted Western military support has helped Ukraine's defence, but it has lacked a strong manoeuvre component and therefore has not substantially aided its offence. For a Ukrainian victory to materialise, Europe in particular would need to do more and do it faster than it is comfortable with. The provision of

Leopard main battle tanks is a case in point. The issue has brought to a head Western policy debates about the risk of further escalation and the need to preserve capabilities if the war spreads to Europe. But Russia has escalated regardless of Western restraint and now is in no position to expand the war. Western inventories and production capacities may not suffice to simultaneously help Ukraine win and keep robust capabilities in reserve.[107] But if the former is deemed vital, the West will have to accept the trade-off and bite the bullet, as it were.

It may now be difficult to envision either side organising sufficiently strong and sustainable offensive-manoeuvre capabilities to win decisively before mid-2023. Circumstances in mid-November indicated that the Russian–Ukrainian war could revert to a war of attrition, straining both sides. Russia has greater indigenous resources, but is hobbled by old equipment, recalcitrant recruits and structural problems in forging them into adequate forces. Ukraine has soldiers more motivated to fight, but lacks equipment and depends on both Western goodwill and Russian kit salvaged from the battlefield, neither of which is an entirely reliable source of supply. The war, however, has unified NATO and imbued it with a renewed sense of purpose. US leadership, drawing on excellent intelligence and patient diplomacy, has galvanised the Western response. The Kremlin will try to deepen the remaining internal fault lines of the transatlantic alliance, with uncertain prospects of success.

If a large-scale war of attrition becomes normalised, Russian security services' appetite for risk will likely grow.[108] Further attacks on European infrastructure should not come as a surprise. With Europe entering its harshest geopolitical winter in decades, some of its political leaders may not be interested in war. But war will certainly be interested in them.

*   *   *

The war is about the future world order as much as the geopolitical fate of Russia and Ukraine.[109] Some implications are already clear. Firstly, the war heralds the end of the post-Cold War period, and ushers in a new era that may prove both turbulent and dangerous, accelerating a long-percolating great-power competition. Secondly, in launching a war to make Russia great again, Putin has achieved the opposite. Instead of subduing Ukraine, dividing NATO and carving out a Russian sphere of interest, the war has united the Ukrainian nation and made it hostile towards Russia, reinvigorated NATO and made Russia an international outcast with waning power in its near abroad.[110] In Northern Europe alone, Putin's grave miscalculations ended Germany's Russia-friendly Ostpolitik and Sweden's and Finland's neutrality.[111] And the war has unleashed reactions the Kremlin neither anticipated nor desired, undermining Russian influence in the post-Soviet space.[112]

The war has also fundamentally transformed its two antagonists. Ukraine is now clearly linked to the West, with the European Union under-writing its economy and the US sustaining its military. If Ukraine wins, the West will need to integrate it into a reconstituted European security order quickly. Despite political and practical obstacles, such as limited access to technology and potential Western and Russian reactions, Kyiv may be tempted to consider nuclear weapons, as Russia has broken the 1994 Budapest Memorandum's requirement of non-aggression against Ukraine in exchange for its relinquishment of nuclear weapons and attempted to engage in nuclear extortion. While it might seem far-fetched now in light of American reluctance as well as Russian opposition, providing adequate security guarantees to Ukraine might eventually involve considering its membership in NATO, which could evolve as the worst option except perhaps all others.[113]

Regarding Russia, discussions now surfacing of possible regime change or a break-up of the Russian Federation were unthinkable before the war. Looking ahead, Russia lacks most preconditions for liberalisation and democratisation, and a 30-year Western bet on normalising relations has ended horrendously and unequivocally. Instead, a resolutely revanchist Russia may well emerge, determined to rebuild its military power in defi-ance of limitations imposed by economic and technological sanctions. Even a best-case scenario for Russian victory would involve profound military, economic and human costs, and a whopping political and moral bill to the Russian people that will eventually come due.

Finally, the Russian Armed Forces have underperformed dramatically relative to prior expectations.[114] A necessary debate is under way to understand why the West got Russia so wrong on this score.[115] Russia cannot, however, be written off as a geopolitical competitor at this stage, either in the present war or thereafter. The Russian Armed Forces will eventually rebuild, perhaps learning from their mistakes in Ukraine just as Ukraine has learned bitter lessons since 2014.[116] Defeat is a harsher teacher than victory.

Acknowledgements

We are very grateful to our colleague Robert Dalsjö, whose insights have been key to this article in its entirety, from initial design to final edits.

Notes

1   See Carlotta Gall, 'As Ukraine Forces Press Offensive, Front Lines Are Shifting Fast', *New York Times*, 9 October 2022, https://www.nytimes.com/2022/10/09/world/europe/russia-ukraine-forces-borova.html.

2   See, for instance, Michael Kofman and Ryan Evans, 'Russia's Plan to Stay in the War', *War on the Rocks* podcast, 26 September 2022, https://podcasts.apple.com/us/podcast/russias-plan-to-stay-in-the-war/id682478916?i=1000580631532.

3   See, for example, 'Ukraine's Military Success Is Reshaping Russia as Well as the War', *The Economist*, 7 October 2022, https://www.economist.com/briefing/2022/10/06/ukraines-military-success-is-reshaping-russia-as-well-as-the-war.

4   This is on top of the 'Russian lend–lease' – that is, substantial amounts of Russian equipment falling into Ukrainian hands after being abandoned or captured. For instance, of the more than 1,300 main battle tanks that Russia has lost (confirmed by photographic evidence), more than 500 were either abandoned or captured, compared to the approximately 300 tanks Ukraine has lost. See Stijn Mitzer and Jakub Janovsky, 'Attack on Europe: Documenting Russian Equipment Losses During the 2022 Russian Invasion of Ukraine', Oryx, https://www.oryxspioenkop.com/2022/02/attack-on-europe-documenting-equipment.html.

5   See Sam Cranny-Evans, 'Understanding Russia's Mobilization', RUSI Commentary, 28 September 2022, https://www.rusi.org/explore-our-research/publications/commentary/understanding-russias-mobilisation.

6   See, for instance, Lawrence Freedman, 'Putin's Annexation and Lyman's Encirclement', Comment Is Freed, 1 October 2022, https://samf.substack.com/p/putins-annexation-and-lymans-encirclement.

7   See Julian E. Barnes, 'U.S. Sees Opportunity for Ukraine to Capitalize on Russian Weakness', *New York Times*, 20 October 2022, https://www.nytimes.com/2022/10/20/us/politics/us-ukraine-war.html; and Melanie Marlowe, Christopher Preble and Zack Cooper, 'Military Lessons from the War in Ukraine', *War on the Rocks*, Net Assessment Podcast, 29 September 2022, https://warontherocks.com/2022/09/military-lessons-from-the-war-in-ukraine/. Pre-war analyses predicted quick Russian progress, or even outright victory; during the first phase there was talk of Russia's suffering 'unsustainable losses' early on; and over the summer it instead seemed that Russian forces were slowly grinding their way towards victory by virtue of sheer firepower. Then, common wisdom instead assumed that it would settle into attrition along fairly stable lines of contact.

8   See Lawrence Freedman, 'Going Nuclear: On Thinking the Unthinkable', Comment Is Freed, 20 September 2022, https://samf.substack.com/p/going-nuclear; Edward Helmore, 'Petraeus: US Would Destroy Russia's Troops if Putin Uses Nuclear Weapons in Ukraine', *Guardian*, 2 October 2022; and Fred Kaplan, 'Why the US Might Not Use a Nuke, Even if Russia Does', *Slate*, 7 October 2022, https://slate.com/news-and-politics/2022/10/why-the-us-might-not-use-a-nuke-even-if-russia-does.html.

9   See Eliot A. Cohen, 'Russia's Nuclear Bluster Is a Sign of Panic', *Atlantic*, 4 October 2022, https://www.theatlantic.com/ideas/archive/2022/10/putin-nuclear-weapons-threat-us-sanctions-military/671642/.

10 For an in-depth account, see Paul Sonne et al., 'Battle for Kyiv: Ukrainian Valor, Russian Blunders, Combined to Save the Capital', *Washington Post*, 24 August 2022, https://www.washingtonpost.com/national-security/interactive/2022/kyiv-battle-ukraine-survival/?itid=hp-top-table-main-t-2.

11 See James Risen and Ken Klippenstein, 'The CIA Thought Putin Would Quickly Conquer Ukraine. Why Did They Get It So Wrong?', *Intercept*, 5 October 2022, https://theintercept.com/2022/10/05/russia-ukraine-putin-cia/.

12 See Greg Miller and Catherine Belton, 'Russia's Spies Misread Ukraine and Misled Kremlin as War Loomed', *Washington Post*, 19 August 2022, https://www.washingtonpost.com/world/interactive/2022/russia-fsb-intelligence-ukraine-war/?itid=hp-top-table-main; Risen and Klippenstein, 'The CIA Thought Putin Would Quickly Conquer Ukraine'; and Sonne et al., 'Battle for Kyiv'.

13 See Rob Lee, 'The Tank Is Not Obsolete, and Other Observations About the Future of Combat', *War on the Rocks*, 6 September 2022, https://warontherocks.com/2022/09/the-tank-is-not-obsolete-and-other-observations-about-the-future-of-combat/. Military historians will likely find similarities between this phase and the early stages of both the Finnish Winter War and the First Chechen War, insofar as an underestimation of their opponent led Soviet/Russian forces to suffer major setbacks after being encircled.

14 For an analysis of the first two months of the war, see Robert Dalsjö, Michael Jonsson and Johan Norberg, 'A Brutal Examination: Russian Military Capability in Light of the Ukraine War', *Survival*, vol. 64, no. 3, June–July 2022; and Sonne et al., 'Battle for Kyiv'.

15 See Sonne et al., 'Battle for Kyiv'; and Mark Urban, 'The Heavy Losses of an Elite Russian Regiment in Ukraine', BBC News, 2 April 2022, https://www.bbc.co.uk/news/world-europe-60946340.

16 Of Ukraine's approximately 600,000-square-kilometre territory, Russia controlled some 40,000 prior to the war. After withdrawing from northern Ukraine, Russia still controlled about 120,000 km², or a fifth of Ukraine, of which it lost some 10,000 in late September. Natalie Croker, Byron Manley and Tim Lister, 'The Turning Points in Russia's Invasion of Ukraine', CNN, 30 September 2022, https://edition.cnn.com/interactive/2022/09/europe/russia-territory-control-ukraine-shift-dg/index.html.

17 See, for instance, Thomas Gibbons-Neff, Andrew E. Kramer and Natalia Yermak, 'Shortage of Artillery Ammunition Saps Ukrainian Frontline Morale', *New York Times*, 10 June 2022, https://www.nytimes.com/2022/06/10/world/europe/ukraine-ammo-shortage-artillery.html.

18 See Thomas Gibbons-Neff and Natalia Yermak, 'On Front Lines, Communication Breakdowns Prove Costly for Ukraine', *New York Times*, 28 June 2022, https://www.nytimes.com/2022/06/28/world/europe/ukraine-army-russia.html; and Andrew E. Kramer and Maria Varenikova, 'As Russia Moves on Another Province, Ukrainians Leave Ghost Towns Behind', *New York Times*, 7 July 2022, https://www.nytimes.com/2022/07/05/world/europe/ukraine-war-donbas.html.

19 See Elliott Ackerman, 'A Whole Age of Warfare Sank with the Moskva', *Atlantic*, 22 May 2022, https://www.theatlantic.com/ideas/archive/2022/05/ukraine-russia-moskva-military-marine-corps/629930/.

20 See Michael Schwirtz, 'Last Stand at Azovstal: Inside the Siege that Shaped the Ukraine War', *New York Times*, 24 July 2022, https://www.nytimes.com/2022/07/24/world/europe/ukraine-war-mariupol-azovstal.html.

21 See Tyson Wetzel, 'Ukraine Air War Examined: A Glimpse at the Future of Air Warfare', Atlantic Council, 30 August 2022, https://www.atlanticcouncil.org/content-series/airpower-after-ukraine/ukraine-air-war-examined-a-glimpse-at-the-future-of-air-warfare/.

22 See Mike Peitrucha, 'Amateur Hour Part 2: Failing the Air Campaign', *War on the Rocks*, 11 August 2022, https://warontherocks.com/2022/08/amateur-hour-part-ii-failing-the-air-campaign/.

23 See Maximilian K. Bremer and Kelly A. Grieco, 'In Denial About Denial: Why Ukraine's Air Success Should Worry the West', *War on the Rocks*, https://warontherocks.com/2022/06/in-denial-about-denial-why-ukraines-air-success-should-worry-the-west/; and Christopher Miller and Paul McLeary, 'Ukraine Has Hobbled Russia's Black Sea Fleet. Could It Turn the Tide of the War?', *Politico*, 29 August 2022, https://www.

politico.com/news/2022/08/29/
russias-black-sea-fleet-stuck-struck-
and-sinking-00054114.

24   See Andrew S. Bowen, 'Russia's War
in Ukraine: Military and Intelligence
Aspects', Congressional Research
Service, R47068, 14 September 2022,
https://crsreports.congress.gov/
product/pdf/R/R47068.

25   See John Ismay, 'The American
Guided Rockets Helping Ukraine
Destroy Russian Forces', *New York
Times*, 9 September 2022, https://www.
nytimes.com/2022/09/09/us/ukraine-
weapons-rockets.html.

26   Important kit that has been used
includes *Bayraktar* TB2 drones; *Javelin*
and NLAW anti-tank weapons; high-
end howitzers; *Gepard*, *Iris*-T and
NASAM air-defence systems; HARM
and *Harpoon* missiles; *Excalibur*
and GMLRS artillery munitions;
and *Switchblade* and *Ghost* loitering
munitions. Possible future entrants
include Western main battle tanks
such as the German *Leopard* or the
American *Abrams*, F-16 fighter aircraft
and longer-range artillery munitions.

27   See Ismay, 'The American Guided
Rockets Helping Ukraine Destroy
Russian Forces'; and Eric Schmitt and
John Ismay, 'Advanced U.S. Arms Make
a Mark in Ukraine War, Officials Say',
New York Times, 1 July 2022, https://
www.nytimes.com/2022/07/01/us/
politics/himars-weapons-ukraine.html.

28   See Dan Lamothe, 'U.S. Dials
Up Shipments of Radar-hunting
Missiles for Ukraine', *Washington
Post*, 8 September 2022, https://
www.washingtonpost.com/
national-security/2022/09/08/
ukraine-harms-missiles/.

29   See Michael Kofman and Ryan Evans,
'What Will Be Ukraine's Pre-winter
Gains?', *War on the Rocks* podcast, 10
October 2022, https://warontherocks.
com/2022/10/what-will-be-ukraines-
pre-winter-gains/.

30   See Anton Troianovski, 'Putin
Supporters Are Enraged by the Russian
Retreat from Lyman', *New York Times*,
1 October 2022, https://www.nytimes.
com/2022/10/01/world/europe/lyman-
russia-retreat-putin.html.

31   See Kofman and Evans, 'What Will Be
Ukraine's Pre-winter Gains?'

32   In 2017, the independent Russian
newspaper *Novaya Gazeta* reported
that the Wagner Group included an
artillery battalion, a tank company,
a reconnaissance company, an engineer company and staff-support
units, comprising some 2,000 men.
See Irek Murtazin, 'Ikh prosto net.
Rasledovanie' [They simply don't
exist. Investigation], *Novaya Gazeta*, 9
October 2017, https://novayagazeta.ru/
articles/2017/10/09/74125-ih-prosto-net.

33   See David Axe, 'As the Russian Army
Digs In, a Pro-Kremlin Mercenary
Company Goes on the Attack in
Ukraine – and Begs for Credit', *Forbes*,
15 October 2022, https://www.forbes.
com/sites/davidaxe/2022/10/15/
as-the-russian-army-digs-in-a-pro-
kremlin-mercenary-company-goes-
on-the-attack-in-ukraine-and-begs-for-
credit/?sh=4e294bcd51d0.

34   See Gustav Gressel, 'Mob Unhappy:
Why Russia Is Unlikely to Emerge
Victorious in Ukraine', European
Council on Foreign Relations, 21
October 2022, https://ecfr.eu/article/
mob-unhappy-why-russia-is-unlikely-
to-emerge-victorious-in-ukraine/.

35 See Barnes, 'U.S. Sees Opportunity for Ukraine to Capitalize on Russian Weakness'.

36 As of late October, the Ukrainian Ministry of Defence estimated that almost 68,000 Russian troops had been killed. Ukrainian Ministry of Defence, 'The Total Combat Losses of the Enemy from 24.02 to 24.10', 25 October 2022, https://www.mil.gov.ua/en/news/2022/10/24/the-total-combat-losses-of-the-enemy-from-24-02-to-24-10/. Western estimates have been more conservative, but assuming there are 2.5 to three wounded for every soldier killed, it is clear that Russia has lost a significant portion of its original invading force, with Western estimates pegged at 80,000 killed and wounded as of early August. See Bowen, 'Russia's War in Ukraine', p. 16. If 40,000 Russian soldiers were killed by October, total losses including wounded should be in the range 140,000–160,000, of the original force of some 190,000. See also 'How Heavy Are Russian Casualties in Ukraine?', *The Economist*, 24 July 2022, https://www.economist.com/europe/2022/07/24/how-heavy-are-russian-casualties-in-ukraine; and Alan Yuhas, 'Thousands of Civilian Deaths and 6.6 Million Refugees: Calculating the Costs of War', *New York Times*, 24 August 2022, https://www.nytimes.com/2022/08/24/world/europe/russia-ukraine-war-toll.html.

37 See Kofman and Evans, 'What Will Be Ukraine's Pre-winter Gains?'

38 Ukrainian authorities report that more than 2,500 Russian main battle tanks are out of action, of which some 1,400 can be visually confirmed. Mitzer and Janovsky, 'Attack on Europe'. See also Illia Ponomarenko, 'How Many Tanks Does Russia Really Have?', *Kyiv Independent*, 1 September 2022, https://kyivindependent.com/national/how-many-tanks-does-russia-really-have.

39 Individual units may well buckle, as they have been severely decimated. Russian documents captured in eastern Ukraine show that some units were operating at 20% strength, and that morale and discipline were breaking down. See Mari Saito, Maria Tsvetkova and Anton Zverev, 'Abandoned Russian Base Holds Secret of Retreat in Ukraine', Reuters, 26 October 2022, https://www.reuters.com/investigates/special-report/ukraine-crisis-russia-base/.

40 See 'Russia Sends Mobilized Men to Ukraine Front After Days of Training – Activists', *Moscow Times*, 27 September 2022, https://www.themoscowtimes.com/2022/09/27/russia-sends-mobilized-men-to-ukraine-front-after-days-of-training-activists-a78911.

41 Kateryna Stepanenko, 'Russian Offensive Campaign Assessment, October 28', Institute for the Study of War, 28 October 2022, https://www.understandingwar.org/backgrounder/russian-offensive-campaign-assessment-october-28.

42 See Lawrence Freedman, 'Cannon Fodder', Comment Is Freed, 28 September 2022, https://samf.substack.com/p/cannon-fodder; and Doug Klain, 'Mobilization Can't Save Russia's War', *Foreign Policy*, 4 October 2022, https://foreignpolicy.com/2022/10/04/mobilization-russia-ukraine-war/.

43 See Gressel, 'Mob Unhappy'.

44 According to Ukrainian Ministry of Defence numbers, 11,670 Russian soldiers were killed in October, approximately a third more than the monthly average. Ukrainian Ministry of Defence, 'The Total Combat Losses of the Enemy from 24.02 to 24.10'.

45 See, for example, the account of defected Russian paratrooper Pavel Filiatiev in Dan Biletsky and Ivan Nechepurenko, 'A Russian Paratrooper Seeking Asylum in France Describes Disarray in Putin's Military', *New York Times*, 1 September 2022, https://www.nytimes.com/2022/09/01/world/europe/russian-defector-france-book.html.

46 See 'Ukraine War: Ukraine Will Treat Deserters Fairly, Zelensky Vows', BBC News, 25 September 2022, https://www.bbc.co.uk/news/world-europe-63025039.

47 See, for instance, 'Rob Lee on Why Attrition Will Be a Critical Factor in the Battle for Donbas', *The Economist*, 30 April 2022, https://www.economist.com/by-invitation/rob-lee-on-why-attrition-will-be-a-critical-factor-in-the-battle-for-donbas/21808954. In late August, AFU commander-in-chief Valerii Zaluzhny stated that Ukraine had suffered almost 9,000 killed. Bowen, 'Russia's War in Ukraine', p. 16.

48 See Barnes, 'U.S. Sees Opportunity for Ukraine to Capitalize on Russian Weakness'; and Gibbons-Neff and Yermak, 'On Front Lines, Communication Breakdowns Prove Costly for Ukraine'.

49 See Johan Norberg and Fredrik Westerlund, 'Russia's Armed Forces in 2016', in Gudrun Persson (ed.), *Russian Military Capability in a Ten-year Perspective – 2016*, Swedish Defence Research Agency, FOI-R--4325--SE, December 2016, p. 23, https://www.foi.se/rest-api/report/FOI-R--4326--SE.

50 See Robert Dalsjö and Johan Norberg, 'Why We Got Russia Wrong', in Jenny Lunden (ed.), *Another Rude Awakening – Making Sense of Russia's War Against Ukraine*, Swedish Defence Research Agency, FOI-R--5332--SE, June 2022, pp. 19–24, https://www.foi.se/rest-api/report/FOI-R--5332--SE.

51 See David Axe, 'Russia's War Mobilization Is Pointless as Long as Its Army Lacks Trucks', *Forbes*, 23 September 2022, https://www.forbes.com/sites/davidaxe/2022/09/23/russias-war-mobilization-is-pointless-as-long-as-its-army-lacks-trucks/?sh=718a7f2b69b4.

52 See Suriya Jayanti, 'Putin's Blackout Blitz: Russia Aims to Freeze Ukraine into Surrender', Atlantic Council, 17 October 2022, https://www.atlanticcouncil.org/blogs/ukrainealert/putins-blackout-blitz-russia-aims-to-freeze-ukrainians-into-surrender/.

53 See Katrin Bennhold, '"Naked Fear": A Pipeline Attack Fans Anxiety in a German Village, and Beyond', *New York Times*, 1 October 2022, https://www.nytimes.com/2022/10/01/world/europe/germany-pipeline-damage-fear.html; and Keir Giles, 'Putin Needs a Drawn-out War – The West's Timidity Gives Him One', *Guardian*, 28 June 2022, https://www.theguardian.com/commentisfree/2022/jun/28/putin-ar-the-west-zelenskiy-ukraine-russia.

54 See David E. Sanger and Julian E. Barnes, 'The CIA Had Warned European Governments of Potential

Attacks on Pipelines', *New York Times*, 27 September 2022, https://www.nytimes.com/2022/09/27/world/europe/cia-nord-stream-pipelines-attack.html.

55 See John Ismay and Lara Jakes, 'Meeting in Brussels Signifies a Turning Point for Allies Arming Ukraine', *New York Times*, 28 September 2022, https://www.nytimes.com/2022/09/28/us/politics/ukraine-weapons-nato.html; and Eric Schmitt, 'Pentagon Plans to Set Up a New Command to Arm Ukraine, Officials Say', *New York Times*, 29 September 2022, https://www.nytimes.com/2022/09/29/us/politics/pentagon-command-ukraine.html.

56 See Paul McLeary, 'NATO Is Rushing Equipment to Ukraine as Troops Hunker Down for the Winter', *Politico*, 19 October 2022, https://www.politico.com/news/2022/10/19/ukraine-nato-russia-winter-equipment-00062596; and Valerii Zaluzhny and Mikhail Zabrdodski, 'Perspektivy obespechenia voennoi kampanii 2023 goda: ukrainskii vzgliad' [The prospects for supplying the military campaign in 2023: A Ukrainian view], *Ukrinform*, 9 September 2022, https://www.ukrinform.ru/rubric-ato/3566431-perspektivy-obespecenia-voennoj-kampanii-2023-goda-ukrainskij-vzglad.html.

57 See, for instance, Dmytro Kuala, 'How Ukraine Will Win: Kyiv's Theory of Victory', *Foreign Affairs*, 17 June 2022, https://www.foreignaffairs.com/articles/ukraine/2022-06-17/how-ukraine-will-win.

58 See Lawrence Freedman, 'Retribution and Regime Change: The Consequences of Putin's Weakness', Comment Is Freed, 20 September 2022, https://samf.substack.com/p/retribution-and-regime-change?utm_source=profile&utm_medium=reader2; and Timothy Snyder, 'How Does the Ukrainian War End?', Thinking About…, 5 October 2022, https://snyder.substack.com/p/how-does-the-russo-ukrainian-war.

59 See Croker, Manley and Lister, 'The Turning Points in Russia's Invasion of Ukraine'.

60 See Risen and Klippenstein 'The CIA Thought Putin Would Quickly Conquer Ukraine'; and Sonne et al., 'Battle for Kyiv'.

61 See Alexander Crowther, 'Russia's Military: Failure on an Awesome Scale', Center for European Policy Analysis, 15 April 2022, https://cepa.org/article/russias-military-failure-on-an-awesome-scale/.

62 See, for instance, Simon Shuster and Vera Bergengruen, 'Inside the Ukrainian Counterstrike that Turned the Tide of the War', *Time*, 26 September 2022, https://time.com/6216213/ukraine-military-valeriy-zaluzhny/; Snyder, 'How Does the Ukrainian War End?'; and Sonne et al., 'Battle for Kyiv'.

63 See Julian E. Barnes and Helene Cooper, 'Ukrainian Officials Drew on U.S. Intelligence to Plan Counteroffensive', *New York Times*, 10 September 2022, https://www.nytimes.com/2022/09/10/us/politics/ukraine-military-intelligence.html; Lawrence Freedman, 'Why War Fails: Russia's Invasion of Ukraine and the Limits of Military Power', *Foreign Affairs*, vol. 101, no. 4, July/August 2022, pp. 10–23; and Shuster and Bergengruen,

'Inside the Ukrainian Counterstrike that Turned the Tide of the War'.

64 See Freedman, 'Why War Fails'.

65 See Julian E. Barnes et al., 'As Russian Losses Mount in Ukraine, Putin Gets More Involved in War Strategy', *New York Times*, 23 September 2022, https://www.nytimes.com/2022/09/23/us/politics/putin-ukraine.html; and Austin Wright, 'Why Russia Keeps Losing Generals', *Foreign Policy*, 20 July 2022, https://foreignpolicy.com/2022/07/20/why-russia-keeps-losing-generals-ukraine/.

66 See 'Who Is Sergei Surovikin, Russia's New Commander in Ukraine?', *The Economist*, 13 October 2022, https://www.economist.com/the-economist-explains/2022/10/13/who-is-sergei-surovikin-russias-new-commander-in-ukraine.

67 See David M. Herszenhorn and Paul McLeary, 'Ukraine's "Iron General" Is a Hero, but He's No Star', *Politico*, 4 August 2022, https://www.politico.com/news/2022/04/08/ukraines-iron-general-zaluzhnyy-00023901.

68 Freedman, 'Why War Fails'.

69 See Barnes and Cooper, 'Ukrainian Officials Drew on U.S. Intelligence to Plan Counteroffensive'.

70 See *ibid.*; Paul McLeary, 'Ukraine in Direct Contact with Musk Amid Starlink Drama', *Politico*, 20 October 2022, https://www.politico.com/news/2022/10/20/ukraine-elon-musk-starlink-00062841; and Mansur Mirovalev, 'How Ukraine Turns Cheap Tablets into Lethal Weapons', Al-Jazeera, 22 August 2022, https://www.aljazeera.com/news/2022/8/26/how-ukraine-turns-cheap-tablets-into-lethal-weapons.

71 For a sobering account from the battle for Sievierodonetsk, see Gibbons-Neff and Yermak, 'On Front Lines, Communication Breakdowns Prove Costly for Ukraine'.

72 See *ibid.*; and McLeary, 'Ukraine in Direct Contact with Musk Amid Starlink Drama'.

73 See 'Rob Lee on Why Attrition Will Be a Critical Factor in the Battle for Donbas'.

74 See Liana Fix and Michael Kimmage, 'What if Ukraine Wins? Victory in the War Would Not End the Conflict with Russia', *Foreign Affairs*, 6 June 2022, https://www.foreignaffairs.com/articles/ukraine/2022-06-06/what-if-ukraine-wins; and Andriy Zagorodnyuk, 'Ukraine's Path to Victory: How the Country Can Take Back All Its Territory', *Foreign Affairs*, 12 October 2022, https://www.foreignaffairs.com/ukraine/ukraines-path-victory.

75 See Robbie Gramer and Amy Mackinnon, 'Baltic States Wanted German Tanks in Ukraine Yesterday', *Foreign Policy*, 27 September 2022, https://foreignpolicy.com/2022/09/27/baltic-states-ukraine-war-russia-germany-military-aid/.

76 See Lara Seligman, Paul McLeary and Erin Banco, '"These Are Not Rental Cars": As Ukraine Pleads for Tanks, the West Holds Back', *Politico*, 22 September 2022, https://www.politico.com/news/2022/09/22/ukraine-requests-american-tanks-counteroffensive-00058303.

77 See Gustav Gressel, Rafael Loss and Jana Puglierin, 'The Leopard Plan: How European Tanks Can Help Ukraine Take Back Its Territory', European Council on Foreign Relations, 9 September 2022, https://

ecfr.eu/article/the-leopard-plan-how-european-tanks-can-help-ukraine-take-back-its-territory/.

78 In Western armies during peacetime, it is routinely assumed that setting up new units can take up to ten years.

79 See Andrew E. Kramer, 'With Western Weapons, Ukraine Is Turning the Tables in an Artillery War', *New York Times*, 29 October 2022, https://www.nytimes.com/2022/10/29/world/europe/ukraine-russia-war-artillery.html.

80 See Tony Lawrence, 'Russia's War in Ukraine: The Early Air War', International Centre for Defence and Security, 15 June 2022, https://icds.ee/wp-content/uploads/dlm_uploads/2022/06/ICDS_Brief_Russia%C2%B4s_War_in_Ukraine_No5_Tony_Lawrence_June_2022.pdf.

81 See Kateryna Stepanenko et al., 'Russian Offensive Campaign Assessment, 24 October 2022', Institute for the Study of War, 24 October 2022, https://www.understandingwar.org/sites/default/files/Russian%20Offensive%20Campaign%20Assessment%2C%20October%2024%20PDF.pdf.

82 See Barnes, 'U.S. Sees Opportunity for Ukraine'.

83 See Mark Cancian, 'Is the United States Running Out of Weapons to Send to Ukraine?', Center for Strategic and International Studies, 16 September 2022, https://www.csis.org/analysis/united-states-running-out-weapons-send-ukraine; and Gramer and Mackinnon, 'Baltic States Wanted German Tanks in Ukraine Yesterday'.

84 See Cancian, 'Is the United States Running Out of Weapons to Send to Ukraine?'; and Mislav Tolusic, 'Ukraine

Makes It Obvious DoD Has to Change How It Buys Weapons', *Defence News*, 13 October 2022, https://www.defensenews.com/opinion/commentary/2022/10/13/ukraine-makes-it-obvious-dod-has-to-change-how-it-buys-weapons/.

85 See Julian E. Barnes, 'Russia Is Buying North Korean Artillery, According to U.S. Intelligence', *New York Times*, 5 September 2022, https://www.nytimes.com/2022/09/05/us/politics/russia-north-korea-artillery.html.

86 See Oleg Zhdanov, 'Daily Commentary About the War, 25 October 2022', YouTube.com, 25 October 2022, https://youtube/ZSMnjoSStz8.

87 See Croker, Manley and Lister, 'The Turning Points in Russia's Invasion of Ukraine'.

88 Vladimir Putin, 'Ob istoricheskom edinstve ruskikh i ukraintsev' [On the unity of Russians and Ukrainians], Kremlin, 12 July 2021, http://kremlin.ru/events/president/news/66181. Putin's statements in late October 2022 likewise reinforced this impression. See Institute for the Study of War, 'Russian Offensive Campaign Assessment, October 27', 27 October 2022, https://www.understandingwar.org/backgrounder/ukraine-conflict-updates.

89 'Putin: diktatura Zapada napravlena protiv vsekh obschestv, ona priobretaet cherty satanizma' [Putin: The dictatorship of the West is directed against all societies, it acquires the features of satanism], TASS, 30 September 2022, https://tass.ru/politika/15921463.

90 See, for instance, Rafael Reuveny and Aseem Prakash, 'The

Afghanistan War and the Breakdown of the Soviet Union', *Review of International Studies*, vol. 25, no. 4, October 1999, pp. 693–708.

91 See Emma Bubola, 'Ukraine Acknowledges That the "Ghost of Kyiv" Is a Myth', *New York Times*, 1 May 2022, https://www.nytimes.com/2022/05/01/world/europe/ghost-kyiv-ukraine-myth.html; and Tanya Goudsouzian, 'How Ukraine Won the Information War', *National Interest*, 23 October 2022, https://nationalinterest.org/feature/how-ukraine-won-information-war-205428.

92 See Jakub Bornio, 'As War Rages in Ukraine, the German–Polish Schism Deepens', *Eurasia Daily Monitor*, Jamestown Foundation, 26 October 2022, https://jamestown.org/program/as-war-rages-in-ukraine-the-german-polish-schism-deepens/; and 'France Under Fire over Ukraine Weapons Deliveries', France 24, 7 October 2022, https://www.france24.com/en/live-news/20221007-france-under-fire-over-ukraine-weapons-deliveries.

93 See Gressel, 'Mob Unhappy'.

94 Ukrainian Ministry of Defence, 'The Total Combat Losses of the Enemy from 24.02 to 24.10'.

95 See David Axe, 'Ukraine Is Collecting a Lot of Russia's Old T-62 Tanks', *Forbes*, 27 October 2022, https://www.forbes.com/sites/davidaxe/2022/10/27/ukraine-is-collecting-a-lot-of-russias-old-t-62-tanks/?sh=121c8bf230a5; and International Institute for Strategic Studies, *The Military Balance 2021* (Abingdon: Routledge for the IISS, 2021), p. 192.

96 See Zhdanov, 'Daily Commentary About the War, 25 October 2022'.

97 Gibbons-Neff, Kramer and Yermak, 'Shortage of Artillery Ammunition Saps Ukrainian Frontline Morale'.

98 Mitzer and Janovsky, 'Attack On Europe'; and Jeff Schogol, 'Dramatic Video Shows Why Russian Helicopters Are Sitting Ducks in Ukraine', *Task & Purpose*, 1 November 2022, https://taskandpurpose.com/news/russian-helicopter-shot-down-ukraine-video.

99 See Chester A. Crocker, 'Endings and Surprises of the Russia–Ukraine War', *Survival*, vol. 64, no. 5, October–November 2022, pp. 183–92.

100 See Siobhán O'Grady, Anastacia Galouchka and Paul Sonne, '"They're in Hell": Hail of Russian Artillery Tests Ukrainian Morale', *Washington Post*, 3 June 2022, https://archive.ph/FLiOI.

101 See 'Russian MoD: 50 Ukrainian Officers Killed in Long-range Strike', teleSUR, 19 June 2022, https://www.telesurenglish.net/news/Russian-MoD-50-Ukrainian-Officers-Killed-in-Long-Range-Strike-20220619-0023.html.

102 See Olga Ivshina, 'Mobilized and Special Forces: What Is Known About Russia's Losses in Ukraine by October', BBC News, 14 October 2022, https://www.bbc.com/russian/features-63250129?ocid=wsrussian.social.in-app-messaging.telegram..russiantelegram.

103 Anecdotal evidence also suggests that during the run-up to the offensive, Ukrainian forces specifically targeted command posts to amplify the disarray of already depleted units. See Saito, Tswetkova and Zverev, 'Abandoned Russian Base Holds Secret of Retreat in Ukraine'.

104 See Bremer and Grieco, 'In Denial About Denial'; and Miller and McLeary, 'Ukraine Has Hobbled Russia's Black Sea Fleet'.

105 See 'Factbox: Where Have Russians Been Fleeing to Since Mobilization Began?', Reuters, 6 October 2022, https://www.reuters.com/world/europe/where-have-russians-been-fleeing-since-mobilisation-began-2022-10-06/.

106 See Felicia Schwartz and Kiran Stacey, 'Ukrainian Officials "Shocked" as Republicans Threaten Tougher Line on Aid', *Financial Times*, 19 October 2022, https://www.ft.com/content/188401b5-229e-490a-9254-42167735d030.

107 See Bornio, 'As War Rages in Ukraine, the German–Polish Schism Deepens'; and 'France Under Fire Over Ukraine Weapons Deliveries'.

108 See Keir Giles, 'Ukraine Won Back Territory and Support, but Russia Will Test the West's Resolve Again', *Guardian*, 5 October 2022, https://www.theguardian.com/commentisfree/2022/oct/05/ukrainian-advances-russia-vladimir-putin.

109 See Crocker, 'Endings and Surprises', p. 184.

110 See *ibid.*, p. 190; and Fiona Hill and Angela Stent, 'The World Putin Wants: How Distortions About the Past Feed Delusions About the Future', *Foreign Affairs*, vol. 101, no. 5, September/October 2022, pp. 108–22.

111 See William Alberque and Benjamin Schreer, 'Finland, Sweden and NATO Membership', *Survival*, vol. 64, no. 5, October–November 2022, pp. 67–72; and Angela Stent, 'Germany and Russia: Farewell to Ostpolitik?', *Survival*, vol. 64, no. 5, October–November 2022, pp. 27–38.

112 See Elnur Alimova, 'Central Asian Leaders Meet Amid Russia's "Declining Role" in the Region', Radio Free Europe/Radio Liberty, 20 June 2022, https://www.rferl.org/a/central-asia-russia-decline-brick-interview/31952425.html; and 'Renewed Fighting in the Caucasus Shows Russia's Waning Influence', *The Economist*, 22 September 2022, https://www.economist.com/europe/2022/09/22/renewed-fighting-in-the-caucasus-shows-russias-waning-influence.

113 A security compact reminiscent of the Budapest Memorandum, 'permanent neutrality' along the lines of post-war Finland, and the West German model all have serious problems of their own. See 'On What Terms Could the War in Ukraine Stop?', *The Economist*, 10 November 2022, https://www.economist.com/briefing/2022/11/10/on-what-terms-could-the-war-in-ukraine-stop.

114 See 'NATO Should Avoid Learning the Wrong Lessons from Russia's Blunder in Ukraine, Says Michael Kofman', *The Economist*, 7 June 2022, https://www.economist.com/by-invitation/2022/06/07/nato-should-avoid-learning-the-wrong-lessons-from-russias-blunder-in-ukraine-says-michael-kofman.

115 See Dalsjö, Jonsson and Norberg, 'A Brutal Examination'.

116 Kofman, 'NATO Should Avoid Learning the Wrong Lessons from Russia's Blunder in Ukraine, Says Michael Kofman'

Copyright © 2022 The International Institute for Strategic Studies

What Kind of NATO Allies Will Finland and Sweden Be?

William Alberque and Benjamin Schreer

Barring a Turkish veto, Finland and Sweden will join NATO as full members prior to the Alliance's Vilnius Summit in June 2023. As we have argued, their membership will be a great asset to the Alliance given their geostrategic locations, military capabilities and political congruence with the other allies.[1] Sweden will help NATO consolidate the defence of the Baltic Sea, including secure sea lines of communication. It will also contribute considerable experience in Arctic and undersea warfare; coastal-defence systems; a highly modern air force; sophisticated military simulation, testing and evaluation capabilities; largely inter-operable forces; and the critical geostrategic asset of Gotland. Finnish forces, for their part, will facilitate NATO's defence of its northeastern flank, which stretches from the Baltic Sea to opposite the Kola Peninsula in the Arctic. Finland will also contribute strategically located coastal defences; a highly capable air force, including, from 2026, a large fleet of F-35 Joint Strike Fighters; a sizeable land force by today's standards; long-range artillery systems such as the High Mobility Artillery Rocket System (HIMARS); and significant Arctic-warfare capabilities.[2]

Understandably, both Nordic countries are inclined to focus primarily on the defence of their own national territories and immediate surroundings. The ability to defend one's territory fulfils Article 3 of the North

---

William Alberque is IISS Director of Strategy, Technology and Arms Control. **Benjamin Schreer** is Executive Director of IISS–Europe.

Survival | vol. 64 no. 6 | December 2022–January 2023 | pp. 123–136 https://doi.org/10.1080/00396338.2022.2150430

Atlantic Treaty and enhances the defence of NATO's populations and territory. However, key allies – in particular, the United States – are likely to
expect Finland and Sweden to contribute to allied defence beyond their
own borders, consistent with NATO's '360-degree' approach to security.[3]
Much will depend on whether and how the new allies transition from their
heretofore self-defence-focused mindset to that of members of a collective-
defence organisation. Therefore, Sweden and Finland will have to consider
and define how they can contribute to the defence of all of NATO.

This article explores the benefits and opportunity costs of these different
choices for the two countries and the Alliance. It acknowledges that while
all allies subscribe to the fundamental principle of collective defence, their
respective levels of political and military ambition vary substantially. The
United States remains the indispensable backbone of the Alliance, given
its commitment and ability to project significant military power across the
entire Euro-Atlantic theatre of operations. But many smaller allies pursue
a more limited role, in terms of both geographic focus and power projection. At the low end of the spectrum, Iceland has no standing army and is
valued for its strategic location and amenability to the operational use of
its territory. Differing levels of ambition among the members have stoked
long-standing debates about burden-sharing, of which Finland and Sweden
will now be a part.[4]

Political, military and defence-industrial choices

In the political realm, Finnish and Swedish policymakers confront three
main choices about their contribution to NATO's defence. The first concerns
their level of commitment to Alliance defence beyond their territories. The
second is about the future of their approach to NATO–European Union
defence cooperation, and could have major political and bureaucratic consequences for the EU's security and defence initiatives.

The third choice involves nuclear weapons. NATO will continue to be a
nuclear alliance for as long as nuclear weapons exist, and Russian threats
to use nuclear weapons against Ukraine have underscored the need for the
Alliance to bolster its nuclear deterrent. But Finland and Sweden are non-
nuclear-weapons states under the Nuclear Non-Proliferation Treaty, and

have strong traditions of supporting nuclear-arms control, non-proliferation and disarmament. Now they are faced with sharp choices regarding their role in fielding NATO's nuclear deterrent, as well as in future changes to the balance between NATO's nuclear and conventional war-fighting postures as members of the Nuclear Planning Group (NPG) and the High Level Group of the NPG (HLG).

In the military sphere, Finland and Sweden have three main choices in translating their respective political levels of ambition into specific changes. Firstly, as a front-line state, Finland will have to decide whether to host a NATO Force Integration Unit (NFIU) on its territory. NFIUs are now located in Bulgaria, Estonia, Hungary, Latvia, Lithuania, Poland, Romania and Slovakia, and help facilitate the rapid deployment of allied forces and support NATO defence planning, exercises and training, as well as local logistical networks, transportation routes and infrastructure.[5] Further questions include whether Finland or Sweden will request permanent or rotational NATO peacetime stationing on their territories; host NATO regional or functional military commands or headquarters; harbour NATO or allied military-equipment stockpiles as Norway does; and host centres of excellence or training and logistical centres.

Secondly, Helsinki and Stockholm must determine how to organise their military exercises, including whether they integrate them into NATO, host NATO exercises or participate in NATO and allied national exercises conducted elsewhere. More particularly, they will have to decide whether and which of their own national exercises will be handed over to the Supreme Allied Commander Europe (SACEUR) to be run by NATO and open to allied participation, or conducted independently. In addition, they will have to determine to what extent they will participate in NATO exercises conducted outside their immediate neighbourhood, whether to open their exercises to NATO partners and whether to participate in NATO exercises in allied countries.

Thirdly, Finland and Sweden need to decide what types of forces, if any, they will contribute to NATO's deterrence and defence postures in other allied countries. Will they deploy forces to the NATO enhanced-forward-presence (eFP) units in Eastern Europe? Will they contribute to or oversee an enhanced Baltic Air Policing deployment? What command-and-control arrangements will they establish between Finnish and Swedish forces and among NATO force commands across all domains? How will they integrate their national defence plans into NATO defence plans? Which Finnish and Swedish forces will be assigned to SACEUR in times of crisis and war?

Finland and Sweden will also have to make defence-industrial choices. Once inside the Alliance, they will be part of NATO's Conference of National Armaments Directors (CNAD) and the subordinate army, air-force and navy Main Armaments Groups (MAG). This will enable Finland and Sweden to submit bids for NATO procurement projects and to advertise their own defence industries' capabilities, yielding enhanced opportunities for selling, purchasing and manufacturing, and for less expensive procurement through the NATO Support and Procurement Agency. There will also be an increased need for force generation, sustainability (spare parts, ammunition stockpiles, ammunition and the like) and national infrastructure to support military operations. Moreover, should Finland and Sweden adopt high levels of ambition as NATO members, they would need to either increase their own defence-industrial capacity and output and advance bilateral or multinational defence cooperation, or rely more on off-the-shelf procurement. While both Sweden and Finland have a hands-off stance on their defence-industrial policy, this may change with NATO membership.

Three levels of ambition

Sweden's and Finland's political and military choices will be informed by whether they select a low, medium or high level of ambition for their membership in NATO.

Low: The Nordic/territorial-defence option

A low level of ambition would dictate a contribution to NATO focused primarily on the defence of national territory and proximate land and sea areas. Finland might argue that defending the largest land border with Russia of any NATO member, as well as a focus on its Arctic territory close to the Russian stronghold on the Kola Peninsula, would make a major and sufficient contribution to allied deterrence and defence. It could also conclude that its land forces, while highly capable, must remain within Finland and cannot make significant contributions to the defence of other NATO allied territories.

Sweden might emphasise the need to defend what will become the largest NATO Baltic Sea coastline, to work with Denmark and Norway to deny Russia access to the southern end of the Baltic Sea, and to use Gotland as an unsinkable command ship to support allied Baltic Sea operations and interdict potential Russian air and sea deployments. It might also highlight its willingness to provide support for High North contingencies – for instance, as part of a future Nordic air strike force with Finland and Norway.

At this low level of ambition, both Sweden and Finland would commit to NATO operations and deliberations under Articles 3 (national and collective resilience), 4 (consultations if an ally feels threatened) and 5 (collective defence), but their focus would remain on the defence of their own national territories. They could also impose restrictions on the deployment of NATO forces on their territories – say, by opting out of any permanent or rotational stationing on their territories.

Such an inward focus would curtail their overall power and positioning within NATO decision-making, resulting in limited responsiveness to threats and challenges across the land, air, maritime, cyber and space domains in allied territory beyond the Nordic region. It would translate into only minor assistance to Southern European allies contending with terrorism, illegal migration and other challenges emanating from the Middle East, Africa and beyond. At this level of ambition, Finland and Sweden would be reluctant to contribute to similar missions, or, for instance, to naval operations in the Eastern Mediterranean and near the Horn of Africa. Contributions to EU- or NATO-led deployments, defence-cooperation and partner-cooperation projects would also be limited.

At such a low level of ambition, Sweden's or Finland's probable role in NATO's nuclear deterrent would be distinctly low-key. They could establish strict constraints on hosting NATO nuclear weapons on their territories in peacetime, as have Denmark, Iceland, Lithuania and Norway. They might make a minimal staffing contribution to the NPG and HLG, but overall they would take a passive position on nuclear planning, while not ruling out nuclear deployments or stationing on their territories.[6] They would not seek to make any political or military contributions to NATO's nuclear-deterrent posture or plans, the Support of Nuclear Operations with Conventional Air Tactics (SNOWCAT) programme, or the annual nuclear exercise *Steadfast Noon*. There would be no practical political and military implications for either Sweden or Finland, aside from the need to develop a small cadre of nuclear-policy specialists within their respective bureaucracies; a wider national nuclear ecosystem would not be forthcoming.

There would be strict limitations on Swedish and Finnish contributions to NATO's force posture. They would rely on coordination with Supreme Headquarters Allied Powers Europe (SHAPE) for the planning and execution of exercises or deployments on Finnish and Swedish territories. They would conduct force planning and generation exclusively in consideration of the defence of national territory, and NATO membership would not be the primary driver of their defence-investment decisions. On command-and-control arrangements, Stockholm and Helsinki would be reluctant to transfer command authority over their national forces to SACEUR even in times of war, and would instead focus on advancing exclusively Nordic command-and-control arrangements, such as deepened integration among the Finnish, Swedish and Norwegian air forces. Swedish and Finnish contributions to NATO exercises outside their own territories would be kept at a minimum. Lastly, the two newest NATO members would baulk at making major contributions to NATO's force posture outside of their national borders.

Both allies would probably meet NATO's defence-spending target of 2% of GDP. In April 2022, Sweden's defence budget stood at around 1.3%, but the new government of Prime Minister Ulf Kristersson has committed to achieving the 2% target 'as soon as possible, but no later than 2026'.[7] Meanwhile, thanks to an extra boost to defence spending of around €2 billion after Russia invaded Ukraine, Finnish spending as a percentage of GDP was about 2% in 2022.[8] But at a low level of ambition such spending levels could be reduced, or at least not increased significantly.

At that level, Swedish and Finnish governments might look to profit from NATO's process of multinational capability cooperation, which favours the acquisition and purchase of inter-operable, cutting-edge and cost-effective equipment. But this process would be largely industry-driven rather than part of an integrated government–industrial strategy intent on building a larger defence-industrial base.

Medium: Nordic–Baltic defence options

Under a medium level of ambition, in the political domain, Sweden and Finland would focus not only on the defence of their national territories and the High North but also on defending Baltic allies. They would perceive the High North and Baltic Sea regions as increasingly integrated strategic theatres to defend alongside their Nordic and Baltic allies as well as Germany, Poland, the United Kingdom and the United States.

In Finland's case, this could mean expanding its military capability and commitment to defend Estonia given the two countries' geographic proximity, growing defence cooperation and commitment to joint coordination of coastal defences across the Gulf of Finland. In Sweden's case, it could include contributing to the maritime and air defence of Poland, particularly in a scenario involving the need to degrade Russian capabilities in Kaliningrad. It also would entail facilitating the secure movement of allied forces to defend the Baltic nations by sealift and airlift – including, in particular, the reinforcement of Lithuania by Germany via sealift through NATO's Baltic Maritime Component Command in Rostock. Sweden and Finland would thus commit to contributing directly to NATO's emerging forward defence posture for the Baltic states and Poland.

Both Finland and Sweden would probably remain hesitant to invest significant resources for new NATO deployments outside the Baltic–Nordic region. Instead, they might choose to contribute to non-traditional security challenges through the EU. In the nuclear domain, they could contribute personnel to the NPG and HLG, and build political and military expertise in their respective bureaucracies to enable their constructive participation in NATO nuclear consultations, improve outreach to parliaments and publics, advance the integration of conventional and nuclear planning and exercises, and decline to rule out NATO nuclear stationing or deployments on their territories. Nevertheless, they would remain passive with respect to

NATO's nuclear force posture, assuming no role in SNOWCAT, *Steadfast Noon* or nuclear war-fighting plans.

A medium level of ambition would see an NFIU established in Finland. Both new allies would focus on the planning of NATO exercises and the logistics and deployment of NATO forces on their territories. In addition, Swedish and Finnish naval and air forces would play a significant role in defending the Baltic countries and Poland, and participate in the enhanced Baltic Air Policing mission. They might also consider the establishment of a NATO command-level structure on their territories. For example, Sweden could offer to host a NATO sub-component of a combined air-operations centre for the High North and Nordic–Baltic area of operations, given its excellent air capabilities. Finland could offer to establish a NATO centre of excellence on Arctic warfare, potentially co-hosted with Norway. Both new allies would have to agree to the permanent or rotational deployment of conventional NATO forces on their territories.

In addition, Finnish and Swedish defence-capability development would focus on contingencies beyond their national territory and its immediate approaches to enable national forces to conduct operations in defence of the Baltic allies. Assets would need to include airlift and sealift capabilities, air-to-air refuellers to enable long-range air-combat operations for NATO, and longer-range anti-air, anti-ship and land-attack cruise missiles and artillery. Military infrastructure and stockpiles to support such missions would also need to be significantly enhanced. Furthermore, Sweden and Finland would likely seek to participate selectively in 360-degree defence, providing support for the southern flank through NATO and EU initiatives by coordinating and maximising the impact of any future (likely modest) deployments in the Mediterranean, Middle East and North Africa.

At this level, Sweden and Finland would still be loath to commit to large-scale NATO exercises or deployments outside the Nordic–Baltic region. But they would be open to contributing forces to eFP deployments in Baltic countries as a visible commitment to NATO's forward defence and to facilitate force integration with other key allies. In terms of command-and-control arrangements, both allies would be required to fully integrate their intelligence, surveillance and reconnaissance assets and commit their naval and air forces to execute SACEUR's defence plans in the region. They would also assign some land contingents operating in Baltic states to SACEUR to reinforce the eFP in times of war, although they would likely retain full national control over the bulk of their land forces.

Here Sweden and Finland likely would spend at least 2% of GDP on defence, but not much more. However, their defence-industrial aspirations would be higher. They would aim to reduce critical NATO capability shortfalls and create depth in logistical assets such as ammunition stockpiles as part of their host-nation support arrangements. They would also seek to become a NATO arsenal for operations in the Nordic–Baltic area of operation by supporting increased defence-industrial capacity in areas where they have comparative advantage, such as anti-tank weapons, artillery, aerospace and air defence. Moreover, they would drive the development of NATO niche capabilities by actively utilising and shaping CNAD activities so as to support Swedish and Finnish defence needs. This would imply a more active role for their respective defence industries, which would call for stronger national-government direction and support.

High: All-of-NATO defence

At this level, Sweden and Finland would fully commit to Article 5 missions across NATO territory through the NATO and EU frameworks, with a leading role in supporting and organising integrated Nordic–Baltic defence while also supporting the defence of the southern flank. At the nuclear level, both allies would play an engaged and active role in the HLG and NPG, and directly participate in the military mission. This would involve contributions to integrated conventional–nuclear war planning, a robust potential commitment to SNOWCAT and *Steadfast Noon*, and a future commitment to NATO's nuclear-sharing arrangements. Regarding the latter, for instance, Finland might consider certifying its F-35s for the carrying ('fitted for, but not with') of tactical nuclear weapons, Sweden could explore a role for its current *Gripen* fighters or their successor platforms, and both countries could examine the potential for NATO nuclear deployments on their respective territories in peacetime and war. Swedish and Finnish governments would also actively foster the evolution of a nuclear ecosystem within their governments and publics to support this ambition by, for instance, creating a Nordic version of the Project on Nuclear Issues.[9]

In this framework, Swedish and Finnish armed forces would pursue major capability investments to enable them to provide significant assets for NATO operations across the entire theatre. Enhancements to host-nation arrangements in both countries would ensure logistical support (including pre-positioning of materiel) for NATO operations from Finnish and Swedish territories in the land, air and sea domains. Moreover, both allies would furnish significant force elements for exercises across the entire NATO expanse and remain open to contributing force packages to NATO eFP forces on the entire eastern flank – for instance, in Romania or Bulgaria. Aside from hosting NATO command posts (such as a sub-component of a combined air-operations centre) on their territories, their command-and-control arrangements would entail the assignment of all forces to SACEUR during war, including command authority for targeting Swedish and Finnish forces to NATO cells.

The financial resources required for this option would be considerable, entailing defence spending of 2–3% of GDP at a minimum. During the Cold War, NATO allies routinely spent over 3% of GDP on defence to ensure high levels of readiness and sustainability. In our judgement, the implementation of NATO's ambitious force-development goals set at the 2022 Madrid Summit will require military spending in allied countries well above 2%. The defence-industrial implications would be significant too. Aside from aiming to reduce all critical NATO capability shortfalls, Sweden and Finland would seek to minimise their dependence on other allies for critical defence capabilities and enablers. In addition, they would become NATO arsenals for important weapons and key sources of other military capabilities. Even more, both allies would use their membership to advance their positions as drivers of military-technological innovation across the Alliance, taking a lead role in programmes such as the Defence Innovation Accelerator for the North Atlantic. To do so, Sweden and Finland would require government-led strategies and resourcing for defence innovation and a very closely coordinated government–industrial approach to NATO membership.

Which way?

Whatever level of ambition Sweden and Finland choose for their member-ship of NATO, defence of national territory will be the priority for both, as it is in most allied countries. An initial decision would not be etched in stone. They could, over time, build out their involvement in the Alliance from a nucleus of preferred partners, starting with their Nordic neighbours, the UK and the US at the lowest level, adding the Baltic states, Poland and Germany at the medium level, and finally the entire Alliance at the highest level. The defence budgets for both countries should increase, at first marginally and then, perhaps, substantially.

For both Stockholm and Helsinki, the US dimension will be critical regarding major decisions on NATO participation. Washington is a central, long-term defence partner of both countries, and one way to reinforce the transatlantic bond is to provide high-end, high-readiness forces to reduce the United States' burden. Both Democrats and Republicans would like Europe to free up the US to operate in Asia in a potential confrontation with China. This does not mean that either Finland or Sweden would be unusu-ally deferential to the US in the Alliance, but they are likely to work closely with Washington wherever possible. The proximate reason they are joining NATO is a major external threat from Russia. Countries facing such threats tend to court greater burden-sharing within alliances.[10]

It will be tempting for politicians in Sweden and Finland to focus on the low-end territorial/Nordic-defence option as their preferred model for NATO membership in lieu of taking on broader commitments. It would require the least change in current policies, and it would be domestically uncontroversial and less resource-intensive. It would also cater well to a distinct strategic culture in which large segments of society consider the primary role of the armed forces to be the defence of national territory rather than the defence of other nations.[11] Both countries could focus on working with Scandinavian neighbours, particularly Norway, with which they are geographically and culturally close, while maintaining close defence cooperation with the UK and the US. Examples include initiatives such as a potential Swedish–Finnish–Norwegian joint land division to defend the sparsely populated common Nordic realm.[12] Finally, Finland and Sweden would be able to avoid political and philosophically difficult quandaries, such as that over allowing the deployment of NATO nuclear forces on their territories in peacetime (while not foreclosing that option) or reconsidering their approach to nuclear deterrence.

Yet a narrow focus on Nordic defence could create frictions with other NATO allies, particularly the United States and the two new members' Baltic neighbours. Washington is likely to register a strong preference for Finland and Sweden to play a central role in the defence of what is now essentially an integrated High North–Nordic–Baltic strategic space, and in particular to entertain the possibility of turning the Baltic Sea into a 'NATO lake' by establishing air and maritime dominance vis-à-vis Russian forces. Indeed, given their respective geographic locations, it is difficult to imagine that the prospective allies would remain outside NATO defence planning for the Baltic states and Poland. Even before NATO membership, their security became increasingly linked to that of their Baltic neighbours and to NATO calculations because of evolving Russian capabilities, including Russia's deployment of missile systems in Kaliningrad and elsewhere.[13] Now, the availability of Swedish and Finnish territories will significantly increase NATO's operational flexibility for the defence of its eastern flank. Their participation in eFP missions in the Baltic states would add operational capability and send a strong political signal of Swedish and Finnish willing-ness to participate in collective-defence efforts beyond their own borders.

In any case, greater nuclear literacy and preparedness within the NATO context will be required of both nations. Russia's nuclear-capable *Iskander* missiles are deployed in Kaliningrad and capable of targeting Sweden as well as other NATO allies. Finland borders the Kola Peninsula, where the bulk of Russia's nuclear submarines are based. For these reasons, Helsinki and Stockholm will be highly likely to participate in NATO's nuclear delib-erations to a significant extent. A feasible middle course might be for them to flag the possibility of certifying their fighter aircraft for potential nuclear roles, leaving open the possibility of hosting nuclear weapons in wartime. More broadly, playing a key role in Nordic–Baltic defence would enhance their political influence within the Alliance, especially with Germany, Poland, the UK and the US.

*　　　*　　　*

It is prudent to assume that once they join as full members, both Sweden and Finland will adopt a medium level of ambition in NATO, opening up a range of new areas for cooperation with other allies and strengthening the Alliance as a whole. A high level of ambition is not likely in the short term, given their strategic needs and the substantial political, financial and personnel costs it would entail. Nevertheless, such a disposition could eventually materialise. For instance, Sweden might consider the deployment of force elements to an eFP at NATO's southeastern flank in order to demonstrate its commitment to the defence of the whole Alliance, while at the same time showcasing its advanced defence-manufacturing capability. In any event, Sweden and Finland are likely to become cornerstones of NATO's integrated deterrence and defence posture for the Arctic–Nordic–Baltic area, and thus key members in the new Alliance of 32.

Notes

[1] See William Alberque and Benjamin Schreer, 'Finland, Sweden and NATO Membership', *Survival*, vol. 64, no. 3, June–July 2022, pp. 67–72.

[2] See Matti Pesu and Samu Paukkunen, 'Finland Will Bolster NATO's Northeastern Flank', *National Interest*, 4 October 2022, https://nationalinterest.org/feature/finland-will-bolster-nato%E2%80%99s-northeastern-flank-205130.

[3] See Christelle Calmels, 'NATO's 360-degree Approach to Security: Alliance Cohesion and Adaptation After the Crimean Crisis', *European Security*, vol. 29, no. 4, July 2020, pp. 416–35.

[4] See Keith Hartley and Todd Sandler, 'NATO Burden-sharing: Past and Future', *Journal of Peace Research*, vol. 36, no. 6, November 1999, pp. 665–80.

[5] NATO, 'NATO Force Integration Units (NFIU)', https://shape.nato.int/operations/nato-force-integration-units.

[6] See Jonas Olsson, 'FOI-expert: Att avstå från kärnvapen kan uppfattas som undfallenhet mot Ryssland' [FOI expert: giving up nuclear weapons can be perceived as surrender to Russia], SVT, 1 November 2022, https://www.svt.se/nyheter/inrikes/foi-expert-att-inte-tillata-karnvapen-i-fredstid-skulle-kunna-uppfattas-som-undfallenhet-mot-ryssland.

[7] Government of Sweden, 'Statement of Government Policy Delivered by Prime Minister Ulf Kristersson', 18 October 2022, https://www.government.se/speeches/2022/10/statement-of-government-policy/.

8   Kati Pohjanpalo, 'Finland Makes 70% Defense Spending Increase in Shadow of War', Bloomberg, 5 April 2022, https://www.bloomberg.com/news/articles/2022-04-05/finland-adds-2-2-billion-defense-spending-in-shadow-of-war.

9   In other NATO countries such as the United Kingdom and the United States, such projects have engendered networks for facilitating exchanges among security professionals and expert scholars on contemporary nuclear issues.

10   See Brian Blankenship, 'The Price of Protection: Explaining Success and Failure of US Alliance Burden-sharing Pressure', *Security Studies*, vol. 30, no. 5, December 2021, pp. 691–724.

11   See Gunnar Aselius, 'Swedish Strategic Culture After 1945', *Cooperation and Conflict*, vol. 40, no. 1, March 2005, pp. 25–44; and Tuomas Forsberg, 'Finland and NATO: Strategic Choices and Identity Conceptions', in Andrew Cottey (ed.), *The European Neutrals and NATO: Non-alignment, Partnership, Membership?* (London: Palgrave Macmillan, 2018), pp. 97–127.

12   See 'Division to the Defence of the Common North', *Corporal Frisk*, 27 May 2022, https://corporalfrisk.com/2022/05/27/6-division-to-the-defence-of-the-common-north/; and Mikael Holmström, 'Hultqvist: skapa gemensam armé i norr' [Hultqvist: create a joint army in the north], *Dagens Nyheter*, 27 October 2022, https://www.dn.se/sverige/hultqvist-skapa-gemensam-arme-i-norr/.

13   See Robert Dalsjö, Christofer Berglund and Michael Jonsson, *Bursting the Bubble: Russian A2/AD in the Baltic Sea Region: Capabilities, Countermeasures, and Implications* (Stockholm: Swedish Defence Research Agency, March 2019).

Copyright © 2022 The International Institute for Strategic Studies

War and Arms Control: When to Pursue Cooperation

Suzanne Claeys and Heather W. Williams

Since the beginning of Russia's war against Ukraine, Moscow has been issuing nuclear threats. On 24 February 2022, within hours of starting a new invasion, Russian President Vladimir Putin warned:

> No matter who tries to stand in our way or all the more so create threats for our country and our people, they must know that Russia will respond immediately, and the consequences will be such as you have never seen in your entire history … All the necessary decisions in this regard have been taken. I hope that my words will be heard.[1]

Seven months later, on 21 September, he stated that 'if the territorial integrity of our country is threatened, we will without doubt use all available means to protect Russia and our people – this is not a bluff'.[2] In October, senior Russian military leaders reportedly had a conversation about 'when and how Moscow might use a tactical nuclear weapon in Ukraine'.[3] Putin's nuclear bullying has blurred the nuclear and conventional domains. It has also intensified the challenge for arms control to constrain a determined authoritarian willing to use nuclear capability for coercive purposes.

Survival | vol. 64 no. 6 | December 2022–January 2023 | pp. 137–152 https://doi.org/10.1080/00396338.2022.2150432

The breakdown of existing agreements and the worsening geopolitical environment are causes for pessimism about arms control, suggesting that the best we can hope for are informal risk-reduction measures.[4] American and Russian negotiations on arms control in the near future would seem incongruous with Russia's clear effort to change the international and nuclear orders.[5] On 8 August 2022, Russia announced the suspension of inspections under the New Strategic Arms Reduction Treaty (New START), the last remaining bilateral US–Russia arms-control agreement. At the same time, active and looming crises also highlight the need for arms control, and the United States and Russia, along with other nuclear-weapons states, have an obligation under the Nuclear Non-Proliferation Treaty (NPT) to pursue a 'cessation of the arms race' and 'general and complete disarmament'. Furthermore, abandoning arms control entirely could diminish American leadership and strategic stability. When, then, should the United States resume active pursuit of arms control with adversaries, such as Russia and China?

On 27 October 2022, the US Department of Defense released its National Defense Strategy, including a Nuclear Posture Review (NPR). The NPR essentially portrays the current security environment as an arms-control hiatus in which the United States 'will prepare for engagement and realistic outcomes in dialogues with both governments [China and Russia] as this remains in our national interest'.[6] In January 2022, the Center for Strategic and International Studies (CSIS) produced a report on 'integrated arms control' that recoupled arms control and deterrence, acknowledging the increasingly diverse range of technologies, domains, risks and actors in the current security environment.[7] In that report, we argued that arms control should be tailored to the geopolitical environment. We also argued that as deterrence becomes more integrated across domains and actors, so should arms control.

An uncertain and rapidly changing strategic landscape calls for a more flexible approach to arms control. Now is not the time to begin negotiations with Russia or China towards formal treaties, but there are other potentially constructive initiatives the United States can pursue immediately, and certainly when the war in Ukraine ends. Post-conflict resolution efforts on Ukraine, in particular, may present an opportunity both for formal efforts to reduce nuclear forces, especially tactical nuclear weapons, and for new, informal risk-reduction measures. Obviously, the extent of the opportunity and the feasibility of measures will depend on the outcome of the conflict and the strategic interests of Kyiv's and Washington's European allies. But formal and informal arms-control efforts are not mutually exclusive, and both should be priorities for the foreseeable future.

Arms control and US nuclear posture

The post-war theorists of arms control have identified its objectives as improving security, reducing economic costs and preventing the 'militarization of society'.[8] Arms control has historically allowed for cooperation between potential adversaries to promote strategic stability.[9] Narrowly defined, strategic stability arises when two adversaries have a survivable second-strike nuclear capability, there are limited incentives to use nuclear weapons first in a conflict (crisis stability) and there are limited incentives to build up nuclear forces (arms-race stability).[10] But arms control has consistently sat at the intersection of competition and cooperation.

Today's strategic security environment is far more complex, multifaceted and competitive than it was in the dyadic days of the Cold War and immediate post-Cold War years, calling into question assumptions about escalation and how a crisis might unfold. Future conflicts are unlikely to evolve in a clear, linear fashion that presents a sharp distinction between pre-conflict activity and conflict termination. Neither is a clear delineation between nuclear and non-nuclear crises sustainable when, as now, conventional and nuclear capabilities are commingled, capable of more diversified strategic effects and increasingly vulnerable to detection, disruption or disablement.[11]

The fundamental purposes of arms control – to stabilise nuclear rivalries and reduce nuclear danger – remain valid and more urgent than ever.[12] A prioritisation of arms control and reducing nuclear risks has been salient in all US NPRs. The Clinton administration completed the first NPR in 1994, establishing the articulation of the role of nuclear weapons as an element of US national-security strategy. Although the 1994 NPR was classified, it led to a congressional mandate for future NPRs at the beginning of a new president's term.

The George W. Bush administration submitted its NPR to Congress on 31 December 2001, with an unclassified executive summary published in January 2002.[13] This NPR came on the heels of the 9/11 attacks and a changing security environment defined by threats from terrorists as well as peer competitors.[14] The document downplayed past arms-control agreements in favour of maximum flexibility.[15] Moreover, in some cases, such as the Anti-Ballistic Missile (ABM) Treaty, the 2002 NPR called for the United States to withdraw from agreements that were no longer consistent with the administration's assessment of the current security environment and its desire for flexibility. Nevertheless, the United States and Russia continued to negotiate the Strategic Offensive Reductions Treaty (SORT), which entered into force in June 2003 and cut the number of deployed strategic warheads over the course of ten years.

The 2010 NPR came after an attempted 'reset' with Russia and reflected Barack Obama's determination to move towards 'the peace and security of a world without nuclear weapons'.[16] The document opened by acknowledging that the 'international security environment has changed dramatically since the end of the Cold War', and that the 'threat of global nuclear war has become remote' while 'the risk of nuclear attack has increased'.[17] This statement captured the NPR's goal of maintaining strategic deterrence and stability at lower nuclear levels, with priority placed on preventing nuclear proliferation and nuclear terrorism. The term 'arms control' only appears seven times in the 2010 NPR, whereas 'reductions' appears 61 times, typically in the context of New START and future agreements. Thus, the 2010 NPR envisioned post-New START arms-control objectives, including further reductions in nuclear weapons, and other forms of cooperation as means of promoting non-proliferation and reducing risks of nuclear terrorism.[18]

The 2018 NPR described a world in which American efforts to reduce the role and number of nuclear weapons had not been reciprocated, and potential adversaries continued to develop their arsenals qualitatively and quantitatively.[19] Uncertainty, in turn, necessitated flexibility, diversity and resilience in America's own strategic capabilities.[20] The 2018 NPR specifically called out Russia's continued non-compliance with arms-control agreements such as the Intermediate-Range Nuclear Forces (INF)

Treaty, stating that 'the status quo, in which the United States continues to comply while Russia continues deployments in violation of the Treaty, is untenable'.[21] The 2018 NPR asserted that 'arms control can contribute to US security by helping to manage strategic competition among states. It can foster transparency, understanding, and predictability in adversary relations, thereby reducing the risk of misunderstanding and miscalculation.'[22] Thus, while arms control was a useful tool for managing strategic competition, progress on arms control was not an end in itself, and depended on the security environment and participation of partners.

The 2022 NPR depicts an increasingly competitive and volatile security environment, underscored by the expansion and diversification of China's nuclear-weapons programme and Russia's invasion of Ukraine. It acknowledges that by the 2030s the United States will, for the first time, face two major nuclear powers as strategic competitors and potential adversaries.[23] In response to this challenge, the NPR states that the United States will pursue a 'comprehensive and balanced approach' that places a renewed

The 2018 NPR called out Russian non-compliance

emphasis on arms control, nuclear non-proliferation and risk reduction to strengthen stability, head off costly arms races and signal desire to reduce the salience of nuclear weapons globally.[24] The document specifically notes US willingness to negotiate a replacement for New START if Russia is willing and acting in good faith, and when conditions allow. Moreover, the NPR states that the US remains ready to engage China on a full range of strategic issues. At the same time, the document recognises challenges to mutual and verifiable arms control, commenting that the US will 'prepare for engagement and realistic outcomes in dialogues with both governments as this remains in our national security interest'.[25] Accordingly, the 2022 NPR signals an arms-control hiatus in which arms-control efforts will be constrained by Russia's history of non-compliance, the ongoing war in Ukraine and competition with China.

All four unclassified NPRs cast arms control as a balance of competition and cooperation on nuclear issues, but they prescribe different policies for pursuing this. They all contemplate a gradual broadening of the concept of strategic stability, to include non-nuclear capabilities and additional actors.[26] But they differ on what they envision arms-control agreements as encompassing. The 2002 and 2010 NPRs focus on specific arsenal reductions or types of systems, while the 2018 and 2022 NPRs zone in on managing nuclear risks. These differences are attributable to both internal political shifts, especially in US administrations, and changes in the geopolitical climate. The 2022 NPR underlines the current challenges of pursuing arms control, such as the lack of a willing partner and a changing strategic landscape. Rather than offering an overly ambitious arms-control agenda, it endorses a US policy marked by preparation and openness to future opportunities.

When to pursue arms control

The conventional wisdom is that arms control is possible when we don't need it and impossible when we do. But historical examples demonstrate this has not always been the case, and that arms control can happen even amid turmoil.[27] While geopolitics might determine what is possible within arms-control agreements, arms control in some format is possible at nearly all stages of conflict and can contribute to strategic stability and security, during peacetime or as part of post-crisis efforts. There are at least four relevant phases on the continuum of conflict: peacetime, the 'twilight struggle', crises and direct conflict. Arms control is possible and common during the first two phases. While it is rare during crises or war, arms control often plays an important role in post-crisis and post-conflict phases. Although we can no longer be confident that a given crisis will proceed through these stages along an escalation ladder, as technological developments have created wormholes of sorts that allow crises to jump across them, they remain reasonably realistic benchmarks.

There are a host of historical cases in which effective arms control arose in a placid geopolitical climate. In the lead-up to the collapse of the Soviet Union, the INF negotiations paved the way for START, signed in 1991, which limited the number of nuclear warheads to 6,000 and the number of nuclear-delivery systems to 1,600 per party. The treaty also provided verification and transparency measures, such as data exchanges and on-site inspections.[28]

After the break-up of the Soviet Union, in March 1992, the United States, Russia, Canada and over 20 European nations signed the Open Skies Treaty, which allowed parties to conduct short-notice observation overflights by unarmed fixed-wing observation aircraft to collect data on military forces and activities, although it did not enter into force until January 2002.[29] In May 1992, the Lisbon Protocol committing the newly independent states of Belarus, Kazakhstan and Ukraine to the transfer of Soviet nuclear weapons to Russia and accession to the NPT as non-nuclear-weapons states was successfully concluded.[30] This list is not exhaustive, but it demonstrates that arms-control agreements can often piggyback on each other during peacetime to take advantage of a spirit of cooperation.

There have also been important bursts of arms control during what Hal Brands calls 'twilight struggles', defined as 'competitions in the no-man's-land between peace and war, although the danger of military conflict is growing'.[31] This stage can also be described as 'unpeace'. In the late 1950s, the superpowers were actively expanding their arsenals as other states pursued nuclear weapons. Yet NPT negotiations began at the United Nations in 1959 to establish an international framework to curb proliferation, and continued through a period of intense and sustained strategic competition. The NPT was opened for signature in 1968 to 'prevent the spread of nuclear weapons and weapons technology, promote cooperation in the peaceful uses of nuclear energy, and further the goal of achieving nuclear disarmament and general and complete disarmament'.[32] The Soviet Union, the United Kingdom and the United States signed the treaty in 1968 and it entered into force in 1970. Furthermore, the success of the NPT and a general thawing of relations between Washington and Moscow led to the opening of Strategic Arms Limitation Talks (SALT) in 1969. The negotiations culminated in the signing of the SALT I Interim Agreement and the ABM Treaty in 1972.[33] Arms control could not 'forever stabilize a relationship that remained competitive',[34] but it did manage that competition, particularly in improving crisis communication and moderating the arms race, and helping to consolidate detente. As the United States enters a new 'twilight struggle', arms control could conceivably play a similar role.

There is little if any historical precedent for arms-control agreements concluded during an ongoing crisis. But there are rich examples of post-crisis arms control that could help identify opportunities for future arms-control initiatives. The arms race in the 1950s and the Cuban Missile Crisis in 1962, for example, gave rise to increased interest in arms control. In 1957, the Soviet Union successfully tested its first intercontinental ballistic missile and launched the first man-made satellite, *Sputnik 1*, into orbit.[35] These accomplishments kick-started the space and missile races, along with extensive nuclear testing. The Soviet Union, the UK and the US detonated more than 100 devices in 1958 alone.[36] As a result of burgeoning atmospheric radiation, all three countries agreed to voluntarily pause nuclear testing while discussing a permanent test ban, which would result in the Limited Test Ban Treaty of 1963, spurred by the Cuban Missile Crisis.[37] The treaty banned nuclear explosions in the atmosphere, outer space and underwater, and significantly restricted underground testing.[38] As a direct result of the missile crisis – the archetypal Cold War close call – the treaty also established a 'hotline' between US and Soviet leaders to mitigate the risk of accidental warfare.[39] Similarly, the United States and Soviet Union initiated a series of unilateral arms-control measures in 1991 following an attempted coup in Moscow that placed the security of the Soviet nuclear arsenal at risk. The Presidential Nuclear Initiatives undertaken by George H.W. Bush and Mikhail Gorbachev subsequently cut both countries' nuclear arsenals.[40]

Post-war circumstances often present important opportunities for arms control as part of a wider peace settlement to manage rearmament and in response to the trauma often associated with large-scale war. A paramount example of this is the negotiation, at the end of the First World War, of the Geneva Protocol, which prohibited the use of poisonous gases on the battlefield and forbade Germany from manufacturing or importing them.[41] In addition, there have been arms-control negotiations following formal conflict resolution in the Balkans, Northern Ireland and Rwanda, among other locales.

This historical framework provides useful guidance as to when arms-control efforts might be plausible and serve the US national interest. While an ongoing crisis or war is generally unpropitious, its aftermath can often be a promising moment in which to capture shared interests in preventing future crises. Arms control is also directly tied to geopolitics.[42] The strategic landscape will shape countries' national interests and strategic priorities, which will set boundaries on what is desirable and possible by way of arms control. But arms control itself can also facilitate political negotiation. As historian Marc Trachtenberg observed at the end of the Cold War: 'If war can be a continuation of politics by other means, then so can arms control, and political negotiations can be conducted in the guise of arms control talks.'[43]

Historical trends cannot rigidly dictate when the United States can or should pursue arms control with its adversaries. But they do indicate that the current arms-control hiatus ought to be used to prepare the ground for renewed arms control. The United States should continue to focus on the overarching objective of avoiding nuclear war.[44] Preparations should acknowledge, as the NPR does, that arms control is a balance of competition and cooperation, and works in tandem with deterrence, as outlined in the integrated arms-control framework.[45] US officials and analysts should also understand that, given the current era of rapid and substantial geopolitical and technological change, strategic stability is becoming an increasingly complex proposition, and that it will require a more inventive approach to arms control than is traditionally provided by legally binding bilateral agreements alone.

Cooperation and competition

When should the United States pursue new arms-control agreements and engage Moscow or Beijing in dialogue? And what can leaders in Washington do during this preparation stage to lay the groundwork for future arms control? Firstly, the US can work on arms control now by continuing to implement New START. Only days after the *New York Times* reported Russian officials' deliberations on the use of tactical nuclear weapons in Ukraine, the US and Russia announced plans to meet in the Bilateral Consultative Commission (BCC), the bilateral mechanism for discussing New START implementation.[46] The agreement continues to provide some transparency and predictability regarding Russia's strategic forces, and the BCC may prove a useful forum for future dialogue.

A second window of opportunity for arms control may open when the war in Ukraine ends. But post-crisis arms-control options will depend on a variety of factors. Key among them are when the war in Ukraine ends, who emerges as the victor, and the preferences of Ukraine's and America's European allies. If the Ukrainians continue to push back Russian advances, the leadership in Kyiv may be reluctant to negotiate and instead want to focus on strengthening the country's borders and rebuilding its forces in the expectation of a frozen conflict, similar to those in Georgia and Moldova. If Russia successfully seizes and holds parts of Ukraine, it may be reluctant to negotiate, or the US may be unwilling to engage Moscow until troops are withdrawn.

More militarily ambiguous circumstances may, however, produce a mutual desire for arms-control arrangements as part of a larger conflict-resolution agreement. Such arrangements could include a combination of formal reductions or limits on strategic forces and informal risk-reduction measures. Because Moscow's nuclear threats have played a dangerous role in the crisis, Russian tactical nuclear weapons should be prominently included in any post-crisis arms-control discussions. It will be crucial for the United States that Russian tactical nuclear weapons be included in any future agreement.[47] One option might be to exchange verifiable reductions in Russian tactical nuclear weapons for limits on US missile defences in Europe. No future arms-control agreements with Russia are likely unless they somehow incorporate limits on US missile defences.[48] The conclusion of the war in Ukraine, depending on the shape of a settlement, might also increase the scope for limiting conventional forces and curtailing arms races in the region.

Finally, this hiatus is an important chance to set the tone for future arms-control and nuclear-deterrence issues. As the United States enters an era of competition with two near-peer competitors – Russia in the strategic-nuclear realm, and China more generally – a top priority should be identifying options for a New START follow-on agreement that are aligned with any new nuclear-employment guidance. Such an agreement might include a common warhead ceiling, but it should be driven by force posture and requirements, and not the other way around.[49] Another priority for deterring two peer competitors should be more risk-reduction measures. These could be especially salutary for drawing China into broader arms-control efforts. One short-term option would be a joint agreement among the five permanent members of the United Nations Security Council to keep a 'human in the loop' in nuclear decision-making.[50]

In 2019, Alexei Arbatov cautioned against abandoning formal arms-control treaties in favour of more informal dialogues, noting that

> granular and pragmatic arms-control negotiations cannot be replaced by recently proposed surrogates, such as discussion forums on 'strategic stability and predictability' and 'creating an environment for nuclear disarmament'. The advocates of this method do not understand that it was the ceilings, sub-ceilings and qualitative limits of the past INF and SALT/START treaties that served as concrete guarantees of stable mutual deterrence, transparency and predictability. Arms-control negotiations that do not focus on specific types of weapons and verification methods are doomed to be merely scholastic exercises.[51]

Some scepticism is warranted. But arms-control efforts are about the management of weapons, and formal and informal tools are not mutually exclusive. More recently, former UK national security adviser Stephen Lovegrove, among others, has argued that 'given the enduring domestic and international challenges of formal arms control with Russia or China, there is no immediate prospect of all the major powers coming together to establish new agreements. So, as we agreed in the NATO Strategic Concept, our immediate focus should be getting on with the work of strategic risk reduction.'[52] These two lines of effort – formal treaties and informal risk-reduction measures – are not inherently at odds, and indeed will need to work in tandem.

One of the most crucial tasks during the arms-control hiatus will be for the United States and its allies and partners to build capacity for future arms-control efforts. This includes training arms-control negotiators and inspectors, along with developing new verification technologies. In May 2022, US National Nuclear Security Administrator Jill Hruby outlined a vision for the Arms Control Advancement Initiative that stands to 'advance our capability for new types of warhead monitoring and verification by maturing new technologies, maintaining expert engagement, and advancing modeling'.[53] Congressional support and allied partnership will be needed to power this effort. The hiatus is also a time to enhance and refine the understanding of wider nuclear issues among US domestic stakeholders, particularly on Capitol Hill and among US allies. Improving 'deterrence IQ' requires a conceptual understanding not only of deterrence and strategic stability, but also of adversaries' thinking and how the strategic landscape looks from Moscow and Beijing.

*   *   *

The 2022 NPR does not offer a revolutionary vision for arms control. Rather, it takes a sober approach to the endeavour in light of the ongoing war in Ukraine and the larger context of great-power competition, with an eye to preparation in the short term. For now, Washington and other capitals should work to convince Moscow to continue to implement New START alongside the United States, notwithstanding the two sides' strategic opposition over Ukraine and Putin's nuclear sabre-rattling. At the same time, they can also begin to envision and shape future agreements for reducing Russian tactical nuclear weapons if and when the war in Ukraine ends in circumstances that make them possible. Longer-term arms-control preparations could contemplate risk-reduction mechanisms with China.

There are obvious challenges to this extended approach to arms control, whereby formal and informal mechanisms are conjoined. For one, to be durable, any future formal agreements would require the advice and consent of the US Senate, which remains heavily polarised and relatively inexperienced on these issues. Given Russia's history of non-compliance, it will also be difficult for arms-control advocates to convince senators and other key American stakeholders to support a future agreement, placing on such advocates a heavy burden of persuasion. Another difficulty is that Moscow and Beijing have shown little regard for norms and are actively working to change the nuclear order. Accordingly, US officials in favour of informal as well as formal arms-control arrangements will need to manage expectations about the real impact of risk-reduction efforts, and ensure that proposed measures are paired with strong deterrence frameworks.

In recent decades, nuclear weapons had substantially receded from public consciousness. Putin's nuclear threats, along with China's rapidly growing arsenal, have brought them back. Moscow and Beijing are likely to continue to leverage their possession of nuclear weapons to advance their strategic priorities. Nuclear weapons are not going away any time soon, and as long as they exist, arms control might once again offer important means of managing associated risks – provided it is adapted to strategic realities.

Notes

1 President of Russia, 'Address by the President of the Russian Federation', 24 February 2022, http://en.kremlin.ru/events/president/news/67843.

2 Quoted in Guy Faulconbridge, 'Putin Escalates Ukraine War, Issues Nuclear Threat to West', Reuters, 21 September 2022, https://www.reuters.com/world/europe/putin-signs-decree-mobilisation-says-west-wants-destroy-russia-2022-09-21/.

3 Helene Cooper, Julian E. Barnes and Eric Schmitt, 'Russian Military Leaders Discussed Use of Nuclear Weapons, U.S. Officials Say', *New York Times*, 2 November 2022, https://www.nytimes.com/2022/11/02/us/politics/russia-ukraine-nuclear-weapons.html.

4 See William Alberque, 'The New NATO Strategic Concept and the End of Arms Control', IISS Analysis, 30 June 2022, https://www.iiss.org/blogs/analysis/2022/06/the-new-nato-strategic-concept-and-the-end-of-arms-control.

5 See Alexander K. Bollfrass and Stephen Herzog, 'The War in Ukraine and Global Nuclear Order', *Survival*, vol. 64, no. 4, August–September 2022, pp. 7–32.

6 US Department of Defense, '2022 National Defense Strategy of the United States of America', p. 16, https://media.defense.gov/2022/Oct/27/2003103845/-1/-1/1/2022-NATIONAL-DEFENSE-STRATEGY-NPR-MDR.PDF.

7 See Rebecca K.C. Hersman, Heather Williams and Suzanne Claeys, 'Integrated Arms Control in an Era of Strategic Competition', Center for Strategic and International Studies, January 2022, https://csis-website-prod.s3.amazonaws.com/s3fs-public/publication/220121_Hersman_Arms_Control.pdf?_jBrYoBv1jWodpXQCKsFJq6A-EGCxWvmz.

8 Hedley Bull, 'Arms Control and World Order', *International Security*, vol. 1, no. 1, Summer 1976, p. 4. See also Bernard Brodie, 'On the Objectives of Arms Control', *International Security*, vol. 1, no. 1, Summer 1976, pp. 17–36; and

Thomas C. Schelling and Morton H. Halperin, *Strategy and Arms Control* (New York: Twentieth Century Fund, 1961).

9 See Colin Gray, 'Arms Control Does Not Control Arms', *Orbis*, vol. 37, no. 3, Summer 1993, pp. 333–48.

10 See James Acton, 'Reclaiming Strategic Stability', in Elbridge Colby and Michael Gerson (eds), *Strategic Stability: Contending Interpretations* (Carlisle Barracks, PA: U.S. Army War College Press, 2013), p. 117, https://carnegieendowment.org/files/Reclaiming_Strategic_Stability.pdf.

11 See Hersman, Williams and Claeys, 'Integrated Arms Control in an Era of Strategic Competition'.

12 See Michael Krepon, *Winning and Losing the Nuclear Peace: The Rise, Demise, and Revival of Arms Control* (Stanford, CA: Stanford University Press, 2021), p. 3.

13 See Charles D. Ferguson, 'Nuclear Posture Review', Nuclear Threat Initiative, 31 July 2002, https://www.nti.org/analysis/articles/nuclear-posture-review/.

14 See Heather Williams, 'Strategic Stability, Uncertainty, and the Future of Arms Control', *Survival*, vol. 60, no. 2, April–May 2018, pp. 45–54.

15 See Ferguson, 'Nuclear Posture Review'.

16 White House, 'Remarks by President Barack Obama in Prague as Delivered', 5 April 2009, https://obamawhitehouse.archives.gov/the-press-office/remarks-president-barack-obama-prague-delivered.

17 US Department of Defense, 'Nuclear Posture Review Report', April 2010, p. iv, https://dod.defense.gov/Portals/1/features/defenseReviews/NPR/2010_Nuclear_Posture_Review_Report.pdf.

18 *Ibid.*, p. vi. The full quote is: 'By promoting strategic stability with Russia and China and improving transparency and mutual confidence, we can help create the conditions for moving toward a world without nuclear weapons and build a stronger basis for addressing nuclear proliferation and nuclear terrorism.'

19 See US Department of Defense, 'Nuclear Posture Review', 2018, p. v, https://media.defense.gov/2018/Feb/02/2001872886/-1/-1/1/2018-NUCLEAR-POSTURE-REVIEW-FINAL-REPORT.PDF.

20 See Williams, 'Strategic Stability, Uncertainty and the Future of Arms Control', p. 47.

21 US Department of Defense, 'Nuclear Posture Review', 2018, p. 74.

22 *Ibid.*, p. xvii.

23 US Department of Defense, '2022 National Defense Strategy', p. 4.

24 *Ibid.*, p. 1.

25 *Ibid.*

26 See Williams, 'Strategic Stability, Uncertainty, and the Future of Arms Control'.

27 See Naomi Egel and Jane Vaynman, 'Reconsidering Arms Control Orthodoxy', *War on the Rocks*, 26 March 2021, https://warontherocks.com/2021/03/reconsidering-arms-control-orthodoxy/.

28 See Colleen Moore, 'From SALT to START: A Timeline of U.S.–Russia Arms Control Talks', Global Zero, 23 April 2020, https://www.globalzero.org/updates/from-salt-to-start-a-timeline-of-u-s-russia-arms-control-talks/.

29 See Amy F. Woolf, 'The Open Skies Treaty: Background and Issues', Congressional Research Service, 7

June 2021, https://sgp.fas.org/crs/nuke/IN10502.pdf.

30 See Council on Foreign Relations, 'Timeline: U.S.–Russia Nuclear Arms Control', https://www.cfr.org/timeline/us-russia-nuclear-arms-control.

31 Hal Brands, *The Twilight Struggle: What the Cold War Teaches Us About Great-power Rivalry Today* (New Haven, CT: Yale University Press, 2022), p. 1.

32 United Nations Office for Disarmament Affairs, 'Treaty on the Non-Proliferation of Nuclear Weapons (NPT)', https://www.un.org/disarmament/wmd/nuclear/npt/.

33 See Moore, 'From SALT to START'.

34 *Ibid.*, p. 146.

35 *Ibid.*

36 Arms Control Association, 'The Nuclear Testing Tally', https://www.armscontrol.org/factsheets/nucleartesttally.

37 Council on Foreign Relations, 'Timeline: U.S.–Russia Nuclear Arms Control'.

38 See US Department of State, 'Treaty Banning Nuclear Weapon Tests in the Atmosphere, in Outer Space, and Under Water', https://2009-2017.state.gov/t/avc/trty/199116.htm.

39 *Ibid.*

40 See Eli Corin, 'Presidential Nuclear Initiatives: An Alternative Paradigm for Arms Control', Nuclear Threat Initiative, 29 February 2004, https://www.nti.org/analysis/articles/presidential-nuclear-initiatives/.

41 See US Department of State, 'Protocol for the Prohibition of the Use in War of Asphyxiating, Poisonous or Other Gases, and of Bacteriological Methods of Warfare (Geneva Protocol)', https://2009-2017.state.gov/t/isn/4784.htm.

42 See Heather Williams and Nicholas Adamopoulos, 'Arms Control After Ukraine: Integrated Arms Control and Deterring Two Peer Competitors', CSIS Occasional Paper, Center for Strategic and International Studies (forthcoming).

43 Marc Trachtenberg, 'The Past and Future of Arms Control', *Daedalus*, vol. 120, no. 1, Winter 1991, p. 213.

44 *Ibid.*, p. 203.

45 See Center for Strategic and International Studies, 'The Future of Arms Control, Strategic Stability, and the Global Order: A Conversation with Sir Stephen Lovegrove, UK National Security Adviser', 27 July 2022, https://www.csis.org/events/future-arms-control-strategic-stability-and-global-order.

46 See Simon Lewis, 'Russia, U.S. to Hold First Talks Under Nuclear Treaty Since Ukraine War – State Dept', Reuters, 21 September 2022, https://www.reuters.com/world/russia-us-discuss-first-nuclear-talks-since-ukraine-conflict-kommersant-2022-11-08/.

47 See, for example, US Department of State, 'New START Treaty: Resolution of Advice and Consent to Ratification', https://2009-2017.state.gov/t/avc/rls/153910.htm.

48 See Austin Long, 'Russian Nuclear Forces and Prospects for Arms Control', Testimony Presented Before the US House of Representatives Committee on Foreign Affairs, Subcommittee on Terrorism, Nonproliferation, and Trade, 21 June 2018, p. 115, available at https://www.rand.org/content/dam/rand/pubs/testimonies/CT400/CT495/RAND_CT495.pdf.

49 See Williams and Adamopoulos, 'Arms Control After Ukraine'.

50 Lauren Kahn, 'Mending the "Broken Arrow": Confidence Building Measures at the AI–Nuclear Nexus', *War on the Rocks*, 4 November 2022, https://warontherocks.com/2022/11/mending-the-broken-arrow-confidence-building-measures-at-the-ai-nuclear-nexus/.

51 Alexey Arbatov, 'Saving Strategic Arms Control', *Survival*, vol. 62, no. 5, October–November 2020, p. 98.

52 Center for Strategic and International Studies, 'The Future of Arms Control, Strategic Stability, and the Global Order: A Conversation with Sir Stephen Lovegrove, UK National Security Adviser'.

53 National Nuclear Security Administration, 'NNSA Administrator Hruby's Remarks at the 16th Annual Strategic Weapons in the 21st Century Symposium', 26 May 2022, https://www.energy.gov/nnsa/articles/nnsa-administrator-hrubys-remarks-16th-annual-strategic-weapons-21st-century.

Copyright © 2022 The International Institute for Strategic Studies

Review Essay

Castroism in Crisis

Russell Crandall

The Cubans: Ordinary Lives in Extraordinary Times
Anthony DePalma. London: Bodley Head, 2020. £20.00. 352 pp.

For half a century, perceptions of Cuba both outside and inside the country have been dominated by the enduring influence of Fidel Castro, something that veteran *New York Times* foreign correspondent Anthony DePalma makes clear in his new book *The Cubans: Ordinary Lives in Extraordinary Times*. External observers regularly referred to 'Fidel Castro's Cuba' during *el comandante*'s lifetime, as if the island nation were his very own, and when he died in 2016 state media declared 'Fidel es Patria' ('Fidel is the Homeland') while the country's teachers instructed their students to chant 'I am Fidel' (p. 6). In Cold War America, the army-fatigue-wearing, cigar-smoking Castro was the perfect communist bogeyman, and DePalma admits that in the early stages of his career, he was captivated by images of Fidel 'shouting, snarling, and pointing his accusing finger straight at the United States' (p. 329).

There is, of course, good reason for this elision of leader and country. As DePalma says, 'everyone knows that Fidel remade Cuba's political, economic, and social structures, putting the state in charge of everything and everyone but him' (p. 6). Yet Castro's towering influence obscures both the

Russell Crandall is a professor of American foreign policy and international politics at Davidson College in North Carolina, and a contributing editor to *Survival*. His latest books are *Drugs and Thugs: The History and Future of America's War on Drugs* (Yale University Press, 2020) and, with Britta Crandall, *"Our Hemisphere"?: The United States in Latin America, from 1776 to the Twenty-first Century* (Yale University Press, 2021).

Survival | vol. 64 no. 6 | December 2022–January 2023 | pp. 153–166 https://doi.org/10.1080/00396338.2022.2150433

multifaceted society that existed before the revolution and the complex one that exists today, one which finds itself increasingly ill at ease with the strictures of the revolution.

DePalma's solution – to explore the country by listening to its 'ordinary' citizens – allows us to regain a sense of Cuba as a whole. Yet he admits that this is difficult work, for personal expression in Cuba is fraught with danger, meaning ordinary Cubans have remained largely unheard:

Their voices have few outlets inside Cuba, and fewer still outside the island.

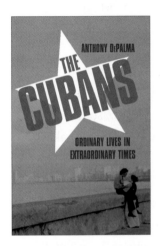

When they speak out it usually is in small rooms where they hope that the whoosh of a table fan or the tinny sound of an old TV keeps their remarks from prying ears. Most never get involved in public protests for fear of retribution from a state system of surveillances that they believe watches over their every move. Only the bravest or most desperate risk everything to join the small number of outspoken dissidents that the government stalks, harasses, and sometimes imprisons. But it is undoubtedly the complicated silence of their ordinary lives – their personal histories of living with an interminable revolution, their changing priorities and shifting alliances, their triumphs and their tragedies from one moment to the next in an endless stream of warm days under a brilliant sun – that tell the remarkable story of Cuba best. (p. 8)

As the reader discovers at the end of the book, DePalma has a personal stake in Cuba (something he might have flagged at the get-go), his Cuban wife Miriam having been taken into exile as a youngster in 1960 by her grandmother, who thought Fidel's revolution would last half a year. DePalma recalls a tattered, late-1950s Kodachrome photo of a young Miriam in a *barrio* (neighbourhood) that decades hence is only a ruin. For DePalma, the 'arched windows and double doors of a grand old house' evoked the 'elegance, dignity, and history' of a Cuba that is no longer (p. 329).

Yet DePalma's book is not about misty-eyed yearning for the pre-revolutionary past, but rather an attempt to capture the real Cuba of today in places such as the gritty township of Guanabacoa: 'broken streets, collapsing buildings, more garbage than flowers. Hot. Smelly. Noisy. Raw' (p. 6). We meet several residents of Guanabacoa and learn, in often excruciating detail, about their chaotic lives, their courage and their cowardice. DePalma is adamant that their sense of place is essential to their actions and agency, for Guanabacoa is a place where

> old cars are not prized classics, but just ugly hunks of battered metal, held together by wire and running on hope. Where rum is cheap and comes in small cardboard boxes. Where there are no robocalls, no fad diets, no supermarket flyers or commercial billboards. Where daily life depends not on tourist dollars but on the courage, confidence, and inventiveness of people living in an excess of prohibitions and a minimum of inhibitions. Where people have become masters at masking their misery with vibrant music and rapturous dancing, disguising their frustrations with layers of disrespectful mocking, making a joke of almost everything and taking nothing so seriously that it merits protest. (p. 7)

It is a picture far removed from the Cuba of the Buena Vista Social Club so beloved by the global left, yet for DePalma there is much to admire in the remarkable tenacity of Cubans, their 'indomitable adaptability' and 'bottomless capacity to make do' (p. 8). This is why, DePalma contends, the US embargo will never succeed: 'People who can turn a plastic soda bottle into a gas tank for a motorcycle, or use an old piston heated in a kitchen stove to repair a flat tire, see the world differently from other, more conventional societies' (p. 8).

El Período Especial

Given his willingness to look beyond the Cuba of leftist lore and fleeting tourist encounters, it may surprise some readers to find that DePalma is no anti-Castroite ideologue, at least in the eyes of this reviewer. The author shows admirable nuance and balance in acknowledging that, in its first decades in power, the revolutionary government made 'unmatched strides' against social inequities, including entrenched poverty and racism (p. 119).

The rub, as DePalma sees it, is that the gains came at the expense of preventing some citizens from earning more than others, which might have initially seemed desirable but is now universally recognised (except, perhaps, among the dinosaurs of the Cuban Communist Party) as counterproductive, at least in economic terms.

The fundamentally flawed nature of the Cuban economic model was dramatically exposed after the abrupt end of the Cold War, which saw $4–5 billion in annual Soviet subsidies evaporate. Trade receipts also plunged, given that Moscow had been Havana's main export market after the US embargo was imposed in 1962, buying 80% of Cuba's sugar harvest. This loss of export income triggered a 'tsunami of shortages' (p. 69), including critical inputs such as oil to keep power plants operational. Having run out of other people's money (as Margaret Thatcher might say), Cuba suddenly lacked the means to import enough foodstuffs to prevent its people from starving. (This was a nation, DePalma reminds us, that before 1959 produced 80% of the food it ingested.) Overnight, vegetables became as unavailable as meat.

Faced with this barrage of challenges, Castro told his compatriots in September 1990 that the *patria* had commenced a 'Special Period in Time of Peace' – surely one of history's great euphemisms. In a speech on 29 September he attempted to steel their resolve: 'What are we going to do? Give up? Never. Renounce socialism? Renounce independence? Never. What we have to do is resist and fight. We must resist, fight, and, of course, win' (p. 68).[1] But the crisis was unrelenting. Life in Cuba was reduced to the basic imperative of gathering enough to eat each day. From the revolution's onset, Cubans had relied on their *libreta* (ration card) to buy essential goods each month: rice, beans, sugar, vegetable oil, bread. In the Special Period, such cards continued to list the goods due to their carriers, but store shelves were bare. Gasoline rationing and a dearth of spare parts meant that buses, trucks and the country's stock of classic American cars were sidelined, replaced by imported Chinese bicycles with curious names such as 'Flying Pigeon' and 'Follow Me'. (An estimated 300,000 *habaneros* alone, in a city of 2 million residents, were issued *bicis*, which led to unwelcomed further weight loss and a surge in accidents.[2]) By the time the crisis wound down in 1995 (some experts contend it lasted another five years), Cuba's economy had shrunk by a third.

Confronted with such harrowing circumstances, ordinary Cubans demonstrated incredible ingenuity: 'they flattened and tenderized grapefruit rinds and fired them as if they were steaks. Banana peels ground up and mixed with spices became another pale substitute for meat' (p. 69). A man called Pipo recounts in *The Cubans* how he would pedal his Chinese *bici* 60 kilometres from his Guanabacoa neighbourhood to a farm where he would 'barter a pair of old shoes or a ripped shirt for a few plantains and some root vegetables' (p. 69). Even rum, a substance so indispensable to the nation that citizens often call it 'Vitamin R', was nowhere to be found, leading neighbours to contribute any residue at the bottom of rum bottles to a collective container. Apartment residents throughout Guanabacoa used their tiny back patios as a place to raise piglets, feeding them already scarce food scraps until they grew into passably fattened pigs. (As the crisis grew more severe in 1994, the Castro regime made the killing of a cow without state authorisation a felony equal to killing a human.) Power blackouts became so frequent and so lengthy that residents rejoiced when the electricity came back on for brief periods that they exuberantly called *alumbrones*.

13 de Marzo

The year 1994 proved to be the nadir of the Special Period, which, cruelly, coincided with one of the hottest summers in Cuban history. Fidel refused to deviate from his chosen path, and ratcheted up the repression of Cubans who dared to dissent.[3] Even for people who didn't openly oppose the regime, life was next to insupportable:

> People were being packed like cattle into long trailers called 'camels' to get to and from work. Elevators in high-rise buildings stopped working, converting sweltering apartments into prisons. Women were breaking open old batteries and using the black paste inside for hair dye. (p. 129)

Around 30,000 Cubans – as well as an unknown number who drowned making the perilous sea crossing – fled Cuba by raft, an overwhelming share of them being intercepted at sea by the US Coast Guard and transferred to the US naval base at Guantanamo Bay, Cuba, before eventually becoming US citizens.

Jorge García, a protagonist in *The Cubans,* had deep roots in Guanabacoa, his extended family having lived there for generations. In 1977 he was shipped off to be a civilian media adviser in Angola, where 75,000 Cuban soldiers were backing a communist insurgency (then aged 33, Jorge was considered too old to fight). His return to Cuba in spring 1980 coincided with the infamous Mariel boatlift – the mass emigration to Florida that ultimately saw 125,000 Cubans flee to the US. He refused to join the Communist Party, a fraught decision to say the least. By 1994, Jorge and his family were among those whose disillusionment with a failed revolution was becoming overwhelming. They decided to take drastic action: together with other family members and friends, they seized a tugboat, the *13 de Marzo,* and sailed for Florida.

Fatefully, Jorge ultimately opted not to participate in the scheme, allowing someone else to take his seat – a decision that was to save his life but bring him untold grief. On 13 July 1994, Cuban Coast Guard vessels rammed the *13 de Marzo* about 11 km offshore, sinking it. Out of the 68 adults and children on the tug, 37 perished, including 11 children, the youngest just five months old.[4] All told, 14 members of Jorge's family, including his son and grandson, died. His daughter, María Victoria, survived to give her father the awful news upon her return to land. She later described how the Coast Guard had attempted to ensure that no one was left alive to be an eyewitness to its crime.

Granma, the newspaper of the Communist Party and at that time the main source of information in Cuba, reported that a squad of armed 'antisocial elements' – a catch-all phrase for 'anyone acting outside expected standards of discipline, loyalty, and revolutionary fervor' – had stolen the tugboat in 'an irresponsible act of piracy' (p. 103). It added that the Cuban authorities had acted 'heroically' to rescue the survivors from the 'capsized' boat. 'A BITTER LESSON FOR IRRESPONSIBLE PEOPLE' blared the headline of a rare full-page *Granma* editorial.

By contrast, the US-government-sponsored anti-regime broadcaster Radio Martí exhaustively reported on the killings as one more sign that the Castro regime was in terminal decline.[5] Undaunted by the mountain of evidence and testimonials – including from the Organization of American States – that there had been an official cover-up, Raúl Castro, brother of Fidel, came out swinging: 'We reject with all our energy the hypocritical and venomous anti-Cuban campaign orchestrated around this incident. And we reject any interference in the internal affairs of our sovereign country by the United States or any other government' (p. 128). Still, the story did not go away. In 1997, Amnesty International issued a report concluding that there was considerable reason to question the veracity of Havana's account of the 13 *de Marzo* incident, noting that witnesses had testified to a coordinated, aggressive operation against unarmed citizens who could not have resisted capture. If these reports were true, then 'those who perished in the incident were victims of extrajudicial execution'.[6]

In the weeks and months following the tragedy, party loyalists loitered outside Jorge's residence, condemning him and his family for putting the children's lives at risk. 'Worms!' they taunted him, 'antisocial revolutionaries!' They alleged that he was part of the 'Miami Mafia' – the infamous exile community that would stop at nothing to ruin the revolution (p. 105). Eventually, Jorge was charged with the vague crime of 'illegal economic activity' and banned from driving, teaching or holding any state employment (p. 150). María Victoria, his surviving daughter, was fired from her job. By the time Hurricane Irma ravaged Cuba in September 2017, Jorge García had put more than 300 km between himself and Guanabacoa, having sought refuge 'in a dumpy ranch house across the street from a Miami boatyard' (p. 5).

Maleconazo

Miriam Díaz, another resident of Guanabacoa, was 47 in 1994, making her 'old enough to remember when the fancy stores along Obispo, Galiano, and San Rafael in Havana were well stocked with the latest fashions from all over the world' (p. 110). By 1994 such grand emporia were a thing of the past, but DePalma explains that Miriam had long since developed a sense of equanimity about the revolution's hardships: 'She'd come to accept that there would be trade-offs in life, and until the special period ended, she'd simply have to make do with what they had. The consolation was that everyone else had to do the same' (p. 110). At least in the early years, the revolution that had spelled the end of glamorous shopping destinations had still appeared to deliver on its promises of literacy, healthcare and dignity for all.

On 5 August 1994, however, Miriam stumbled across a particularly disruptive protest on Havana's Malecón, the city's legendary esplanade, an uprising that would later become known as the Maleconazo and that was directed at the unbearable privations of the Special Period. 'The crowds were protesting the hundreds of days without electricity overhead, overheated apartments, bad food, dirty clothes, mind-numbing television – when there was electricity' (p. 112). Yet the significance and intent of the gathering was hotly disputed. As DePalma explains:

> State media played down the protest, attributing it to a few delinquents who were stared down by local construction workers, and focused on the moment when Fidel's green army jeep pulled up to the Malecón and the comandante himself waded into what quickly transformed from an angry mob into an adoring audience. (p. 115)

But Miriam knew the state was lying; these protests were not mere troublemaking by delinquents or drug addicts, as per state television, but a genuine, spontaneous revolt against the Castro government.

Cary, another true believer in the revolution who had risen to a senior position in the textile industry, had long mocked her mother Zenaida's scepticism and cynicism, until mother and daughter happened to stroll past a tourist-hotel lobby where CNN was showing violent scenes of the Maleconazo. Predictably, Cary was dismissive. 'You know what the enemy [the United States and its population of Miami-based exiles] can do. It's just a montage of images that they found to make it look like a protest. But it's not real.' By contrast, Zenaida – a beneficiary of and fervent believer in much of the revolution's early social gains – now saw the protests as proof of the revolution's sclerosis. In the end, Cary realised that her *mamá* was right: 'There was only one national news program in Cuba, and what was being reported about that day was simply not true. And if this report was a lie, [Cary] had to consider, what about all the things she'd heard on TV or read about in *Granma* but hadn't seen for herself? What about the hijacked ferries? What about the tugboat?' (p. 112).

'¡Raúl Castro es un capitalista!'

The Maleconazo's political impact can best be judged by the fact that in its wake Fidel eased up on some of his revolution's 'extreme idealism' (as DePalma deftly phrases it, p. 133). In particular, he loosened state restrictions on private enterprise and the use of once-denounced US dollars, including at new specialty stores that carried a range of foreign consumer goods – items that were naturally unavailable at state-run Cuban-peso *tiendas* (stores). Havana also opened some industries – notably hospitality and tourism – to foreign investment, provided the foreigners in question were Canadians, Italians, Russians, Spaniards – anyone but Americans.

In 2006, Raúl, now acting president due to his older brother's incapacitation through illness, was more inclined to embrace greater economic pragmatism (read, capitalism), in large part due to his decades of running the Cuban military, in which pragmatism and logistics outweighed ideological purity. He even tried to cut one million 'non-productive' workers from state jobs, a number that had to be severely curtailed given the social disruptions it threatened to unleash. There were numerous (though still maddeningly slow and opaque) ways that Cubans could work in the 'private sector', although a profusion of red tape meant that many such undertakings were doomed to fail before they could even begin. Nevertheless, by 2020, 13% of the country's workforce, or 600,000 Cubans (one-third of whom were women and one-third under 30 years of age), were employed in this 'free market' – a dramatic increase from 3% a decade prior.[7] Of course, the nature of Cuba's 'private-sector' jobs was quite different than in the capitalist world, with licence-holders being allowed to run single-person 'businesses' such as peeling fruit, cleaning car sparkplugs or operating a horse-pulled cart. 'In reality', DePalma argues, 'the government was offering its people not freedom to better themselves, but permission to eke out a level of survival the government could no longer provide' (p. 180).

Even so, there were cases in which access to capitalism allowed some Cubans to insulate themselves to some degree from the political system.

DePalma introduces us to a talented Guanabacoa artist, Arturo Montoto, who had left Cuba to live in Santiago, Chile, and Mexico City.[8] During this time he became an internationally renowned painter, with his canvases fetching sums that would astonish most of his fellow Cubans living under communism (one was listed on eBay at the time of writing for $16,500). Nevertheless, Arturo decided to return to his native land. His motivation was that he missed not the country's political system or its shortages, but rather its legendary sunshine – he simply had to paint in the 'splendid Cuban sun' (p. 193). Having had little interest in the kind of anti-Castroite political art produced by some exiles in Miami, he was equally uninterested in the state-sanctioned art produced back home: 'He remained as distant as ever from the regime and its philosophies, and with the fear of retaliation removed because of his fame, his scorn for the system grew' (p. 194).

Cuba *libre*?

As with any critical account of Cuba, *The Cubans* will probably agitate the advocates of Castroism, who may allege that DePalma is cherry-picking his Guanabacoa subjects to make Castroism seem universally despised, and misrepresenting the source of Cuba's social ills, which in their eyes is the US embargo. Yet it is hard to argue with the author's assessment of the country's current predicament: 'endless sun, gorgeous white-sand beaches, and beautiful people, but without petroleum, modern technology or a commitment to democracy and individual rights'. The country's desperate economic situation has seen little improvement, with the government raiding the very people it should be sustaining: 'It skims 10 percent off every U.S. dollar traded for its worthless Cuban convertible pesos. And it squeezes every peso it can out of its new generation of entrepreneurs' (p. 333).

In summer 2021, Cuba suffered another of its not-infrequent crises. Health facilities were swamped by a surge in COVID-19 cases; there were interminable lines for already severely rationed foodstuffs and medicines; and the electrical grid was plagued by a series of blackouts. To make matters worse, the island nation was in the grip of an especially brutal heatwave. It was an explosive atmosphere waiting for a spark.

On 11 July 2021, protests broke out across Cuba, from the streets of Havana to the provincial cities in the east. Organising via social media, tens of thousands of citizens took to the streets chanting 'Libertad!' and 'Patria Y Vida!' ('Motherland and Life!' – a reference to a song by musicians in Cuba and the US that challenges the post-1959 Cuban government's ubiquitous slogan, 'Motherland or Death').[9] The protests represented the most significant anti-regime action since the Maleconazo, but unlike in that event, the July 2021 protesters were not simply demanding more goods and services, but also political freedom and reform.[10]

That same day, President Miguel Díaz-Canel – a hardliner's hardliner who had taken over from Raúl Castro earlier in the year as first secretary of the Communist Party – urged the nation's 'revolutionary' civilians and security agencies to repel the 'vulgar criminals' who sought to 'discredit the revolution and fracture the unity of our country'.[11] 'The order to combat has been given', he declared.[12]

To staunch the embryonic insurrection, Díaz-Canel deployed police commandoes and club-wielding undercover operatives, including the special units known as the Boinas Negras (Black Berets), to arrest dissidents and marchers, and intimidate anyone still only thinking about revolting. The government also blocked access to social media and messaging services. Cuban and foreign human-rights activists estimated that more than 1,400 people were detained, many of whom could not be located.[13] In June 2022, the regime stated that almost 300 people, including many youths aged 16 or 17, had received prison sentences of between five and 25 years for their participation in the unrest.[14] Following the July 2021 eruption, hundreds of dissidents, journalists and other civil-society actors emigrated, adding to the surging exodus from Cuba, with some 100,000 Cubans crossing into the United States via the Mexican border in 2021 alone.[15]

Fidel and Raúl are no longer 'universal symbols of resistance', and the mythology of the revolution means little to Cuban youths who, with their tattoos, smartphones and seething nihilism, see the old men of the Sierra as impossibly out of touch (p. 333). Díaz-Canel, heir to the Castros' legacy, is as 'unrecognizable around the world as the leader of any small country' (p. 333). As proof of how far the revolution has fallen since the heady years of the 1960s, DePalma cites the fact that each prescription in Cuba announces: 'HEALTH CARE IN CUBA IS FREE, BUT IT COSTS MONEY' (p. 333).

It is somewhat surprising, given his criticism of the Castros and their revolution, that DePalma does not profile any political dissidents. It may be that he simply did not encounter any during his reporting stints in Guanabacoa, or that he feared talking to them would put them in jeopardy. It may also have been worth spending more time on the broader context in which the ordinary Cubans he does profile have lived their lives. Like the island's rum, the Castroite ideology pitting a Cuban David against a *Yanqui* Goliath can be intoxicating, though both sides have played their part in creating a rigid stand-off that has lacked nuance and sometimes involved overstating the malignancy of the other side. Barack Obama made overtures that were rolled back by Donald Trump, displaying two contrasting methods of managing the US–Cuba relationship that are equally worthy of scrutiny. The American embargo of Cuba rolls on, raising the question of how much longer the Cuban regime will be able to survive, despite the support of influential American friends such as Hollywood celebrities Oliver Stone and Sean Penn, Democratic Senator Bernie Sanders, diplomatic historian Greg Grandin and former reporter Stephen Kinzer.

Perhaps the deeply personal nature of DePalma's investigation, which emphasises the bravery and dignity of ordinary Cubans trying to survive in impossible circumstances, necessarily excludes much consideration of more abstract political questions. After all, as DePalma so eloquently argues, any discussion of the island's political destiny must be mindful that Castroism is not synonymous with Cuba and its people.

Notes

[1] For the full text of Castro's speech, see 'Castro Gives Speech on 30th CDR Anniversary', Havana Domestic Radio and Television Services, 29 September 1990, http://lanic.utexas.edu/project/castro/db/1990/19900929.html.

[2] Richard Boudreaux, 'Havana, in a Crunch, Pedals Toward Future', *Los Angeles Times*, 24 September 1991, https://www.latimes.com/archives/la-xpm-1991-09-24-wr-3226-story.html.

[3] See Human Rights Watch, 'Human Rights Watch World Report 1994: Cuba', 1 January 1994, available at https://www.refworld.org/docid/467fca7e17.html.

4   See Anthony DePalma, 'As in 1994, Cubans Protest Against a Regime's Mortal Threat', *Washington Post*, 13 July 2021, https://www.washingtonpost.com/opinions/2021/07/13/1994-cubans-protest-against-regimes-mortal-threat/; Tod Robberson, 'Story of Tug's Sinking Incited Cubans', *Washington Post*, 11 September 1994, https://www.washingtonpost.com/archive/politics/1994/09/11/story-of-tugs-sinking-incited-cubans/94be9de7-c5c5-43d7-89ff-118ff5ebb4c3/; and Amnesty International, 'Cuba: The Sinking of the "*13 de Marzo*" Tugboat on 13 July 1994', AMR 25/013/1997, 30 June 1997, https://www.amnesty.org/en/documents/amr25/013/1997/en/.

5   See Jeffrey Feltman, 'Voice of America's New Radio Station to Cuba', *Fletcher Forum*, vol. 9, no. 1, Winter 1984, pp. 81–90.

6   Amnesty International, 'Cuba: The Sinking of the "*13th de Marzo*" Tugboat on 13 July 1994', p. 1.

7   'Cuba's Government Approves Small and Medium-sized Enterprises', *The Economist*, 12 August 2021, https://www.economist.com/the-americas/2021/08/12/cubas-government-approves-small-and-medium-sized-enterprises.

8   See the artist's website at https://www.arturomontoto.com/.

9   See José Miguel Vivanco, 'Cuba Responds to Landmark Demonstrations with Brutal Repression', Human Rights Watch, 14 July 2021, https://www.hrw.org/news/2021/07/14/cuba-responds-landmark-demonstrations-brutal-repression.

10 Nick Miroff, 'Cuba's Communist Authorities Have Long Feared Change. Street Protests Show the Risk of Resisting It', *Washington Post*, 22 July 2021, https://www.washingtonpost.com/world/2021/07/22/cuba-protests-economy/.

11 Anthony Faiola, 'Cubans, Broken by Pandemic and Fueled by Social Media, Confront Their Police State', *Washington Post*, 12 July 2021, https://www.washingtonpost.com/world/2021/07/12/cuba-anti-government-protests/.

12 Freedom House, 'Cuba: Authorities Must Refrain from Inciteful Language, Use of Force Against Peaceful Protestors', 13 July 2021, https://freedomhouse.org/article/cuba-authorities-must-refrain-inciteful-language-use-force-against-peaceful-protests.

13 Human Rights Watch, 'Prison or Exile: Cuba's Systematic Repression of July 2021 Demonstrators', 11 July 2022, https://www.hrw.org/report/2022/07/11/prison-or-exile/cubas-systematic-repression-july-2021-demonstrators#_ftn3.

14 Julio Antonio Fernández Estrada, 'A Year After Cuba's Uprising, the Aftershocks Continue', *Americas Quarterly*, 11 July 2022, https://americasquarterly.org/article/a-year-after-cubas-uprising-the-aftershocks-continue/.

15 *Ibid.*

Copyright © 2022 The International Institute for Strategic Studies

Book Reviews

United States
David C. Unger

The Rise and Fall of the Neoliberal Order: America and the World in the Free Market Era
Gary Gerstle. Oxford: Oxford University Press, 2022.
£21.99/$27.95. 406 pp.

In this admirably ambitious book, Gary Gerstle aims to develop a broader definition of neo-liberalism than previous analysts have managed. Beyond that, he seeks to explain how neo-liberalism became what he calls a political order, an ideology so dominant, so hegemonic, that even nominal opposition parties accepted its basic assumptions. In both these goals, he substantially succeeds.

Gerstle has invoked the concept of a hegemonic political order before, notably in a 1990 volume he co-edited with Steve Fraser, *The Rise and Fall of the New Deal Order, 1930–1980*. A theme of that book was that the New Deal political order had become so hegemonic by the 1950s that even a Republican president like Dwight D. Eisenhower subscribed to its main elements – social security, steeply progressive tax rates, the regulatory state, labour-union rights and Keynesian macroeconomics. In this new book, Gerstle argues that the same hegemonic pattern recurred with the neo-liberal order, this time with Bill Clinton serving as the Democrat's Eisenhower.

The underlying concept of ideological 'hegemony' draws on the thinking of Antonio Gramsci, the early Italian communist whose ideas later influenced the American New Left. In the hands of a skilled and nuanced historian like Gerstle, it can be an illuminating construct. But to the extent that 'hegemony' posits that dominant ideologies shape and define their historical epochs, it risks slipping into determinism.

Survival | vol. 64 no. 6 | December 2022–January 2023 | pp. 167–174 https://doi.org/10.1080/00396338.2022.2150435

Gerstle's assertion in this book that elite fears of the potential appeal to workers of communist ideas helped bring about the class compromises of the New Deal order better fits the American realities of the 1930s, or those of Europe and the Third World, than those of the contemporary United States, and it risks slighting the self-agency of worker and minority movements. That said, the capitalist sense of triumphalism that accompanied the demise of the Soviet Union did shape the neo-liberal ideology of subsequent decades.

Gerstle portrays neo-liberalism as a true descendant of classical nineteenth-century liberalism, from its faith in the constructive potential of unfettered markets to its emancipatory promises of individual freedom. He argues that Franklin D. Roosevelt and the Democrats who came after him hijacked the traditional term 'liberalism' to describe something new and less liberal than the old classical-liberal creed. That left later generations of classical liberals in need of a new name for their not-so-novel doctrines. Neo-liberalism was classical liberalism renamed and reborn – into a world much transformed.

In Gerstle's account, the neo-liberal ideology nurtured in the 1950s and 1960s employed three main strategies: 1) building institutions and practices designed to shield market relations from political interference (think Milton Friedman and Alan Greenspan); 2) applying market principles and ideology beyond the traditional confines of economics to other areas of civic and political life (think Gary Becker); and 3) insisting that personal liberation and unleashing creative genius required smashing the New Deal administrative and bureaucratic order (think Friedrich Hayek and Ayn Rand, but also the *Whole Earth Catalog*'s Stewart Brand and Apple's Steve Jobs). In Gerstle's account, neo-liberalism's natural habitat stretched from early libertarian New Agers on the fringes of the New Left to old-fashioned classical-liberal critics of the New Deal order.

Crucially, he argues, neo-liberalism wasn't just an intellectual movement of discontented anti-New Deal classical liberals. Had neo-liberalism remained confined to the purist intellectual precincts of the Mont Pelerin Society or the University of Chicago's economics department, it never could have become hegemonic.

Neo-liberalism's rise to hegemony required enlisting well-connected business leaders such as Lewis Powell and charismatic politicians such as Ronald Reagan. In 1971 (the year before Richard Nixon appointed Powell to the Supreme Court) the future justice circulated an influential memo summoning corporate America to a counter-attack on the New Deal in order to save the American free-enterprise system from imminent demise. Soon after, Reagan successfully forged a new electoral majority by melding the anti-regulatory grievances of business leaders with growing white-working-class discontent over a stalled post-1970s economy.

Those white workers weren't themselves neo-liberals. Many of them, or their generational successors, later flocked to the illiberal banner of Donald Trump. But, Gerstle argues, Reagan's skill at mobilising these working-class votes for his neo-liberal policies made the neo-liberal order hegemonic in the 1980s and 1990s.

This is a bold and well-argued book that is sure to enrich debate on one of the liveliest topics in modern US politics.

Wildland: The Making of America's Fury
Evan Osnos. New York: Farrar, Straus and Giroux, 2021.
$30.00. 480 pp.

After 12 years of reporting from Iraq, China and other foreign lands, Evan Osnos, a staff writer for the *New Yorker*, returned to the United States in 2013. He soon realised that something fundamental had changed during his time away. Using the reporting skills that had won him acclaim in his foreign assignments, he set out to investigate what had happened at home, centring his account on three very different American locations, linked by the fact that Osnos had lived or worked in each of them before moving abroad.

One was Greenwich, Connecticut, the wealthy New York suburb – its 'Golden Triangle' the home of hedge-fund billionaires – where Osnos had grown up in the 1980s and 1990s. The second was Clarksburg, West Virginia, where he had worked in the late 1990s as a reporter for the local newspaper. Clarksburg was once a mid-sized coal-country boom town, but by the 1990s its environmentally devastated, jobs-poor economy was, like the *Exponent Telegram* itself, barely keeping afloat. After Clarksburg, Osnos took a reporting job with the *Chicago Tribune*, starting on what he described as the lowest rung of the paper's city desk. Chicago, America's third most populous city, seemed to him like two separate and unequal cities, its booming downtown distinct from its economically and demographically bleeding (and predominantly African-American) South and Near West sides. That division grew even sharper in the first decade of the new century when the puncturing of the subprime mortgage bubble devastated broad swathes of South Side Chicago, uprooting and impoverishing tens of thousands of already struggling households.

The result of Osnos's parallel investigations is this readable and insightful book. In some of the most compelling sections, he traces the startling direct links between the twenty-first-century fortunes of these three places. He shows how lives so geographically and sociologically distant from each other they seemed to be lived on different planets were, in fact, closely entwined. Greenwich hedge-fund billionaires reaped megaprofits from the corporate hollowing out of Appalachian coal companies. That compounded Clarksburg's miseries by allowing those restructured companies to legally walk away from their former workers' health-insurance and pension claims. Hedge-fund megaprofits flowing to some of Greenwich's most affluent billionaires were further boosted by the creative financial engineering Wall Street used to market more than a trillion dollars' worth of mostly unsustainable subprime mortgages. The predictable collapse of those mortgage-backed securities left thousands of South Side Chicagoans – along with millions elsewhere – homeless, hopeless and indebted.

The author's interviews with local people show readers what is often invisible from the class-segregated urban and suburban enclaves of blue America, affording us a close-up and personal view of the making of the American carnage and its attendant build-up of rage and desperation that fuelled Donald Trump's two presidential runs. For tens of millions of Americans in tens of thousands of cities and neighbourhoods across Appalachia, the Midwest rust belt, and the empty rural towns of the Great Plains and South – that vast red-state expanse condescendingly dismissed by Manhattan and Silicon Valley sophisticates as 'fly-over country' – the United States' economic engine had stalled and government at every level looked indifferent, incompetent, corrupt or some combination of all three.

In the book's final chapters Osnos looks for signs that might point to a happier, post-Trump future based on the historic strengths of the American character. He notes the post-prison repentance and reform of a Greenwich hedge-fund mogul, the modest grassroots electoral successes of two West Virginia political reformers and the grit of South Side survivors trying through sheer force of will to imagine a better future for themselves and their neighbours.

The strengths of such individuals are real and moving. But will they prove powerful enough to reverse the mighty engines of destruction so well described by Osnos in the rest of this book?

The End of Ambition: The United States and the Third World in the Vietnam Era
Mark Atwood Lawrence. Princeton, NJ: Princeton University Press, 2021. £28.00/$35.00. 386 pp.

This useful diplomatic history traces internal debates within the Kennedy, Johnson and Nixon administrations over the goals and practices of US foreign policy toward five significant countries in what we now call the Global South: Brazil, India, Indonesia, Iran and the former Southern Rhodesia (now Zimbabwe). These successive American administrations presided over sharp policy swings toward each of the five countries. Mark Atwood Lawrence argues that these shifts were as much a function of the changing international context circumscribing American power as they were of the differing policy preferences of the successive presidents.

The 'End of Ambition' referred to in the book's title doesn't just describe the fading of American liberal ambitions from the robust and confident international idealism of John Kennedy and his New Frontiersmen to the more defensive and cynical realpolitik of Lyndon Johnson, Richard Nixon and Henry Kissinger. It also sets that story amid the growing erosion of America's post-Second War World hegemony – an erosion accelerated by the self-inflicted material and political constraints of the Vietnam War – which increasingly foreclosed the options and ambitions available to any American president.

The five case studies are well chosen. Each of these countries was a major concern of Washington policymakers during these decades, and while the details of US policy varied country by country, combining them in one study helps the reader to grasp the larger picture of American purposes and methods. We get a sense of the results these presidents hoped to achieve (pro-American governments, no matter whether they were democratic or authoritarian); what they hoped to prevent (military or diplomatic alignment with Moscow or Beijing); and what policy tools they were prepared to contemplate or use (including regime change with the assistance of American military or intelligence assets). We also see the extent to which Washington's chosen policies succeeded or failed in their intended goals. The historical record turns out to be mixed, with proclaimed successes in Brazil, Indonesia and, for a time, Iran, but little visible impact in the cases of India and Southern Rhodesia.

Lawrence, who teaches history at the University of Texas, doesn't dwell on what lessons, if any, Washington may have learned from these experiences. For the most part, he lets the archives speak for themselves. Apart from the dissenting views of the losing bureaucratic players, there is not much explicit questioning of Washington's predilection for bullying other governments into its diplomatic orbit, whether they or their people like it or not, nor of pressing for models of liberal modernisation imposed from above that were academically and politi-cally fashionable in 1960s Washington. Nor are harsh judgements passed on America's deep involvement in overthrowing civilian governments (Brazil, Indonesia), condoning systematic torture (Brazil, Iran, Southern Rhodesia) and conditioning humanitarian development aid on loyal support of Washington's chosen policy goals, especially, in the Johnson years, support for the disastrous Vietnam War.

The reader will have to look elsewhere for such critiques, and they are not hard to find. The value of this book is its granular dissection of the process through which actual policies are debated and decided on, only to sometimes be overwhelmed by external forces beyond the ken or control of policymakers. More such books are needed to flesh out our understanding of American foreign policy in the second half of the twentieth century.

The Wilson Circle: President Woodrow Wilson and His Advisers
Charles E. Neu. Baltimore, MD: Johns Hopkins University Press,
2022. £37.00/$49.95. 273 pp.

Countless books have been written about Woodrow Wilson, America's 28th president. Charles Neu, emeritus professor of history at Brown University, takes a potentially promising new approach by viewing Wilson and his presidency through the eyes of ten political and personal associates. These include Wilson's first wife, Ellen, who died in 1914; his second wife, Edith, who took charge of the White House after Wilson's 1918 stroke; navy secretary (and mentor to Franklin Roosevelt) Josephus Daniels; treasury secretary (and Wilson son-in-law) William Gibbs McAdoo; White House political secretary Joseph Tumulty; and international-policy adviser Colonel Edward House. The remaining members of this 'Wilson circle' are White House physician Cary Grayson, war secretary Newton D. Baker, War Industries Board chairman Bernard Baruch and Ray Stannard Baker, Wilson's spokesman at Versailles and later his authorised biographer. All were strong admirers of Wilson, though not always of each other. The variety in their viewpoints and vantage points is helpful for a fuller understanding of Wilson's personality and presidency.

This would, however, have been a better, more useful book if Neu, a recognised authority on Wilson and his era, had chosen to write with greater critical distance from the Wilson circle, especially on the pronounced white-supremacist views (and practices) of so many of them. Much of the recent historical debate on Wilson's legacy has revolved around whether and how much his racial biases affected his thinking about applying his doctrine of national self-determination to non-European peoples.

Revealingly, America's leading sponsor of liberal internationalism was also the re-segregator of official Washington and an active promoter of D.W. Griffith's pro-Ku Klux Klan film, *The Birth of a Nation*. It is striking to read how many in Wilson's circle came from southern families, most of whom had served the old Confederacy and identified with its 'lost cause'. Among the most egregious of these was Daniels, who used his proprietorship of Raleigh's *News & Observer* to incite and lead a white-supremacist campaign that culminated in the 1898 white-power insurrection in Wilmington, North Carolina, which some historians consider the only successful armed overthrow (so far) of a democratically elected government in US history. That insurrection led directly to the massacre of between 60 and 300 innocent black people.

Wilson was a complex character best known until recently for the seminal role he played in the formulation of the US liberal-internationalist ideology, still the dominant strain in US foreign-policy thinking today. But Wilson was also the first Southern Democrat in the White House since the Civil War. His southern upbringing and views on white supremacy were significant features of his White House, and of so many in his inner circle. Neu faithfully reports the white-supremacist views and backgrounds of these advisers, but chooses to treat them as incidental features of their political personalities. It's odd to read a book published in 2022 that so notably underplays the white-supremacist dimension that continues to reshape and diminish Wilson's reputation.

Thirteen Cracks: Repairing American Democracy After Trump
Allan Lichtman. Lanham, MD: Rowman & Littlefield, 2021.
£16.99/$21.95. 211 pp.

This is a disappointing book. Allan Lichtman, a Distinguished Professor of History at American University who attracted media attention by publishing one of the few scholarly books that predicted the 2016 presidential-election victory of Donald Trump (followed a year later by *The Case for Impeachment*), has again laid out a would-be prosecutor's case against the Trump administration and its Republican Party allies. These charges are backed up with suitably damning quotes from liberal academics, journalists and advocates.

Though meant to fortify Lichtman's case, the selective sourcing and partisan thrust of many of these citations make it unlikely that this book will change many minds, or win added political support for the various legislative, constitutional and attitudinal changes Lichtman proposes at the end of each chapter.

This is unfortunate, since the accuracy of many of Lichtman's talking points is beyond dispute, and several of his proposed fixes deserve wider discussion and debate. Trump *did* repeatedly ignore or cast aside democratic and institutional norms. Republican leaders, including veterans who once knew better, *did* enable and echo him. The radical Supreme Court majority they worked together to swell *has* embarked on a series of fundamental reinterpretations of constitutional law, the results of which are now starkly evident.

Some of the changes Lichtman proposes to reinforce American democracy are modest and potentially within political reach, such as strengthening the Electoral Count Act and reinforcing and extending whistleblower protections. Others seem more wishful, though worth articulating and fighting for, such as strengthening the power, will and resources of Congress to better rein in a future overweening executive. More radical but potentially beneficial constitutional changes, such as reapportioning the Senate and, consequently, the Electoral College, merit their inclusion on Lichtman's list, even though they seem hopelessly out of reach during the present era of paralysing partisan division.

Lichtman is an accomplished scholar. But this work, despite its repeated – and overly selective – invocation of social-science studies, is more one of advocacy than of scholarship. *Thirteen Cracks* is more likely to rally the liberal faithful than to reach the broader ranks whose participation will surely be needed to seal these cracks and repair American democracy.

Without making a case for the Trump administration's trashing of democratic norms, it should be noted that there is more than one side to some of the issues Lichtman raises. There is, for example, legitimate debate, based both on constitutional text and on more than two centuries of American history, on how far the unitary executive power of the presidency extends, and how it can or should be checked by the institutional resistance of an unelected bureaucratic 'deep state', a debate that Stephen Skowronek, John A. Dearborn and Desmond King illuminatingly explore in *Phantoms of a Beleaguered Republic* (reviewed in the April–May 2022 issue of *Survival*).

There are also serious arguments to be made about the efficacy of fixes based on new regulatory agencies and authorities versus attempts to reinforce what American historians refer to as 'republican' values. In an elision all too typical of this book, Lichtman cites James Madison on the inability of mere 'parchment barriers' to protect liberties in the absence of a culture of republican virtue well planted among the people, then almost immediately resumes his advocacy of solutions relying on essentially legislative or regulatory remedies (p. 176).

Europe
Hanns W. Maull

Turkey Under Erdoğan: How a Country Turned from Democracy and the West
Dimitar Bechev. New Haven, CT: Yale University Press, 2022.
£20.00/$28.00. 263 pp.

'Your country, with 150 years of democratic and social reform, stands as a model to others and as Europe's bridge to the wider world': thus was Turkey praised by George W. Bush during a NATO summit in Istanbul in 2004 (p. 77). That same year, Recep Tayyip Erdoğan, then Turkey's prime minister, promised in a speech delivered at the University of Oxford to make European values Ankara's values, to carry out democratic reforms, to improve human rights and to deliver economic growth. For a while, he did so, but since then the country, still led by now-President Erdoğan, has adopted an elective authoritarian system in which it is difficult to discover any surviving traces of liberal democracy. Ankara has also sought in its foreign policy to navigate its own course between China, Russia and the West, and to exploit its hard power to establish Turkey as a regional great power in the Middle East.

Dimitar Bechev's authoritative account expertly weaves together the two parallel tracks of Turkey's move towards authoritarianism and away from its moorings in the West under Erdoğan, exploring the many linkages that connect these seemingly separate developments. He explains not only what happened, but also why. Erdoğan's political personality is an important part of the answer, but there were also deeper factors at work. Bechev reaches back to the 1980s, to the prime ministership and presidency of Turgut Özal (1983–93) and the rule of his Motherland Party, to identify deep continuities in Turkish domestic politics and foreign policy. Under Özal, the social and cultural cleavages that had resulted from Turkey's top-down, secular modernisation began to fuel political polarisation. A cult of the strong state and an exclusive nationalism harboured by Turkey's established, secular elites were eagerly adopted by the Justice and Development Party (AKP) and shrewdly channelled by Erdoğan to promote his own agenda. Those same elites had failed to meet the expectations of the majority of the Turkish people, but continued to meddle in politics when they saw their interests threatened. This pattern was no longer sustainable in a rapidly changing society, however, resulting in their loss of power. The AKP was the beneficiary of this situation, and Erdoğan cleverly exploited it to turn himself into the leader (*reis*) of a 'New Turkey'. An aborted coup in 2016 highlighted both the power of popular resistance (which played a critical role in defeating the coup) and its subsequent impotence, when Erdoğan quickly imposed emergency rule and used it to suppress not only the masterminds of the coup, but also all other remaining opponents to his personal monopolisation of power.

For all the weaknesses in Turkey's political system and the cleverness of Erdoğan in exploiting them to establish himself as the country's sole source of power, Bechev also blames the West for contributing to recent developments, arguing that the rise of illiberal populism in the West undermined its claim to the moral high ground. 'Instead of us becoming little America, you became a big Turkey', Bechev quotes the political scientist Ersin Kalaycıoğlu (p. 9).

In addition to recounting the story of Turkey's drift away from democracy, the author also charts the evolution of the country's foreign policy from 'zero problems' with its neighbours to the (successful) projection of military power from Libya to Syria and the Gulf. His epilogue offers a glimpse into the future. Twenty years down the road, he predicts, Turkey will still be as Erdoğan has fashioned it: a country that is deeply divided and polarised politically and socially, still torn in a love–hate relationship with the West, and still a major regional power. Yet if it is to exploit its potential to the full, it will have to bring its own house in order by reviving its faltering economy, strengthening its institutions and relaunching its democratisation.

Borderlands: Europe and the Mediterranean Middle East
Raffaella A. Del Sarto. Oxford: Oxford University Press, 2021.
£65.00/$85.00. 208 pp.

This assessment of Europe's relationship with the Middle East casts a rather sobering light on the European Union, which likes to present itself, and to be seen, as a 'normative power' engaged in the worldwide promotion of democracy and human rights. Based on extensive empirical research, *Borderlands* explores two major dimensions of the relationship, trade and the migration–security nexus, during the 20-year period from 1995 to 2015. It does so by treating the EU as an 'empire', with the Middle East as one of its 'borderlands' – areas into which the Union, exhibiting empire-like behaviour, has tended to expand. All empires, including the EU, share certain characteristics, according to author Raffaella Del Sarto: as vast and composite political entities with a core and one or several peripheries, their territorial expanse is often unstable; they rise and expand, but also decline and shrink; and they tend to subordinate surrounding political entities through a combination of direct and indirect rule, co-opting local elites while allowing them a degree of autonomy in exchange for deference and tribute. As the author shows, the EU's relations with the Middle East display all these characteristics.

The EU's behaviour is rooted in the colonial legacies of some of its founding member states (as well as that of the UK, which joined in 1973). European material interests, rather than the Union's self-professed norms of democracy and human rights, determine the relationship. Norms are indeed important, but only those that concern the legal and technical frameworks that the EU has successfully exported to countries in the Middle East and North Africa (together known as the MENA region), rather than those related to democratic governance and human rights. Del Sarto describes the EU's 'relentless efforts to expand various territorial and functional borders to the southern periphery' as 'the essence of European policies' (p. 147). EU officials have persistently shaped economic exchanges to Europe's own benefit, as the author's assessment of the trade relationship shows.

Her analysis of the migration–security nexus focuses on Europe's overriding concern with stability in its neighbourhood. This has resulted in a long history of European support for and collusion with authoritarian governments. In recent years, anxiety in Europe about migrants crossing the Mediterranean have stoked right-wing populism, while the terrible human costs associated with such migration have led to protests and civil unrest, exacerbating the pressures on European governments. In response, European capitals have appealed to governments from Turkey to Libya to stem the flows of people. The result has been to strengthen authoritarian regimes and crony capitalism across the region. Regimes have also sought to exploit Europe's obsession with migration for their own ends – most blatantly in the case of Erdoğan's Turkey, which used Syrian refugees to blackmail the EU.

Del Sarto is relentlessly critical of EU policies towards the MENA region, and she builds a powerful case. Yet she readily admits that it is difficult to establish exactly how much blame Europe deserves for the social inequality and authoritarian governance that has blighted the region. Her analysis includes two outliers, Turkey and Israel, which do not quite fit into her model of dependent development under authoritarian governments. Both countries suggest that peripheral states may have more agency in pursuing their own trajectories than Del Sarto allows. Still, this is a welcome and important contribution to our knowledge about Europe's external relations.

**Europe in an Era of Growing Sino-American Competition:
Coping with an Unstable Triangle**
Sebastian Biba and Reinhard Wolf, eds. Abingdon: Routledge,
2021. £130.00. 213 pp.

China–EU Relations in a New Era of Global Transformation
Li Xing, ed. Abingdon: Routledge, 2021. £120.00. 299 pp.

Europe in an Era of Growing Sino-American Competition is a timely and welcome addition to the burgeoning literature on the new cold war between China and the United States. The editors have brought together an impressive, all-European set of voices to analyse Europe's difficult choices in a world of escalating superpower tensions. Their findings are divided into three parts. The first assesses Europe's agency, with contributions by Øystein Tunsjø and Lieslotte Odgaard that explore the scope and limits of European policy options in dealing with America and China, and Europe's possible role in a 'new US–China bipolar system' (p. 23); and from Tomasz Kamiński and Joanna Ciesielska-Klikowska, who look at sub-national relations between the European Union and China. This chapter unfortunately overlooks the problematic aspects of Chinese sub-national influence in Europe and, in any case, would have been better placed in the volume edited by Li Xing.

The second part looks at geostrategic issues, exploring Europe's position vis-à-vis the United States (Emil Kirchner), its role in the South China Sea (Michael Paul) and its place in the 'North Korean conundrum' (Ramon Pacheco Pardo). Part three explores geo-economic issues, such as trade and technology (Margot Schüller), foreign direct investment (Philipp Le Corre), the Belt and Road Initiative (Claude Zanardi) and climate-change cooperation (Mario Esteban and Lara Lázaro Touza). The editors contribute a thoughtful conclusion that summarises the volume's main findings and pushes the analysis further towards answering the five questions that guided the project: should Europe take a side, or collaborate with both the US and China on an issue-by-issue basis? Should Europe try to salvage an increasingly fragile global order or resign itself to its decline, instead concentrating on building a viable regional order? Should Europe prioritise NATO or enhance its own 'strategic autonomy'? Should it try for a more meaningful role in the Indo-Pacific or concentrate on Europe and its neighbourhood? Finally, will Europe, as the editors put it in their concluding chapter, 'still be able to afford the "luxury" of promoting its values' (p. 203), or should it give precedence to its material interests?

Overall, the answers provided add up, as the editors rightly suggest, to a veritable paradigm shift. Europe will need to strengthen itself, politically and militarily, to meet the geopolitical and geo-economic challenges of the age. If it fails, the editors note that the political consequences could be as grave as those of climate change. They approvingly quote Josep Borrell, the EU High Representative for Foreign Affairs and Security Policy, to the effect that Europe 'must relearn the language of power and conceive of Europe as a top-tier geo-strategic actor' (p. 206). Good advice, but will it? The one glaring oversight in this otherwise comprehensive, thought-provoking analysis is the issue of Taiwan. While the island is mentioned, by my count, in three places (the index strangely identifies only one of them), nowhere do the contributors engage seriously with the most geopolitically dangerous source of tension between the US and China.

Taiwan does not appear even once in *China–EU Relations in a New Era of Global Transformation*, which characterises Europe's relationship with China as 'standing in two boats' (p. 9). This refers to the contradictions between the EU's desire for partnership with China and the scope for conflict, and between the political and security demands of Washington and the economic leverage of China. As a way to 'conceptualize and understand China–EU relations' (p. 9), however, the metaphor is simply too vague to be of much use, and therefore appears very little in the individual contributions. Instead, contributors like Feng Yuan repeatedly express their hope for 'convergence through multilateralism' between the EU and China (p. 60), while rightly raising doubts about whether European and Chinese notions of multilateralism are at all compatible.

Indeed, Beijing appears to prefer a multipolar world to a multilateral one, and seems ultimately to desire unipolarity. The challenge for Europe is thus to determine 'how to multilateralize a multipolar world', as Feng Yuan puts it (p. 72). Anna Caffarena and Giuseppe Gabusi explore how the EU might 'steer' China towards a multilateralised world. Their case studies on European–Chinese cooperation within the Asian Infrastructure Investment Bank (AIIB) and the World Trade Organization (WTO) provide interesting insights into the potential of 'steering' China. Yet they probably underestimate the ability of Beijing to steer the EU, as demonstrated by its ability to defang the Union's human-rights criticisms of China within the United Nations Human Rights Council and even within the EU itself.

In addition to four chapters on the overall relationship between China and the EU, there are three contributions on China's Belt and Road Initiative (BRI) and two on energy and the Arctic. There are also chapters on the Baltic states' relationship with China; on the cultural influence of China in the Balkans; on Sino-European cooperation on sustainable management of the oceans (the so-called 'blue economy'); on mergers and acquisitions in the textile industries; and on tourism. There is much knowledge to be gained from these specialised contributions. Overall, however, as with so many edited volumes, there is a lack of cohesion, substantial redundancies and a heavy dose of theorising that does not lead anywhere. The volume also contains too much Eurocentrism and too little attention to China's influence in Europe. Among the few exceptions is the contribution by Anastas Vangeli on the 'ideational impact' (p. 131) of China's BRI on Europe. He rightly points out that China's mercantilist economic policies have helped to push the EU towards more industrial policies of its own, but he fails to take up the EU's response to China's BRI in its 'Connectivity Strategy' and 'Global Gateway' initiatives, both of which have clearly taken leaves out of China's book. The volume might have benefitted from a concluding chapter to pull the different strands together and provide a broader perspective on the EU's relationship with China. Then again, the book's structure may reflect Søren Dosenrode's conclusion that 'the surprise … is not as much that the EU has a weak and fragmented policy [towards China], but that it has one at all' (p. 55).

European Disunion: Democracy, Sovereignty and the Politics of Emergency
Stefan Auer. London: C. Hurst & Co., 2022. £25.00. 256 pp.

The European Union and its role in international relations have increasingly come under critical scrutiny. Stefan Auer's study of 'European disunion' represents one of the most thorough and interesting revisionist critiques of the European project and its concomitant academic discipline, European Studies. For the author, who was born in Slovakia and now teaches at the University of Hong Kong, the deep troubles now facing the EU ultimately have a single cause: the Union's ambition to replace the nation-state as the ultimate political arbiter. This, Auer tries to show, was not the original intention behind the European project, which was meant to consolidate democracy and the rule of law across Western Europe. Rather, it resulted from the EU's evolution after the end of the Cold War, which subjected ever larger segments of European affairs to the EU's peculiar technocratic and legalistic approach to governance. This approach, Auer argues, lacked the democratic legitimacy of national politics by 'opting for more *governance* instead of *government*' (p. 68, emphasis in original). When the Union was shaken by a series of crises triggered by the collapse of the Wall Street investment bank Lehman Brothers in 2008, it responded with the 'politics of emergency'. Following the brilliant (but also notorious) German political philosopher Carl Schmitt (who, as a public intellectual, contributed to the destruction of the Weimar Republic and the legitimation of the Nazi regime that replaced it), Auer argues that the EU represents an effort to organise a large space (in Schmitt's parlance, a *Grossraum*) but to replace its politics with technocratic governance. In this, the EU has tried to take over important functions of the state, such as providing security and protection for its citizens, but it cannot do so, because it lacks the state's authority (*Souveränität*). Which EU citizen would, after all, be prepared to die for it?

In the EU, it is never clear who is really in charge of a decision, and therefore who bears responsibility. Moreover, as the EU ultimately lacks power to enforce its decisions, it cannot but fail its citizens in emergencies – as it did, in the author's view, in the eurozone and refugee crises, in its efforts to protect Ukraine from Russia, and ultimately even in its attempts to secure democracy and the rule of law within its own borders. The result has been what Auer calls the EU's 'sovereignty paradox': member states have ceded enough of their sovereignty to supranational institutions so as no longer to be able to resolve problems on their own, yet they retain enough of it to resist compromises and veto common decisions. The question for Auer therefore is no longer 'whether more or less Europe is needed, but instead what kind of Europe is best suited to safeguarding democracy, prosperity and political stability' (p. xix). This is a powerful argument, based on thorough research and delivered in elegant, succinct prose. One may not agree with Auer's two core assumptions – that sovereignty is absolute and indivisible, and that national identities are inescapable – and may dislike his reliance on Schmitt to bring his case against the EU. There can be little doubt, however, that Auer has put his finger on a deep sore on Europe's body politic.

Counter-terrorism and Intelligence
Jonathan Stevenson

Western Jihadism: A Thirty Year History
Jytte Klausen. Oxford: Oxford University Press, 2021.
£30.00. 553 pp.

According to a recent CIA report, al-Qaeda has not re-established its transnational operational capabilities in Afghanistan and does not pose a proximate threat to the US homeland. Thus, the Biden administration's posture of armed vigilance appears workable, the targeted killing of al-Qaeda leader Ayman al-Zawahiri with a drone strike in Kabul last July serving as proof of concept. When centrally based jihadism waned in the wake of the post-9/11 counter-terrorism mobilisation, however, home-grown jihadist extremism, though not as lethal overall, gave the movement sustenance and kept the transnational terrorist threat alive. A residual threat remains, and Jytte Klausen, one of the ranking experts on the subject, has written a very accomplished and useful single volume that explains the transnational jihadist phenomenon from soup to nuts. The first 200+ pages of the book is historical exposition from Osama bin Laden's roots through 9/11, sound and assured but nothing especially new. But the book is, of course, explicitly a 'history'.

It gets especially interesting with the seventh chapter, titled 'Homegrown Terrorism', which confronts and helps resolve the much-debated question of whether jihadism, as it has evolved, is essentially 'leaderless' or substantially 'hierarchical'. Marc Sageman is the leading proponent of the former view, Bruce Hoffman of the latter. Klausen systematically takes a hard look at post-9/11 European jihadist networks in London – her featured case study – as well as Belgium, France, Germany, the Netherlands and Spain. Distilling the results of her inquiries, and drawing illustratively on organisation theory, she notes drily: 'The trade-off between growth and quality control is a well-known problem in business, and indeed in any organization. In this case [of jihadism], further difficulties were presented by geography and the constraints of maintaining secrecy' (p. 265). Her primary research, graphically represented, indicates that while the European network was 'considerably more fragmented and diffuse' than those that formed in the 1990s, 75% of the individual activists identified were connected to the core network. She concludes, perhaps a little grandiosely but with empirical support, that home-grown terrorism is 'a myth' (p. 267). Her analysis could resonate in assessments of other extremist networks.

The book also offers an insightful chapter on the intellectual background – including 'just war' theory – of jihadism; a close dissection of, on balance,

Survival | vol. 64 no. 6 | December 2022–January 2023 | pp. 182–188 https://doi.org/10.1080/00396338.2022.2150440

underwhelming jihadist recruitment efforts in the United States, highlighting the importance of online indoctrination; and a somewhat foreboding assessment of the 'ISIS effect'. Regarding the latter, Klausen notes that, despite declining attacks and arrests in Europe since the defeat of the Islamic State's Middle Eastern 'caliphate' in 2018, 'the structural underpinnings for a jihadist come-back are still largely in place. Europe may be more at risk now than at any time since the 1990s' (pp. 444–5). She ends the book on an appropriately balanced note: 'The threat of [jihadist] terrorism at home, to the American public, has been wildly exaggerated. Meanwhile, the threat posed by white supremacists and far-right extremists has long been ignored. But sometimes jihadist terror-ism has too readily been talked down, victory prematurely declared' (p. 473). This suggests the possibility that rising great-power competition, as well as the increasing salience of a genuinely home-grown threat of right-wing extremism, has risked downplaying jihadism.

It Can Happen Here: White Power and the Rising Threat of Genocide in the US
Alexander Laban Hinton. New York: New York University Press, 2021. $29.00. 295 pp.

A great deal has been written in recent years about right-wing extremism, unleashed by Donald Trump, in the United States, and the possibility that it may lead to large-scale civil breakdown. Counter-terrorism experts, historians, political scientists, sociologists and policy analysts have offered constructive and sometimes penetrating analyses of the problems and challenges. Examples include Kathleen Belew's *Bring the War Home,* Cynthia Miller-Idriss's *Hate in the Homeland* and Arie Perliger's *American Zealots.* In *It Can Happen Here,* Alexander Laban Hinton, a distinguished anthropologist at Rutgers, weighs in, sardonically deriving the title of the book from Sinclair Lewis's novel *It Can't Happen Here,* which was inspired by the populist Louisiana demagogue Huey P. Long.

Hinton, a fluid writer working here in a professorial first-person, starts his book with dire stridency:

> If dramatic, Trump was not exceptional. His presidency was a symptom of a long and enduring legacy of systemic white power in the United States, one filled with moments in which genocide and mass violence took place. During Trump's administration, white power merely became more visible, and some of its more extreme and violent aspects were put on public display. (p. x)

That tone does not abate. The author sees insurrection and even civil war as a potential overdue reckoning. He locates the threat in the content of Trump's and his ideological allies' thinly coded racist speech, and matter-of-factly condenses material on the evolution of the American far right's apocalyptic thinking in a long chapter titled 'White Genocide'. But the book, he notes, is primarily a call to '"think beyond" our assumptions' (p. 197) and 'an exercise in moral imagination' (p. 198). Thus, he takes the reader through his own relatively effective pedagogy in an anthropology seminar at an elite university in the American northeast.

The late novelist Larry McMurtry lamented that his books were often embraced as traditional tales of a heroic American West, when he intended to write revisionist westerns that depicted the white Americans who settled and dominated the region as brutal and intolerant, if in some ways virtuous. Hinton risks no such ambiguity. He clearly believes that for Americans to fully appreciate the threat white supremacists pose to democracy, they must starkly admit not only that it can happen here but that it *has* happened here, starting with the country's inception. His concluding prescription is enlightened educational curricula that acknowledge that the most dangerous immigrants arrived in 1492 and take it from there. This seems unrealistic as an overall solution given that such an approach would amount to the kind of 'critical race theory' – a term Hinton does not mention or use – that many right-wing Americans reflexively oppose. By the same token, he is not wrong about the deeply toxic lineage of the American republic and the increasingly daunting challenge of setting the country in a virtuous direction.

Stars at Noon (film)
Claire Denis, co-writer and director. Distributed by A24, 2022.

The eminent French director Claire Denis has explored with unparalleled insight and nuance the way colonialism and geopolitics have contorted human relationships in movies such as *Chocolat* (1988), *Beau Travail* (1999) and *White Material* (2009). In her new film *Stars at Noon*, which won the Grand Prix at the Cannes Film Festival, she skilfully adapts Denis Johnson's almost-eponymous 1986 novel (he included a definite article), rather generically updating late-Cold War Nicaragua to a desolated and inevitably steamy present-day incarnation. The story remains a character-driven one of romance and espionage in a washed-out site of outside intrigue, the main surface difference being the COVID masks. But Johnson wrote his book at a moment when the United States was a galvanised superpower, especially in Latin America. What's new in Denis's film, subtly but pervasively, is America's strategic enervation.

Trish is a lissom freelance-journalist-cum-humanitarian-observer who wants to escape an increasingly dangerous country but lacks sufficient funds for airfare. She's filed a few too many unpublishably impassioned stories with the disinterested travel magazine that once ran her copy, leaving the editor (a gloriously clownish John C. Reilly) unsympathetic with her plight. He cuts her off mid-Zoom. Her default is heavy drinking, casual pilfering and prostitution at $50 a transaction, moving apace from a rough Nicaraguan policeman in a shabby back room to a duplicitous British oil-company honcho named Daniel in a high-end hotel. Both pay for the sex, patiently filmed as if to amplify its utility as refuge and procrastination. The cop confiscates Trish's passport and tells her to fatten up. The Brit falls for her and she for him.

Trish's mien swings between crypto-feminist bravado, in line with the gringo journalist's oft-repudiated presumption of functional immortality, and garden-variety damsel-in-distress despair. This is a difficult span for an actor to traverse with authority, but the immensely talented Margaret Qualley, fully invested here, pulls it off handily. She locks into old-school melodrama, and Denis's characteristically sensualist movie, with its seductively languid jazz soundtrack, needs that electricity to attain sufficient focus. Plus, it's a neat trick to make the sole-proprietor sex trade seem like insouciant fun. Daniel is a Greenean character, weak and forlorn, and Joe Alwyn's vacant performance makes him less engaging than he should be. Even so, given the man's bland good looks, vulnerability, vague conscience and apparent resources, he's credible enough as a repository for Trish's libido, hope and puerile idealism.

The plot is deliberately opaque, the better to privilege Denis's universal point that political instability and intrigue make personal relationships and feelings very hard to navigate. That said, a more specific design is decipherable, if only by generous inference. It transpires that Daniel has been selling information about valuable mineral deposits to players hostile to the United States and its Nicaraguan proxies. The CIA's traction in Nicaragua appears tenuous, so perhaps the agency and its allies are endeavouring to get Daniel to more stable and US-friendly Costa Rica to interrogate him. In the crucial third act, a smarmy case officer, reciting his 'consultant' cover with obvious and self-amused disingenuousness, confronts Trish with a few choice facts. Most pointedly, he has access to a lot of cash, and Daniel is involved in what he describes, with imperious laziness, as a 'rogue state'. It appears that these disclosures insidiously ratchet up her motivation to deliver Daniel, which, by manipulatively appealing to his chivalry, she effectively does.

As the CIA man, Benny Safdie nearly pockets the film. He plays the role with paradoxically dissipated verve, finely calibrated between swagger and resignation, insistence and fatigue. This is the right strain for a contemporary America hard-pressed to manage strategic challenges even in a Western Hemisphere putatively reserved for its hegemony by the Monroe Doctrine. In Cold War-era movies set in Latin America, such as Costa-Gavras's *Missing* (1982) or Roger Spottiswoode's *Under Fire* (1983), the United States, mainly through its covert machinations, loomed as a baleful and omnipotent presence. Now it looks threatening, to be sure, but also unsteady, perhaps on the way to disempowerment. That might make the people it entangles even crazier.

White Malice: The CIA and the Neocolonisation of Africa
Susan Williams. London: C. Hurst & Co., 2021. £25.00. 695 pp.

The CIA's role in a rapidly decolonising Cold War-era Africa has long been portrayed popularly as nefarious, including the charges that it supported, among other intrigues, the assassination of the leftist Congolese nationalist leader Patrice Lumumba, white-supremacist apartheid rule in South Africa for decades, and the installation or maintenance of numerous ideologically convenient but brutal authoritarian rulers. In *White Malice*, British historian Susan Williams provides a vivid account of significant aspects of the agency's activity, informed by declassified material and rendered eminently readable by telling and energetically related anecdotes.

The comprehensive cast of the book's title is mildly deceptive. The CIA's intense two-year involvement with the Belgian Congo (later known as Zaire and then as the Democratic Republic of the Congo) between January 1959 and February 1961, though generously contextualised, occupies most of the book – more than 300 of the text's 518 pages – and the narrative does not extend chronologically too far to the left or right of that time span. But this tight focus could be justified, given that the Congo episode brought together the United States' scramble for strategic resources – to wit, the Congo's rich uranium deposits – and the West's overall political and military mission of containment. It is also clear that, from the author's perspective, the CIA's concerted opposition to Lumumba and involvement in his murder were emblematic of its Cold War approach to Africa.

While Williams's presentation is highly professional, she manages to convey an accusatory sense of irony and indignation by skilfully arraying and describing terrible events that speak for themselves. For example: 'Although Lumumba's murderers had sought to dissolve his body with acid – to eradicate any physical mark of the man – they were unable to destroy what he meant and signified to the people of the Congo and the world' (p. 392). She is careful not to indulge in

self-conscious interjections of explicit indignation, leaving that to direct participants or observers. She notes that John Stockwell, when assigned to command
the CIA's Angola Task Force in 1975, 'was appalled by the stupidity' of the CIA
in singling out Angola's ruling party as an enemy when it 'had not committed a
single act of aggression' (p. 460) against the US. Barack Obama, she comments,
'deplored the prejudice and ignorance in the West' about Africans (p. 515).
Williams's larger purpose is to disabuse readers of what she and others see as
the CIA's retrogressive presumption that Africans are unamenable to democracy and development, and therefore must be coerced. She makes a strong if
selective case.

From Warsaw with Love: Polish Spies, the CIA, and the Forging of an Unlikely Alliance
John Pomfret. New York: Henry Holt, 2021. $29.99. 288 pp.

In his spirited new book, former *Washington Post* reporter John Pomfret brings
journalistic precision and literary flair to an evidently under-appreciated subject:
the long and chequered history of interactions between Polish and American
spies. After setting the tone with the Cold War story of Marian Zacharski, a
Polish machine-tool salesman who became a spy prized by both Warsaw and
Moscow for the US military secrets he inveigled, the author trenchantly nails
down the fundamental geopolitical tension that Poland felt during that era.
'Poland's Communist government used fears of German revanchism to generate support for a forced alliance with Moscow. Poles were taught to distrust
West Germany, and to believe that, if given the chance, a unified Germany
would seek to reclaim territory it had lost' (p. 52).

In addition to the Soviet Union's excesses and eventual collapse, it was the
United States' support and guarantee of protection from Germany that ensured
strong Polish allegiance to the West after the Cold War ended. Pre-existing con-
nections by virtue of America's large Polish diaspora were also key. To usher in
Poland's return to the West, the CIA helped Warsaw build a new intelligence
agency, and senior Polish-American CIA officer John Palevich was an important player. Pomfret notes, however, that the US was sensitive to Polish anxieties
about radical upheaval and allowed the government to 'preserve much of the
Communist infrastructure as it transitioned to democracy' (p. 108) – a lesson that
the US would famously unlearn in dealing with post-Saddam Iraq. By then, the
Polish Office of State Protection (or UOP, the Polish acronym by which it is known)
had made itself increasingly useful to its American counterpart, and the two
countries' special relationship had facilitated Poland's inclusion in NATO's first
post-Cold War expansion in 1999, which made that relationship even stronger.

Poland, which loyally deployed troops to Iraq as part of what then-secretary of defense Donald Rumsfeld called the 'new Europe', was disappointed by US short-sightedness there. But from Pomfret's vantage, it was shabby American behaviour elsewhere that did the most damage to the bond between the two countries. Shaken by the 9/11 attacks, Poland was 'keen to do right by the United States' (p. 199). So, beginning in December 2002, it hosted a 'black site' to which the CIA 'renditioned' terrorist suspects for interrogation and – initially unbeknownst to Polish authorities – sometimes torture. In particular, Khalid Sheikh Mohammed – the architect of the 9/11 operation – was waterboarded there 183 times before the Polish government, always reluctant, shut down the site after nine months. When news of the site's activities leaked and the CIA did nothing to shield Polish officials, the Polish government felt betrayed and the special relationship suffered. One message is that close operational ties between allied intelligence agencies – indeed, governments as a whole – can have political consequences when the stronger partner 'asks for too much' (p. 243). Polish citizens were the only ones in Europe who supported the Europhobic Donald Trump's re-election. Serendipitously, the Russia–Ukraine war appears to have provided an opportunity for a reset.

Copyright © 2022 The International Institute for Strategic Studies

Closing Argument

Woman, Life, Freedom in Iran

Mahsa Rouhi

I

Iranians call my cohort the 'Burnt Generation'.[1] We grew up during the 1970s and 1980s in the abyss of revolution, an eight-year-long war with Iraq, mass executions, pervasive violence and revenge.[2] We took shelter from missile attacks, and heard gunshots and horrific tales of poison gas on the front. Families and friends lost loved ones to combat, death sentences, imprisonment or – if they were lucky – exile.

Strict morality was enforced on the streets, in schools, in universities and in public buildings. Those who did not believe in or practise the values and restrictions of the Islamic Republic were forced nonetheless to abide by them. The fear of state-administered violence – beating, torture or death – made even non-believers internalise a practice of outward submission. Parents of the Burnt Generation started to impose even stricter rules, rules they themselves did not believe in, to protect their children.

We learned the art of quiet dissent. In private, non-religious families led a double life, defying rules for the most normal activities: watching satellite TV and foreign movies, listening to non-approved music, dancing, attending mixed family gatherings, taking secret pleasure in life. In school or other public arenas, we were not to confront authority on issues of

Mahsa Rouhi is Research Fellow at the Institute for National Strategic Studies at National Defense University. The views expressed here are those of the author and are not an official policy or position of the National Defense University, the US Department of Defense or the US government.

Survival | vol. 64 no. 6 | December 2022–January 2023 | pp. 189–196 https://doi.org/10.1080/00396338.2022.2150441

religion, politics and values. Everything about our own identity was illegal. Worse, schools invaded our privacy by 'morally policing' what we could wear, how we could act, what we could think. Non-compliant youths would be turned in to the authorities.

The outside world has seen photos and videos showing that many Iranians have partied, consumed alcohol, loosened their headscarves, listened to Western music and kept dogs as pets. Unseen in these frames is the constant anxiety that these lifestyle choices could produce, risking as they did one's education, career, freedom or even life. While the Islamic Republic did not always strictly implement its morality policies, its citizens remained at the mercy of random luck and arbitrary enforcement.

For many, the best shot was to leave Iran for Europe, North America or elsewhere, which caused a brain drain that made indigenous Iranian society feel all the more depressing.[3] Exiles sought not just to have a materially better life, but also to reclaim their true identity and to enjoy a measure of freedom. A good number have succeeded, but it has taken them years to unlearn panic when seeing police, fear of persecution for what they are wearing, and anxiety about the consequences of their personal lives for their employment and welfare. Politically outspoken exiles feared that the Iranian government would detain them when they returned home to visit loved ones, and that they would be unable to see their parents or even attend their funerals.

Shaped by our traumas of revolution, repression, benighted childhoods and war, my generation found the prospect of another revolution unbearable. This has shaped the reaction of even Iranian liberals to invocations of regime change. They explored all forms of non-violent action available, hoping that peaceful reform would eventually bring real change. There was no naive assumption of short-term, transformative change, nor wishful trust in 'reformists' or 'moderates'. The main calculation was how much one could do without precipitating widespread violence.

The election in 1997 of Mohammad Khatami as president showed that this cautious push for reform could work. The Khatami era brought a new openness to Iranian cinema, literature, newspapers, television and universities. At the same time, greater economic exchange with the outside world created a business constituency for reform. But the reformers could not hold their ground against conservative forces, and the hopes of the 1990s were extinguished in the early 2000s, culminating in the 2005 election of Mahmoud Ahmadinejad. Part of the problem was that the economic engine helping to drive these reforms created concentrated wealth and, with it, widespread corruption, for which Ahmadinejad's 2005 rival, the more pragmatic Akbar Hashemi Rafsanjani, was notorious. This pattern of hope and disappointment was repeated in the candidacy of Mir Hossein Mousavi in 2009, and the presidency of Hassan Rouhani starting in 2013. While reformers sought change, brutal crackdowns continued, notably against university students in 1999, the Green Movement in 2009 and protesters against fuel-price increases in November 2019, when hundreds were killed and thousands imprisoned.[4] Yet, while the Islamic Republic could suppress public demonstrations, it could not address the root causes of popular dissatisfaction or show the flexibility required to ameliorate it.[5]

II

In the months after July 2015, when the Joint Comprehensive Plan of Action (JCPOA) – the Iran nuclear deal – was signed, many in Iran were filled with optimism about the future. They imagined that the agreement would do away with sanctions, promote economic prosperity, end decades of hostility and international isolation, and help turn Iran into a normal member of the international community. Many Iranians believed that these changes would promote domestic political reform as well.

However realistic or unrealistic these prospects may have been, the Trump administration's withdrawal from the deal in May 2018 and subsequent strategy of 'maximum pressure' killed them. Efforts to salvage the deal without the United States failed, so any remaining hope for reform hinged on the prospect of a new administration that would return the US to compliance. During his campaign for the presidency, Joe Biden indicated his intent to return to the deal. For a combination of reasons, however, this did not happen.[6] As a result, the agenda of Rouhani-aligned moderates for normalisation with the West was further discredited.

Then came the June 2021 elections in Iran. The Islamic Republic has long had a hybrid political system: a clerical autocracy with elements of managed democracy. The clerical system always vetted candidates for high office, but typically allowed at least one relatively moderate candidate to appear on the ballot, offering some hope for economic, political and foreign-policy reform. This sliver of hope for Iranian liberals meant the possibility of a peaceful transition to a better system and a better life. Such prospects boosted voter participation, which the Islamic Republic claimed as a sign of public support for the regime itself. Turnout rates typically equalled or exceeded two-thirds of the electorate.[7]

The 2021 election was the first time that the Islamic Republic controlled the process so blatantly as to indicate that it was no longer interested in accommodating the more liberal portion of the population. By barring virtually all competitive candidates – certainly reformists and even some relative hardliners such as Ali Larijani – the Islamic Republic made clear that the optics of democracy no longer mattered. Mostafa Tajzadeh, a reformist candidate barred from running, wrote in a June 2021 tweet that this election shifted from being 'engineered' to being a mere facade for direct appointment.[8] Ebrahim Raisi, a hardline cleric implicated in the 1988 mass executions of political prisoners, was essentially hand-picked. Frustrated and disappointed, more than half of Iranian voters stayed home and another 3.7 million cast blank ballots, marking the lowest voter turnout since the revolution.[9] Once in office, the Raisi government consolidated hardline domestic policies, sanctioning the brutality of the morality police. Meanwhile, with onerous international sanctions still in place, the new government was unable to bring any economic relief. The move to provide drones to Russia for its war against Ukraine, hugely unpopular among Iranians, compounded the anger.[10]

III

On 16 September 2022, Mahsa Amini, a 22-year-old from Iran's Kurdistan region, died in custody after being arrested for improperly wearing her hijab. Her death ignited a national wave of protests that were ongoing at the time of this writing.

The compulsory hijab has become the symbol of gratuitous state oppression bearing down most directly on Iran's women. Yet, unlike earlier protests, these gained broad public support among rich and poor, urban and rural, young and old, female and male. Most striking was the solidarity among ethnic communities and regions across the country, which was unprecedented. In an article for the *Atlantic*, Roya Hakakian reflected that 'no one can predict how a revolution starts. Nor can anyone know when one injustice will be what causes a people's fury to overcome their fear.' It hit so close to home for most Iranians, she noted, because virtually all of them felt that Amini could have been them or at least a female member of their family.[11] To use a popular Persian expression, 'the knife reached the bone' when a woman could be arrested, humiliated and killed simply for the way she wore a headscarf.

Amini's generation came of age under different circumstances than mine. It was less scarred by first-hand experiences of revolution and war, but still burdened with repression, corruption and international sanctions.[12] The oldest of that generation will recall the 2009 Green Movement. A decade later, 'Bloody November' became another formative memory, followed by the shooting down of Ukraine International Airlines Flight 752. The youngest of this generation endured the COVID-19 pandemic in their pre-teen and teen years. Many Iranians feel it was mishandled due to 'ideology-driven policies' that led to insufficient testing, bans of Western vaccines that slowed the roll-out of medications and minimal lockdown precautions.[13] Having faced years of harsh sanctions, the most severe due to Iran's nuclear programme, many Iranians now wonder whether a more prudent political path could have spared them hardship.

Today's information and communication technologies offer this generation unprecedented access to facts, linking them to a global community and providing an outlet for their opposition to Iranian government policies. Unsurprisingly, Tehran's response to the growing influence of social media and internet access has been censorship, shutdown and misinformation, which is only partly effective but still makes Iranians feel deprived and unhappy.[14]

Even though the Burnt Generation grew up traumatised and cautious, they have imparted their hopes for a freer future to a younger generation that is willing to fight against state repression, and they support that fight. There are constraints, however. Iranians of all ages do still fear the prospect of chaotic regime change, having witnessed the experiences of Afghanistan and Syria. But the prospect of continued hardship under the present system is now dire enough for them to court risk. An Iranian merchant told journalist Homa Hoodfar:

> Under the Shah, we had nothing, but we had our mosque and God and Islam. Under this regime, we still don't have anything, but we have lost our Islam and God as well. Nobody wants to go to mosque. Everybody makes fun of Islamic belief. This is what the Revolution has brought for us.[15]

Unlike the 1979 revolution, the protest movement has neither a single charismatic leader nor a centralised structure, and lacks the characteristics typically associated with successful insurgencies.[16] I believe in drawing lessons from history, which suggest that the current inchoate revolution is likely to fail. I have also learned, however, to keep an open mind for exceptions, new precedents and unexpected turns. In the Iranian protests, social media have offset organisational deficits and afforded Iranians an 'opportunity to witness and incentivize solidarity'.[17] The new generation in Iran regards its command of information as an operational asset and, beyond that, an indication of a more progressive framework of revolution than the putative model that relied on an elite for collective wisdom.

Fear and caution have turned to resentment and anger, and a feeling that there is nothing to lose.[18] Until recently, it was only fervent supporters of the regime who were willing to die for their cause. This new generation of dissenters now seems ready to match their will to sacrifice. This is potentially a strategic shift that could drastically change Iran's political landscape. This time, brutal repression has not shut down protest but rather fuelled the grievances underlying it.

I have in the past argued that a strategy of maximum pressure against Iran is doomed because Iranians are more willing to endure hardship than the indignity of capitulation.[19] But the violation of human rights, denial of individual freedoms and economic misery are forms of indignity too. The movement remains leaderless, its arc and durability unknown, the 'day after' question unanswered. But its unprecedented demographic breadth, philosophical commitment and sheer persistence may afford its participants enough time to develop a novel framework for political change, organise and protect themselves, and plan for a new Iran.

On the fortieth day of mourning after Amini's death, even after hundreds of protestors had been killed, tens of thousands more took to the streets across the country.[20] Even if the current uprising is repressed, it is probably only a matter of time before the next wave arises. One 16-year-old girl reflected: 'They can kill us. They can arrest us. But it is the start of their end. Maybe today. Maybe next week or next month. But our revolt is irreversible.'[21]

Notes

1   The term in Persian is 'Nasl-e Sukhteh'.

2   There is no clear or reliable data on how Iranians feel about the regime. Many still support the Islamic Republic to varying degrees. My aim, however, is to represent the beliefs and sentiments of a significant portion of the Iranian population based on what I have observed taking place within and outside the country.

3   See Pooya Azadi, Martin Mirramezani and Mohsen B. Mesgaran, 'Migration and Brain Drain from Iran', Stanford Iran 2040 Project, Working Paper No. 9, April 2020, https://iranian-studies.stanford. edu/iran-2040-project/publications/ migration-and-brain-drain-iran.

4   Human Rights Watch, 'Iran: No Justice for Bloody 2019 Crackdown', 17 November 2020, https://www.hrw. org/news/2020/11/17/iran-no-justice-bloody-2019-crackdown.

5   See Omid Memarian, 'The Green Movement Never Went Away', *Foreign Affairs*, 14 June 2019.

6   Joby Warrick and Anne Gearan, 'Biden Has Vowed to Quickly Restore the Iran Nuclear Deal, but that May Be Easier Said than Done', *Washington Post*, 9 December 2020.

7   'Rate of Voter Turnout for Presidential Elections in the Islamic Republic of Iran from 1980 to 2021', Statista, 21 June 2021, https://www.statista.com/ statistics/692094/iran-voter-turnout-rate/.

8   See Kian Tajbakhsh, Masih Alinejad and Sara Bazoobandi, 'Iran's Presidential Election: Opportunity or Dead End?', Carnegie Endowment for International Peace, 15 June 2021, https://carnegieendowment.org/ sada/84772#tajbakhsh.

9   'Rate of Voter Turnout for Presidential Elections in the Islamic Republic of Iran from 1980 to 2021'.

10 Especially for the Burnt Generation, Iran's support for Russia's war against Ukraine has felt like a deep betrayal. Providing Russia with weapons used to target population centres and kill innocent civilians reminds them of Iraq's conduct in the Iran–Iraq War, and they find it unacceptable for Iran to condone victimising another population in the same way.

11 Roya Hakakian, 'The Bonfire of the Headscarves', *Atlantic*, 24 September 2022.

12 See Holly Dagres, 'Meet Iran's Gen Z: The Driving Force Behind the Protests', *Foreign Policy*, 1 November 2022.

13 Atlantic Council, 'Iran's COVID-19 Deaths "2.5 Times Higher" than Health Ministry Numbers', 1 December 2021, https://www.atlanticcouncil.org/blogs/iransource/irans-covid-19-deaths-2-5-times-higher-than-healthy-ministry-numbers/.

14 Earlier this year, the Regulatory System for Cyberspace Services Bill, informally known as the 'Internet Protection Bill', was reintroduced in the Iranian parliament. The bill sought to criminalise internet-circumvention tools, such as VPNs, and move Iranians towards a scrubbed national internet system. Despite campaigning on protecting internet freedoms and the bill failing to pass in parliament, there are indications that the Raisi administration has been secretly implementing its restrictions. See Golnaz Esfandiari, 'Iran Accused of Secretly Implementing Controversial Draft Internet Bill', Radio Free Europe/Radio Liberty, 9 September 2022, https://www.rferl.org/a/iran-internet-bill-controversy-secretly-implementing/32026313.html; and Kourosh Ziabari, 'Iran's Leaders Are Scared of the Internet', *Foreign Policy*, 6 June 2022.

15 Isaac Chotiner, 'Iranian Feminism and "All These Different Kinds of Veils"', *New Yorker*, 2 November 2022.

16 See Jeff Colgan, 'Measuring Revolution', *Conflict Management and Peace Science*, vol. 29, no. 4, September 2012, pp. 444–67.

17 Jon B. Alterman, 'Protest, Social Media, and Censorship in Iran', Center for Strategic and International Studies, 18 October 2022, https://www.csis.org/analysis/protest-social-media-and-censorship-iran.

18 See Parisa Hafezi, 'Many Young Iranians Lose Their Fear in Struggle for "Freedom"', Reuters, 3 November 2022, https://www.reuters.com/world/middle-east/many-young-iranians-lose-their-fear-struggle-freedom-2022-11-03/.

19 See Mahsa Rouhi, 'Iranians Will Tolerate Hardship But Not Capitulation', *Foreign Policy*, 13 May 2019.

20 See Farnaz Fassihi and Cora Engelbrecht, 'Tens of Thousands in Iran Mourn Mahsa Amini, Whose Death Set Off Protests', *New York Times*, 26 October 2022.

21 Hafezi, 'Many Young Iranians Lose Their Fear in Struggle for "Freedom"'.

Copyright © 2022 The International Institute for Strategic Studies